Praise for *Thank God I Had a Gun*

As one who has been debriefing gunfight survivors for more than 35 years, I was particularly pleased to read Chris Bird's new book, *Thank God I Had a Gun: True Accounts of Self-Defense*. Chris doesn't just push a political agenda in the polarized debate on gun control: he shows the human side of these larger-than-life events in which an armed citizen's where-withal—in terms of both equipment, and personal courage and preparedness—made a profound difference. From the paralyzing terror that many of the survivors had to overcome before they fought back, to the tragic heroism displayed in the Tyler, Texas, incident, to the post-event psychological trauma suffered by the armed citizen in Phoenix who shot it out with a cop-killer, Chris's book shows the reality of this topic.

There is much to be learned from Chris's painstaking, detailed research. I recommend this book highly.

— **Massad Ayoob**, author of *Combat Handgunnery* and director of Lethal Force Institute

The public is bombarded daily with articles, news stories, books and conferences by gun control advocates seeking to disarm law-abiding American citizens. In *Thank God I Had a Gun*, Chris Bird has written a book based on real stories of people who exercised their God-given, constitutionally-guaranteed right to defend themselves with the use of a firearm. He employs the same tactics those on the other side employ chicanery against the citizen who believes in freedom owes it to themselves, their family and their friends to read this book.

— **Bob Barr**, former Georgia congressman and member of the NRA board of directors

Mr. Bird's book is a star in the galaxy of personal protection—a sampling of the importance of freedom to own and lawfully carry firearms. The chapter on New Orleans post Hurricane Katrina, alone, is worth the price of the book.

— **Marion P. Hammer**, past president of the National Rifle Association and executive director of Unified Sportsmen of Florida

The second amendment was not drafted for hunting; the Founding Fathers knew the importance of self-defense against criminals and a possible tyrannical government. Chris Bird has made it very clear that if you believe in gun control, you may be only one incident away from committed support of gun possession for self protection!

— **Ron Paul**, Congressman, Texas 14th district

The subjects of Chris Bird's newest book, ***Thank God I Had A Gun: True Accounts of Self-Defense***, are very ordinary people. They were not SWAT cops, nor were many of them very heavily trained. In the accounts comprising the book, possession and use of guns changed the course of events for these citizens. The stories should serve as both inspiration and caution for the private citizen considering how to defend self and family from the ever-present threat of crime.

— **Gila Hayes**, author of *Effective Defense* and co-owner of Firearms Academy of Seattle

Great true stories that spark a self analytical, 'what would I have done?' The chilling narrative on post Katrina New Orleans should be required reading for those who doubt the Second Amendment's relevance in today's America.

> — **Jerry Patterson**, Texas Land Commissioner
> and former state senator who sponsored
> the Texas Concealed Handgun Law

At Tac Pro Shooting Center, we try to break all the myths out there, so students are more prepared for what can happen in a real gunfight—especially with handguns. We want them to understand that they must see the clues and be aware of their surroundings; that the old .45 is not going to "knock them back" or "throw them to the ground"; that shot placement trumps both velocity and caliber; and that staying in the fight is crucial. Chris's research and investigation in *Thank God I Had a Gun*, provides real-life examples of these fundamental truths.

> — **Bill Davison**, president of Tac Pro Shooting
> Center, former Royal Marine and
> firearms instructor to British Special Forces

Widely traveled, a longtime journalist and retired military officer, Chris Bird is more than amply qualified to write a book like *Thank God I Had a Gun*.

He has thoroughly researched his subject matter to inform the reader of over a dozen incidents involving the use of firearms in defensive situations, and one has only to read the first chapter relating to the New Orleans situation in the aftermath of Hurricane Katrina to realize that this is not another 'thumbsuck,' biased gun book.

If you don't heed the contents of this book, like ignoring history, you will be condemned to repeat it.

Thank God I Had a Gun is a sobering reminder of how society can degenerate in the blink of an eye, protected only by those who are prepared to defend themselves.

> — **Louis Awerbuck**, author of *Tactical Reality* and president of Yavapai Firearms Academy

Chris Bird combines his talents as a trainer and a writer. The gripping accounts of those who have used their firearms in self-defense underscores the importance of awareness and training. Don't just be there. Be alert!

> — **Larry Pratt**, executive director of Gun Owners of America

When someone asks smugly, 'Why does anyone need a gun?' veteran journalist Chris Bird provides 14 irrefutable answers in his masterful retelling of the deadly, true-life experiences of men and women who survived only because they had a gun when suddenly endangered by murderous predators. This is compelling reading, more convincing than any polemic.

> — **Joseph P. Tartaro**, executive editor of *The New Gun Week* and president of the Second Amendment Foundation

Responsible gun ownership is one of the most demanding and important acts an American citizen can pursue. Safe and effective gun handling in the face of vicious criminal assault is the ultimate test of that responsibility. Where can a gun owner go to, to learn the tested skills that save lives? To those citizen-heroes who have already been tested and survived. Chris Bird has collected 14 detailed stories of ordinary men and women who have been forced to face the firestorm. What they did right and wrong, what training worked and what didn't, what equipment saved some and failed others is uncovered in this exceptional text.

Brave men and women have already faced down death to learn these lessons. Chris Bird has put their stories together so their courage and sacrifices shall not be wasted. *Thank God I Had a Gun* is an absolute must read for the responsibly armed man and woman, and needs to be in every serious gun owner's library.

> — **Michael de Bethencourt**, firearms writer and senior instructor for Northeast Tactical Schools

Chris Bird tells the compelling stories of good people who used firearms to save lives. When you read these stories, you too will be grateful that these victims were not defenseless when the predators attacked. As Bird shows, taking guns away from good people will lead to good people being murdered. The book shows the personal, life-saving consequences of gun ownership by responsible citizens, and the deadly perils of gun prohibition.

> — **David B. Kopel**,co-author of *No More Wacos* and research director of The Independence Institute

I like it! This is the kind of information the general public needs to be exposed to, to counter the propaganda they get daily. Nice mix of male/female and outcomes.

Thank God I Had a Gun: True Accounts of Self-Defense is a book long needed. In contrast to the daily propaganda fed to Americans by the mainstream media, here are fourteen accounts of actual honest citizens defending themselves and their families, using guns in the right hands, for the right reasons. With some 12.5 million victims of violent interpersonal crime in the U.S. each year, here are excellent examples of intelligent, proactive people who took back control over their fates.

Chris does an excellent job of providing background on the characters, detail of the incident, and the aftermath of the crisis. This gives the reader valuable insight into the overall picture of self-defense, rather than just a clinical view of the mechanics involved. I highly recommend this book for gun owners, or those who are considering taking steps to avoid becoming a victim.

> — **Tom Givens**, author of *Fighting Smarter* and
> veteran firearms instructor to
> law enforcement officers and civilians

Chris Bird's accounts of "ordinary people using guns to defend themselves"—and his comments on the lessons learned—are "must reading" for every serious gun owner. Unlike the unrealistic "tough talk" of naïve gunshop commandos, the harsh consequences of real-life deadly force confrontations are sobering and highly instructive. If you want a riveting look at truth, not fantasy, this book is for you."

> — **Emanuel Kapelsohn**, vice president of the
> International Association of Law Enforcement
> Firearms Instructors, a charter member of the
> American Society of Law Enforcement
> Trainers, lawyer, and expert witness in the use
> of force

Excellent text, with character and situation development reminiscent of Joseph Wambaugh! It reads well, and I love the conclusions.

— **John Farnam**, author of *The Farnam Method of Defensive Handgunning* and president of Defense Training International

THANK GOD I HAD A GUN

True Accounts of Self-Defense

To Alex, Olga and
Alexander

Remain Undaunted

Chris

Xmas 2006

THANK GOD I HAD A GUN
True Accounts of Self-Defense

Chris Bird

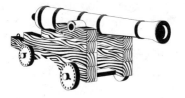

Privateer Publications
San Antonio, Texas

Privateer Publications, +1 (210) 308-8191
Post Office Box 29427, San Antonio, TX 78229 USA
First printing, August 2006.
Printed in the United States of America. Recycled paper.
Impression 10 9 8 7 6 5 4 3 2 1

ISBN: 978-0-9656784-5-2 / 0-9656784-5-8
Library of Congress Control Number: 2006903873

Publisher's Cataloging-in-Publication
(Provided by Quality Books, Inc.)

Bird, Chris.
    Thank God I had a gun : true accounts of self-defense
/ Chris Bird.
    p. cm.
    ISBN 0-9656784-5-8

    1. Firearms--United States--Use in crime prevention--
Case studies. 2. Victims of crimes--United States--
Biography. 3. Self-defense--Case studies. 4. Gun
control--United States.   I. Title.

HV7431.B56 2006   362.88'0973
                             QBI06-600174

Photo Credits: Steve Woods, Dallas; Robert Langham and Tyler
Texas Police Department; Vinnie Pervel and Alastair Jackson,
New Orleans; Charles Heller, Tucson; NRA News; Benjamin Krain
and Arkansas Democrat-Gazette; Robert Lawrence, Tempe; Fort Worth
Police Department; Lee County Florida Sheriff's Office; Indianapolis
Police Department; Rory Vertigan and Manuel Maltos, Phoenix;
Clinton County Michigan Sheriff's Office; US Geological Survey;
Maricopa County Arizona Sheriff's Office; Phoenix Police Department;
Ray Messick, Atlanta.

*To Mum, who put up with so much,
for so long, with so little complaint;
And to my daughters, Katy and Rebecca.*

"Arms in the hands of citizens (may) be used at individual discretion for the defense of the country, the overthrow of tyranny, or in private self-defense."
– John Adams

"To disarm the people is the best and most effective way to enslave them."
– George Mason

"I am a Second Amendment absolutist."
– Condoleezza Rice

CONTENTS

FOREWORD

When Chris Bird called me to ask if I would review his new book, *Thank God I Had a Gun*, I silently thought, 'Good grief, like I don't have other important things to do: shuttle kids to basketball camp, wash clothes, do the dishes, clean the stalls, doctor a horse's eye, mop the floor, get the oil changed, pick up the kids. . . .'

So, I must admit that it wasn't with much enthusiasm that, once his book arrived, I planted myself in the recliner to do a polite but cursory scan. Several hours later, my husband returned from work to find me still firmly planted with my nose buried in the pages.

Wow! 'Riveting' may be an overused word in book and movie reviews, but it is perfectly descriptive of the stories that Chris has compiled in such a readable manner.

I firmly believe that it has always been the personal stories with which folks can identify that have the ability to change public policy. People need to be able to imagine themselves in the situations facing the people in this book, and being forced to make the same choices. The media loves such stories for a reason, too: they sell.

I hope copies of Chris's book eventually end up in the hands of passive individuals who grew up without guns and believe the cops will rescue them from any sticky situation (i.e., most women and many new-age men). Perhaps, they will find themselves empathizing with one or more of the book's real life characters enough to reevaluate their previously anti-gun positions.

Who knows, maybe they will even vote!

— **Suzanna Gratia Hupp**, Texas State
   Representative, District 54

Suzanna saw her parents murdered in the 1991 Luby's cafeteria massacre in Killeen. She subsequently became one of the most com - pelling witnesses in favor of the right of civilians to carry concealed handguns for protection, testifying before many state legislatures and Congress. She was elected to her central Texas district in 1996.

INTRODUCTION

One of the best-kept secrets in the United States is how often and how effectively ordinary citizens defend themselves with firearms against criminal attack or criminal threat.

Criminology professor Gary Kleck of Florida State University estimates that each year about 2.5 million ordinary Americans use firearms in confrontations with criminals. Kleck is not the only researcher in the field to reveal such results. In the book *Armed: New Perspectives on Gun Control*, which he wrote with Don B. Kates, Kleck states there are seventeen national surveys that indicate huge numbers of defensive uses of firearms each year. In the vast majority of cases not a shot is fired, and frequently the incidents are not reported to the police.

A lot of people don't want you to know how effective armed citizens are at preventing crime and deterring criminals. They include federal politicians such as senators Charles Schumer of New York, Edward Kennedy of Massachusetts, and Dianne Feinstein of California. They have sworn to uphold the U.S. Constitution, including the bit about "the right of the people to keep and bear arms shall not be infringed." Some of them are hypocrites: Feinstein used to hold a concealed-handgun permit, but doesn't want you to have one. Kennedy's bodyguard was arrested for trying to take two submachineguns and a pistol into a Senate office building.

National politicians are joined by their big-city colleagues, such as mayors Richard Daley of Chicago and Michael Bloomberg of New York. These are the patronizing politicians who appear to believe that ordinary citizens—the people who elect them—cannot be trusted with firearms. The mayors, of course, are protected by legions of New York and Chicago police officers with guns.

Many government bureaucrats seem to have forgotten that they are the servants of the citizens, not their masters. They include some agents of the federal Bureau of Alcohol, Tobacco, Firearms, and Explosives who set up Randy Weaver, attacked the Branch Davidians at Waco largely as a publicity stunt, and recently harassed law-abiding customers at gun shows in Virginia.

Since the rash of high-profile shootings at middle-class schools in the late 1990s, school officials have taken what they call a "zero tolerance" stance regarding guns. This, to me, is the most troubling. It has resulted in such atrocities as a second grader being chastised for playing war games and a high-school student being denied a photo of him holding his skeet-shooting shotgun in the school yearbook. Ill-informed educators are brainwashing the next generation to believe that guns are evil and people who own guns are bad. Many school children are being pressured into signing pledges never to use violence under any circumstances. Every child who goes through the current American school system is a potential conscientious objector to military service. God help the nation if it is ever invaded.

There are state, national, and international organizations, like the Brady Campaign to Prevent Gun Violence (formerly Handgun Control Inc.), the Violence Policy Center (VPC), and the International Action Network on Small Arms (IANSA), that propagate lies and disinformation dedicated to demonizing guns and the civilians who own them. Many members of and contributors to these organizations are just misinformed members of the public concerned for the safety of themselves and their families and who have bought the lie that guns, rather than criminals, are the cause of violent crime. However, the people who run these organizations, like

Sarah Brady of the Brady Campaign, Tom Diaz of the VPC, and Rebecca Peters of IANSA, have one goal: the confiscation of all privately owned firearms. They cloak it in a shroud of violent-crime reduction, but are part of an elite that believes there is something barbaric and uncivilized about self-defense. There is no question that these people would prefer you to be a dead victim they can exploit, rather than a survivor who used a gun to successfully defend yourself.

The national media, companies like The New York Times, The Washington Post, ABC, CBS, and NBC, buy into this attitude. Big-city newspapers have been almost unanimous in predicting a blood bath that has not come to pass whenever a state enacts a concealed-carry law, and the television networks regularly ignore any story that might show defensive use of a gun in a positive light. So, most defensive uses of guns happen below the public's radar. But they do happen, again and again and again.

This book recounts in detail fourteen incidents that lift the veil surrounding the defensive uses of guns.

If we take Kleck's figures as correct, and they are probably fairly close, in the United States every hour an average of 285 people use guns to defend themselves. This compares favorably to the average of 156 crimes of violence reported to police each hour, according to FBI statistics for 2004.

Most frequently, when a gun is used for self-defense, no shot is fired, as in the cases of Ray Messick of Atlanta and Deanna Eggleston of Arlington, Texas. In the same way that nuclear missiles kept the Soviets from attacking the U.S.A., the threat of a gun in the hands of an ordinary citizen is a powerful deterrent against personal attack.

The most common use of firearms for self-defense occurs when people, like Susan Gaylord Buxton, also of Arlington, Texas, and Judy Kuntz of Indialantic, Florida, defend themselves from intruders in their homes. Many people, like Barbara Thompson of Fort Worth and Clarence Cochrane of Crawfordsville, Arkansas, use firearms to defend themselves at their businesses.

Some people, like Robert Lawrence of Tempe, Arizona, get the rough end of the legal system for trying to defend themselves. Some good citizens, like Mark Wilson of Tyler, Texas, and Rory Vertigan of Phoenix, get involved in shootings while trying to help others.

In each case study presented in this book, I have tried to put the incident into context and provide information about the background and training of the citizen involved. I have dealt with the incident and its aftermath.

Where possible I have interviewed the citizen who defended himself or herself and backed up the information with media reports and information from law enforcement.

I hope this book reveals to some people the positive uses of firearms and helps those who need to defend themselves.

Stay safe and remain undefeated.

Chris Bird

San Antonio

ABOUT THE AUTHOR

Chris Bird has been a journalist for thirty years and a handgun shooter for more than forty. He was born in England, and his interest in shooting steered him through the bureaucratic red tape of owning handguns in England, Canada, and Australia. As a commissioned officer in the Royal Military Police of the British Army in the 1960s, Bird was stationed in Berlin, West Germany, and Belgium, serving as company weapon-training officer and winning awards for shooting in competition. After leaving the military, Bird migrated to Canada, where he worked as a cowboy in British Columbia, while shooting and hunting extensively.

As a journalist he worked as a crime and investigative reporter for the *Vancouver Province* newspaper and the Canadian Broadcasting Corporation. He has also been a salesman, a private investigator, and a shotgun guard for an armored-car company in Australia. In the late 1980s he and his wife, Anita, sailed a twenty-seven-foot sailboat from Vancouver, Canada, to Sydney, Australia, and back to San Francisco.

He arrived in Texas in 1989 and became a police reporter for the *San Antonio Express-News*, covering crime and law enforcement from municipal to federal levels. He is author of *The Concealed Handgun Manual*, which is now in its fourth edition and twelfth printing. The book is on the Texas Department of Public Safety list of approved reading for concealed-handgun instructors and licensees.

Bird is certified in Texas as a concealed-handgun instructor; a director of the Texas Concealed Handgun Association; and a member of the Texas State Rifle Association, the National Rifle Association, the Second Amendment Foundation, and Gun Owners of America.

ACKNOWLEDGMENTS

Most books depend upon a lot of people to make them happen, and this one is no exception. It could not have been written without the help and encouragement of many.

Special thanks are due to each of those who had the courage to share their stories: Susan Gaylord Buxton, Clarence Cochran, Deanna Eggleston, Ron Honeycutt, Habib Howard, Zelda Hunt, Judy Kuntz, Robert Lawrence, Ray Messick, Vinnie Pervel, Barbara Thompson, and Rory Vertigan.

Many others helped me get information and perspective on the incidents I recount here. I apologize if I have omitted anyone. I had more help from more people with Mark Wilson's tragic story than with any other. They include Mark's mother, Lynn Stewart; Detective Clay Perrett, Detective Wayne Thomas, Officer Don Martin, and Sergeant Rusty Jacks, all of Tyler Police Department; Ron Martell; Jim Carter, Robert Lloyd, and John O'Sullivan; and most of all Robert Langham, who gave me a place to work, helped me with interviews, and let me use some of his photographs.

Those who helped me with other accounts include Ginny Simone of *NRA News*, who was a constant help with several stories, and Daryl D'Angelo, known to many as blogger Polimom, who helped me navigate her Hurricane Katrina archives.

Herbie and Tammy Howard helped me tell Habib's story. Ken Heard and Ben Krain of the *Arkansas Democrat-Gazette* gave me their perspectives on Clarence Cochran's shooting, as did his son, Tommy Turner. Thanks also go to Deputy Thomas Martin of Crittenden County Sheriff's Office. Vicki Ganske and Nona Best of the Fort Worth City Attorney's Office were exceptionally pleasant and helpful.

For the stories from Arizona, I had help and support from my friend Alan Korwin of Bloomfield Press and assistance with research from Gary Christensen of Tempe and Barb DeLuca of Tucson. Charles Heller of Liberty Watch Radio helped with Zelda Hunt's story and let me use his photo of her. Defense lawyer Tait Elkie gave me his take on his client Bob Lawrence's cautionary tale.

In Florida prosecutor Jean-Paul Galasso of Fort Myers shared his thoughts on Steve Robey's hotel-room-invasion incident. Agent Lou Heyn of the Brevard County Sheriff's Office was always helpful with Judy Kuntz's case.

In the case of Susan Gaylord Buxton, James Dark and attorney Albert Ross, both of the Texas State Rifle Association, provided valuable information. Christy Gilfour of the Arlington Police Department was always pleasant and helpful, while my friend J.R. Labbe, columnist for the *Fort Worth Star-Telegram,* pointed me in the right direction.

A special thank you goes to Deanna Eggleston and her son Austin for posing for the cover photo and to her husband Lee for his support. Steve Woods of Dallas took the eye-catching photo that graces the cover of this book, while Laura Lindgren of New York put the cover together and provided light-hearted repartee—thank you both.

I received help and encouragement from everyone at Independent Publishers Group of Chicago, but particularly Mary Rowles.

This book would probably have been stillborn if it hadn't been for its midwife, my friend and editor, Suzi Hughes, owner of Wordwright Associates.

Thanks as always to my dear wife, Anita, for her encouragement and forbearance.

THANK GOD I HAD A GUN

True Accounts of Self-Defense

Chapter 1

Remember New Orleans: Vinnie Pervel

When Hurricane Katrina roared ashore on the morning of Monday, August 29, 2005, just east of New Orleans, a lot of things changed. According to contemporary news reports, the Category Four storm first came ashore about 7 A.M., south of the Crescent City between Grand Isle and the mouth of the Mississippi River. It swirled north, crossing land and water, and reached land again about 11 A.M. a few miles east of the city, close to the Louisiana-Mississippi border. Considering the damage it did to the Big Easy and much of the Mississippi coast, a direct hit was not required. Close is good enough, it appears, for horseshoes, hand grenades, and hurricanes.

The storm surge raised the water level in Lake Pontchartrain, and about midday breaches were reported in the levees that had protected the city. Because much of New Orleans is below the level of the lake, the city began to flood. It is obvious a year later that New Orleans will never be the same.

Some residents of the city wisely evacuated before the hurricane arrived, others belatedly assembled at the Louisiana Superdome and the Convention Center hoping to be bused to safety, and others refused to move from their homes.

The following day the media reported mass looting and a complete breakdown of law and order. Human vultures were picking away at the carcass of a once great city. Police officers had no way of communicating with one another. Many did the best they could under the circumstances, trying to maintain order amid chaos. Some police officers were shot, many lost their homes and stayed anyway, but some officers fled the city. There were reports of others actually taking part in the looting.

In the first days after the storm the Big Easy turned into the Big Uneasy, with groups and gangs of looters, robbers, carjackers, and home invaders roaming the streets. The residents who remained had to take care of themselves. Many had guns—others secured arms—and they stood watch to protect themselves and sometimes their neighborhoods.

Firearms Confiscations

New Orleans police officers and law enforcement officers from other jurisdictions and even other states started a campaign to take lawfully owned guns from law-abiding residents.

According to court documents and reports in the media, New Orleans Mayor Ray Nagin ordered law-enforcement officers under his authority to evict people from their homes and confiscate their lawfully owned firearms. Officers went door-to-door confiscating firearms from residents, frequently at gunpoint.

On September 8 television viewers across the United States watched as P. Edwin Compass III, the superintendent of the New Orleans Police Department, announced all guns belonging to residents would be seized. "No one will be able to be armed. Guns will be taken. Only law enforcement will be allowed to have guns," he said. This policy was confirmed by Deputy Police Chief Warren Riley, who later succeeded Compass as superintendent.

As might have been predicted, nary a word of outrage emanated from members of the mainstream media, who seem to believe the Second Amendment and gun owners are throwbacks to prehistoric, knuckle-dragging Neanderthals.

There was little or no criticism from the national media, even after a Fox affiliate from the San Francisco area videotaped several California highway patrolmen and, apparently, a Louisiana state trooper assaulting and forcibly disarming a frail white woman in her own home on Magazine Street. The story from KTVU News showed the woman, 58-year-old Patricia Konie, holding a small revolver by the cylinder in a non-threatening manner. She said, "You're going to have to shoot me, because I'm not going. Well, I don't want to kill you; I don't want to kill you, period."

The next shot is of Konie on the ground with several burly police officers on top of her. She is then led out of her home with officers holding her arms.

When questioned by the anchorman, reporter Ken Wayne appears to act as an apologist for the police behavior. The story ran nationally on Fox News.

Konie was shipped out against her will and ended up in South Carolina for a month before she was allowed to return to her home. According to her lawyer, Konie later underwent surgery for a dislocated and fractured shoulder sustained in the attack. She also filed suit in federal court against California and Louisiana police officers. She accused the officers of various civil-rights violations including assault, kidnapping, and illegally disarming her.

"Patricia Konie had food, plenty of water, and a roof over her head. The police who illegally entered her home and imposed their will on a frail, middle-aged female should have been out apprehending armed, male looters instead," her lawyer Ashton O'Dwyer said.

If the police officers ever testify in a courtroom, it is likely they will invoke the Adolph Eichmann defense: "I was just following orders."

While most members of the national media accepted the disarming of law-abiding residents as normal—even desirable—gun owners and their organizations were outraged. The National Rifle Association (NRA) and the Second Amendment Foundation filed a complaint in the United States District Court for the Eastern District of Louisiana to stop the seizures of legally owned firearms and to get the New Orleans police and the sheriff of St. Tammany Parish to return the seized guns.

The complaint cited the Louisiana Constitution, which states, "The right of each citizen to keep and bear arms shall not be abridged. . . ."

The complaint also cited various rights guaranteed by the U.S. Constitution, specifically:
- The Second Amendment, which states in part, "the right of the people to keep and bear arms shall not be infringed."
- The Fourth Amendment, which provides that "the right of the people to be secure in their persons, houses, papers, and effects, against unreasonable searches and seizures, shall not be violated. . . ."
- The Fourteenth Amendment, which stipulates that no state shall deprive any person of liberty or property without due process of law.

- The equal protection clause of the Fourteenth Amendment, which provides that no state shall deny to any person the equal protection of the laws.

The complaint followed media reports of upscale properties being guarded from looters by private security guards armed with semi-automatic or fully-automatic rifles. Therefore, the complaint stated further that, while Nagin and Compass instituted and executed a policy of confiscating firearms from law-abiding citizens, they "allowed selected wealthy persons to keep their firearms and/or to retain armed private security personnel to protect their more expensive homes and properties." The rich were being granted privileges not available to the majority of the resisdents of New Orleans.

The complaint filed with the court mentioned only one specific instance of guns being seized: on September 9 Buell O. Teel and his brother were operating a boat on Lake Pontchartrain in St. Tammany Parish when sheriff's deputies aboard a patrol vessel stopped them at gunpoint and asked if they had any weapons. Teel said he had two rifles. Deputies boarded Teel's boat and seized the rifles. They refused to give him a receipt. A short time later, Teel's boat was boarded again by St. Tammany deputies, who illegally searched him and his boat for weapons.

On September 23 lawyers for all sides agreed to a consent order signed by U.S. District Judge Jay C. Zaney, which ordered the seizures to stop and the seized guns to be returned to their owners. St. Tammany Sheriff Jack Strain and his deputies honored the federal-court order and returned all seized weapons to their owners. Mayor Ray Nagin, New Orleans Police Superintendent Edwin Compass, and his successor Warren Riley apparently ignored the order.

In February 2006 the NRA and Second Amendment Foundation filed a motion in federal court to have Nagin and Riley held in contempt of court. The memorandum in support of the motion cited several cases, supported by affidavits, of guns being confiscated from law-abiding citizens. These affidavits indicate a pattern of rudeness and a lack of accountability more in keeping with police in countries like Colombia or Zimbabwe than officers in a western democracy who claim to be servants of the public.

- On September 9 Robert Edward Zas, 42, was evacuating his home with four friends and three dogs in a van stuffed with household goods. At Poydras and Barrone Streets, they were stopped by a uniformed officer dressed in black, but with no badge or identification on his clothes. A New Orleans police officer and a Louisiana state trooper were also present. The officers asked if they had any guns. Zas had a rifle, and his friend Lisa Ann Zalewski, 37, had in a suitcase an unloaded .22-caliber pistol that had belonged to her grandmother. According to Zalewski's affidavit, an officer threw her gun on the ground, breaking the grips, while the state trooper searched her "and grabbed my breasts with no reason whatsoever. He told me to go back to NJ [presumably New Jersey]; that we were the scum bringing New Orleans down." The guns were seized before the evacuees were allowed to continue.

- On September 19 Ashton O'Dwyer, 57, the lawyer who later took Patricia Konie's case, got out of his vehicle at his home in Southport, a "bad" neighborhood. He was lawfully carrying a .38-caliber Smith & Wesson revolver from his vehicle to his house when two New Orleans police officers told him to drop the gun and raise his hands. O'Dwyer complied and was handcuffed and put in a patrol car. He was released, but his gun was not returned, and the officers refused to give him a receipt for it. The gun had been given to him by his father as a "house gun."

• On September 21 two roofing contractors from Texas, Joseph Lee Hooper and Jason Klemm, 37, were driving down Canal Street in the French Quarter when they were stopped by four officers in a sports utility vehicle. The two male officers said they were U.S. marshals, one from Chicago and one from Texas. The two female officers wore shirts with "New Orleans Police Department" on them. Klemm asked the officers for their names, which they refused to give. They asked Hooper and Klemm if they had any weapons. Both were wearing handguns in shoulder holsters and had concealed-handgun licenses, Klemm's from Texas, Hooper's from Florida. Both licenses are recognized by Louisiana law. They seized Klemm's 9mm Beretta and Hooper's .40-caliber Glock with a laser sight on it. The officers refused to give them receipts and refused initially to give them the serial numbers of the guns. The officer claiming to be a U.S. marshal from Texas eventually gave them the guns' serial numbers. "They then let us go into that mess with no protection at all," Klemm stated. Hooper said that after two weeks of getting the runaround, and with help from a friend, he was able to get the guns back from the police station in the French Quarter from an officer who refused to give his name. The $400 laser sight was missing. Hooper was convinced that if the friend had not intervened, he would never have gotten the guns back.

According to the memorandum supporting the contempt motion, an investigator working for the NRA and Second Amendment Foundation interviewed several law-enforcement witnesses who were willing to testify. One unnamed New Orleans police officer confirmed that officers at his roll call were ordered to seize any guns from anyone who could not verify ownership. The officer said they were instructed to call the Bureau of Alcohol, Tobacco, Firearms and Explosives (BATF) to get federal agents to pick up the weapons. However, as the agents did not respond for several hours, the officers quit calling them. The officer is then quoted as saying, "I am not real proud of it, but if they were nice, most of the guys kept them; if they were crap, they tossed them in the river or in the canal."

The 2003 annual report of the New Orleans Police Department states, "We Protect And Serve Through Our Core Beliefs: Integrity: We are dedicated to maintaining the highest moral and ethical standards, through the principles of pride, honesty, trust, and courage. Fairness: We are dedicated to treating our employees and citizens with dignity, respect, and equality."

It appears that, by 2005, not everybody in the police department was on the same page.

The memorandum continued, saying that BATF agents refused to accept from New Orleans police any firearms that had not been used in the commission of a crime. Eventually, at federal government expense, BATF rented a storage container for the police to use to secure the seized guns.

While the federal BATF is no friend of gun owners, at least some of its agents were operating with more regard for the law than police officers dedicated to protect and serve the residents of the Crescent City.

Although the lawyer for the city and police department was apprised of the investigator's findings in a letter dated December 6, 2005, no response was received, and apparently the court order was ignored.

In March 2006 lawyers for the City of New Orleans admitted for the first time that the police department had more than a thousand guns seized from residents in the aftermath of the hurricane. The NRA and the Second Amendment Foundation announced that arrangements were being made to return the guns to their owners.

Vinnie Pervel and Algiers Point

Hurricane Katrina changed not only the landscape in and around New Orleans, it changed attitudes. One person who experienced a major change in thinking was Vinnie Pervel, a 49-year-old renovation contractor who lives in Algiers Point.

Algiers Point was founded as a separate city in 1719 across the Mississippi River from New Orleans. The Crescent City has since swallowed it up; it is now in Orleans Parish and within the boundaries of the city. Most of the city is squeezed into the strip of land between Lake Pontchartrain in the north and the sweeping meanderings of the Mississippi River in the south. Algiers and Algiers Point are exceptions. The Point is a historic district, about ten blocks square, on the West Bank of the Mississippi, across the river from the French Quarter. It has a spectacular view of downtown New Orleans.

Vinnie was born in New Orleans and has lived in the city all his life, except for a sojourn in the Navy and another as a Mormon missionary in Australia. He has lived on the Point for a decade with his partner Gregg Harris, 47. They live two blocks from the river on Pelican Street in a fine two-story house that was built in 1871 and is filled

A map of New Orleans dated 1869, two years prior to the construction of Vinnie's home. (From the collec - tion of the UT Austin library)

with antiques. Vinnie's mother, Jennie Pervel, lives right across the street from them. She was 75 years old and is known in the neighborhood as "Miss P."

Each year before hurricane season, Vinnie and Gregg made preparations. They bought supplies, such as gas cans, gasoline, flashlights, and trash bags, and filled containers with clean water. In late August when Hurricane Katrina was headed their way, Vinnie bought almost $700-worth of plastic tarps from Lowe's home improvement store. He had also recently bought a gasoline-powered generator. The house has windows equipped with louvered shutters they close and latch during storms. His mother's house also has plenty of windows. Vinnie covered with plywood any windows without shutters in his home, his mother's house, and a rental house he owned on the Point. He also covered the eight French doors at the back of his house.

There was an old 12-gauge, pump-action shotgun in the house. Gregg's father had given him the gun, but neither Gregg nor Vinnie liked guns, so they had put it in a closet with a box of shells and left it there to gather dust.

Vinnie had fired the shotgun only once—in the woods around Gregg's parents' house in Arkansas—just to see what it was like. "I fired it one time, and I didn't like it. At that time I didn't feel that I needed that gun at all in my home."

In April 2005 Algiers Point was experiencing an increase in crime. A free ferry ran across the river from Canal Street on the edge of the French Quarter to the Point, and young criminals were coming across from the East Bank, stealing and robbing on the West Bank, and using the ferry as getaway transport.

Vinnie has been involved in the neighborhood organization for years. He has been president of the Algiers Point Association a couple of times, as well as treasurer.

The association held a meeting to find a solution to the crime problem. The residents could hire off-duty New Orleans police officers to patrol the neighborhood, or they could get a private security company. Some residents suggested everyone should buy a gun.

Vinnie was appalled at the thought of everyone having guns. It did not fit in with his idea of civilized living. "I was against anybody really having a gun. I didn't see the need for it. You could protect your family in other ways, I thought: an alarm on your house or something like that."

Despite his dislike of guns, Vinnie had joined the National Rifle Association in the 1980s when he was becoming interested in politics. He had done so under the misapprehension that NRA stood for National Republican Association. When he started getting gun magazines he realized his mistake and let his membership lapse.

The Hurricane

In late August, as Hurricane Katrina increased in severity crossing the Gulf of Mexico and headed for New Orleans, Vinnie and Gregg decided not to evacuate. They didn't want their home looted in the aftermath and were afraid that if they left they would not be allowed to return. Vinnie's mother also decided to stay.

By the evening of Sunday, August 28, Vinnie and Gregg were prepared for the storm. The house was battened down, and Jennie Pervel had moved in for the duration.

"The most amazing thing about a storm is when you've got a house with thirty-six windows in it and there's always sunlight coming in, when you close the shutters and board up the back, it's amazing. It's like walking into another environment: it's really dark. You know something's coming," Vinnie said.

The wind picked up during the night, blowing down trees and knocking out the electricity about 2 A.M. However, they had some light in front of the house from three gas lamps on the porch, which kept burning. About 4 A.M. a huge pecan tree in a neighbor's yard was blown down, hitting a brick wall behind them, but missing their house. About 6:30 the eye of the storm passed and the wind changed. It picked up the pecan tree as though it were no bigger than a sheet of plywood and flipped it over in the other direction. "It missed our house a second time," Vinne said.

The house is two stories, with twelve-foot ceilings, and towers above its neighbors. It caught a lot of wind, but the house has stood for more than a hundred years and it suffered little damage.

"You could hear the antique crystals on the chandeliers downstairs just tinkling, because the house was moving that much from the wind," Vinnie said.

He recalled a conversation he had with his mother that morning. "Vinnie, do you hear that?" his mother yelled from her bedroom.

"Yes, Mom, I hear the tinkling. It's the chandeliers and the crystals, but that's a good sign."

"Why's that?"

"Because if it stops, it means the house has fallen down," Vinnie replied.

Despite making light of the movement of the house, he was scared. "It was probably the most scary time I've been involved with, with any kind of hurricane or storm that came through New Orleans."

By 9 A.M. on Monday the worst of the storm had passed, so Vinnie went out and looked around. Algiers Point did not flood, though some other parts of the West Bank in Jefferson Parish did.

"Our yard was just a mess. We have a beautiful garden and it was a mess. We had lost all kinds of plants, and arbors, and everything else. But Gregg takes care of the garden, so I said, 'I'm going to go out and start cutting off some electricity and gas for safety.'"

Vinnie got into his five-year-old white Ford van and started driving through the neighborhood. As a remodeling and construction contractor, he had a lot of tools in the van, including his battery-pack power tools and the plastic tarps. He was well-equipped if he came across any damage to the houses on the Point.

Trees were down everywhere, blocking the streets and severing power lines. Most of the trees that blew down were pines and pecans; the big oaks survived.

About five houses on the Point were demolished. Most of the others were in good shape, with only a few shingles off the roofs. Of the two thousand residents of the Point, Vinnie estimated only about a hundred remained. "You couldn't see anybody in the street."

A Defining Moment

He stopped at the houses of people he knew and who had evacuated. He flipped the main breakers, cutting off the electricity to the houses for safety. He used a pair of pliers to switch off the gas at the meters.

At 3:30 P.M. he was at the corner of Belleville and Evelina Streets, three blocks south of his house. He pulled up at a house he had sold about four years previously. He had remained friendly with the new owners and intended to cut off the gas and electricity.

Vinnie got out of his van and put his keys in his pocket. He noticed that a lavender-colored Geo Prism, driven by a young black woman, had pulled in right behind him. He was paying attention to the Prism when he became aware of two young black men at the front of his van. They were about 19 years old, both wearing white T-shirts that reached to their knees, black jeans, and white tennis shoes. They were about Vinnie's height—five feet eight inches—and a little lighter than his hundred and sixty pounds. Both wore their hair in long cornrows.

The Prism drove off as the men started asking questions. Vinnie recalled the conversation. "How do we get out of here? We want to evacuate," one of the men said.

"If you go right down this road here you can catch the ferry by the ferry landing; they're evacuating free," Vinnie said.

"You don't realize, we have children."

"They take children as well."

At that point, Vinnie noticed that one of the men was holding one hand behind his back, and he could see the end of what looked like a sledge-hammer handle. He was afraid the men meant to harm him, so he turned away from them, intending to yell to a group of about a dozen friends, all members of the neighborhood association, who were at the end of the block. Most of the men were armed with shotguns.

Before he could open his mouth, one of the young men hit him in the back of the head with his fist, and Vinnie went down. As he fell, he hit the front of his head on the edge of a brick planter on the sidewalk. The other guy stood over him with a three-foot maul in his hand. "Just stay down. We want your truck, the keys to your van," the man demanded.

Vinnie told him the keys were in his pocket. One of the men took them, got into the van, and cranked it up. As soon as it was running, the other guy ran to the passenger side and got in, and the van took off south on Belleville. As they drove away, Vinnie's fear gave way to anger.

"At the time I had a pair of pliers in my hand 'cause that's what I was cutting the gas off with. I just stood up, and I flung the pliers and knocked out the back window of the van," Vinnie said.

"I hit right in the middle of the back window and busted it out. The guys both turned around and looked at me, because they thought I was shooting at them. They almost hit a tree, but they just managed to turn left, go down another block, and turn right."

Vinnie yelled to the group of friends and neighbors for help. They piled into a truck and drove towards him, but Vinnie was already chasing after his van and had made it another block when he saw a black police officer, in uniform, sitting in an unmarked white Crown Victoria. He told the officer two men had stolen his van and hit him in the head. The officer said he would go after them.

"He turned around and went the other way," Vinnie said. He was the last police officer Vinnie and his friends would see for ten days.

"I went home, told Gregg what happened, and he freaked out. My mom freaked out, and I guess I freaked out, 'cause I went upstairs, and I got the gun and went on my front porch upstairs off my bedroom. I sat on my second-floor balcony with the gun."

The assault and the hijacking of his van was the defining moment for Vinnie Pervel. In those few minutes, he went from being a supporter of gun control to an ardent supporter of the Second Amendment. He realized why ordinary, law-abiding citizens needed guns to defend themselves. He had just seen that residents could not rely on the police for protection, or even to stop crime when it was happening.

He was hearing random shots being fired, mostly across the river. He knew that with the breakdown of law and order, ordinary citizens would have to provide their own security. And that didn't mean burglar alarms and deadbolts: it meant guns.

"I have no problem with having a gun in my house now," he said.

Vinnie was on the balcony when a young black guy on a bicycle tried to ride past the house. "He freaked me out."

Vinnie told him, "Look, don't take offense in any way, but you need to find another way. Don't come past my house."

The young man said he lived just down the street. "I don't care. I don't know who you are. Find another way," Vinnie replied.

His mother recognized the young man and said: "It's okay, he's good, I know him from church." So Vinnie let him pass, but anyone else who tried to pass in front of the house was stopped. They went the other way, and they didn't make any fuss about it. "When I showed them the gun, that's all they needed," he said.

The West Bank is in the New Orleans Police Fourth District. He called the Fourth District, the mayor's office, and the state police. He was told that no one was coming out to write a report. It was a month before a police-woman took a report of the stolen van. She had to write it on a two-by-three-inch notepad because the computer system still didn't work.

Fort Pelican

The West Bank of the city has its own water, gas, and electrical systems, so on Algiers Point the gas stayed on and the water system retained pressure throughout the storm and its aftermath. Residents were advised not to drink the water, but could use it for showers and shaving. The house on Pelican Street had plenty of fresh water in containers. The gas continued to supply the three lamps on the front porch—the only lights on their street. They were able to take hot showers and use the stove for cooking. They did lose electricity for about two weeks because the falling trees knocked down the power lines. This meant they had no air-conditioning in temperatures over ninety degrees. It also meant the city on the East Bank looked quite different after dark.

"I got a view of downtown New Orleans from my front porch. You could see there was nothing on, even in the city. All the skyscrapers were darkened; it was awful."

They were having dinner that first night when Vinnie got a call from an Algiers Point Association member who had evacuated. She told him there was plenty of information on NOLA.com about what was happening on the East Bank but nothing about the West Bank. She said people from Algiers Point wanted to know what was happening there. Vinnie said she could put his name and phone number on the NOLA web site. NOLA.com is a site about New Orleans that carries news and information from the *Times-Picayune*, the newspaper with the largest circulation in the state.

That night Vinnie stayed up on his balcony in a rocking chair listening to the sporadic gunfire and cradling the shotgun. He noticed that his neighbor across the street spent the night on his porch by himself. The next morning the neighbor, Gareth Stubbs, approached Vinnie in the street between their houses. He asked if he could move in with them, because he was afraid of being caught in a crossfire. Stubbs had lived across the street from Vinnie and Gregg for as long as Vinnie had been living there, but they seldom spoke. They had decided that Stubbs was just rude, but they soon changed their minds.

"We found what the problem was: the guy has a hearing problem, so he couldn't hear you. We became the best of friends. He spent two weeks with us after that on our balcony."

Gareth Stubbs was in his mid-forties and was alone because his wife, a nurse, was stuck in Houston.

Soon they fell into a regular routine. Vinnie hooked up the generator in the back yard and it ran one lamp.

Vinnie also hooked it up to the refrigerator. They ran the generator for only a couple of hours each evening, because they wanted to make the gasoline last as long as possible, and they didn't want to attract unwanted attention.

"We feared if we left it for longer than that people would know we had it. There were people walking up and down the street at night-time so we didn't want that to happen."

The generator kept the fridge cool, but the frozen food started to thaw out. Their stove ran on gas so they were able cook meals. First they cooked the food that was defrosting in the fridge. They all ate together in the evening—Vinnie, Gregg, Miss P, and Gareth—about 6:30 and afterwards stood watch. They had plenty of food from their three houses and about thirty gallons of fresh water in bottles.

Vinnie started getting phone calls as a result of his name and phone number being posted on the NOLA web site. One of these calls was from a woman who grew up in Algiers and still had close connections there. Her name was Daryl D'Angelo, and she ran a blog under the name of Polimom—Political Mom—from her home in Katy, close to Houston. At the time Vinnie didn't know what a blog was. Daryl asked him what he needed. His reply: guns and ammunition. This was quite a step from the pro-gun-control Vinnie of a few days before.

Daryl was able to get local residents who had been evacuated to e-mail her rather than calling Vinnie, who did not have a computer. She never actually asked for guns and ammunition, but on her blog asked for any supplies that might be useful to those remaining on the Point.

"She must have had forty people that contacted her and told her where the house was, where the ammo was, where the gun was, how to get into the house." She called Vinnie every evening to pass on the information, sometimes telling him where the key to a house was hidden or where a window was open.

Every morning Vinnie and Gareth drove around the Point in Gareth's pickup, stopping at the houses and collecting the guns. They ended up with about forty guns: mostly pump and semi-automatic shotguns, but some semi-automatic rifles, three .38-caliber revolvers, and a derringer. They didn't need that many, but people wanted Vinnie to have them rather than have them looted.

One family had just moved into Algiers Point and still had a moving van parked in front of the house. They had a gun safe that was locked. Vinnie and Gareth manhandled the gun safe out of a window, because it wouldn't go through the door. They carted it back to the house on a baby buggy. When they got it home, they broke it open and found a treasure trove of about fifteen guns.

People on the Internet started referring to Gregg's and Vinnie's house on Pelican Street as "Fort Pelican." So they used a piece of sheetrock to make a sign, spray-painted in black, "Fort Pelican," and hung it on the front porch.

Someone on the Internet started referring to the residents of Fort Pelican as the "Algiers Point Militia." Later other residents of the Point also began referring to themselves as the Algiers Point Militia, Vinnie said. There was no central organization; it was just a nickname for the Point residents who stayed and who were armed.

After getting the guns, Vinnie talked to Daryl D'Angelo, the woman with the Polimom blog, about gasoline for their generator. They used it sparingly, but its voracious appetite for gasoline meant they were running low. Daryl and her contacts came through, and Vinnie and Gareth went collecting gasoline from neighbors' homes.

After several days, some of the Point's evacuees asked Daryl if Vinnie could check on pets they had left behind. When they evacuated, most thought it would be for only a few days, so they put out food and water for three days or so. When they recognized they were unable to return, they began to worry.

That started a daily routine with Vinnie and Gareth feeding and watering cats, dogs, guinea pigs, goldfish, and even a parrot. The owner of the parrot warned that the bird was really mean, but Vinnie found it quite friendly. It would perch on his finger when he went to feed it. "It was a sweetheart of a bird." He fed it for about two weeks, but when the owner returned and he went back to visit, the parrot bit him.

"We had one person call us about a snake but we never found it."

During these gun and gas expeditions and pet-feeding runs, Vinnie rode with Gareth, while Gregg stayed home to look after Miss P. After a week, though, Gareth was called back to work by the ship company that employed him. Vinnie continued making the rounds on his bicycle.

Vinnie was surprised that most of the hundred-or-so residents who stayed on Algiers Point were single men who were renting their homes. "The men were all armed. They had shotguns."

The aftermath of the hurricane brought people in the neighborhood closer together. Vinnie got to know quite a few of these neighbors. When he was driving around collecting supplies from the houses, he would see the same people and stop to talk to them in a way he would not have had time to do under normal circumstances.

"There are individuals that I knew of, but never really associated with, but now they make an effort to say, 'Hello, how are you doing? What's going on?' Things like that."

Losing the air-conditioning made living very uncomfortable, Vinnie said. "It was ninety-five degrees at night, a hundred percent humidity, mosquitoes."

They couldn't keep the mosquitoes out of the house because they had to keep the windows open to provide some air circulation, and they had no window screens. Gareth dozed in the rocking chair on the balcony, but Vinnie has a bad back and had to sleep lying flat on the deck of the balcony on a couple of blankets. They kept about half-a-dozen guns each, ready-to-hand. Gareth would stay awake most of the night; Vinnie would wake up from time to time and make sure he was all right.

On Thursday, September 1, Daryl posted a report on her blog saying there had just been a shooting incident in the seven-hundred-block of Pelican Street, the same block as Fort Pelican. She wrote: "Everybody [the residents] were [sic] sitting outside on their porches, and three 'guys' came walking down the street with a gun. Somebody opened fire [no details], and a regular firefight started. They estimate that twenty-five shots were fired."

Usually about half-a-dozen local residents armed with shotguns stood around in the street at the intersection of Pelican and Vallette Streets, just west of Vinnie's house. On this day Vinnie thought there was only one man there when three young black guys approached the intersection.

"There were three young thugs, we call 'em, walking through our neighborhood, and they started removing tree branches, which we put across the street because we didn't want traffic coming through. I heard someone say: 'Don't do that.'

"They said: 'Well, what are you going to do about it?'

"The young thug pulled up his shirt and showed a revolver in his pants. Well, from there it was a gun battle. One of the young thugs got hit in the head, and he ran about a block down and supposedly died in the four-hundred block, the next block up. The other two ran right in front of my house. I was in the back of the house at this time, but my mom and Gregg and Gareth were on the front porch sitting in the rocking chairs, and the young man pointed the pistol at them but didn't fire. He ran down the street, and people ran after him shooting at him."

Vinnie estimated about fifteen shots were fired, but only the one thug was hit. The guy who was shot ran south. He collapsed and died on Vallette, at the corner of Alix Street.

The residents involved in the gunfight were not vigilantes, just honest people trying to defend their neighborhood, Vinnie said. Sometime after the shooting, police officers, some apparently from Texas, drove by and started asking questions about the incident and about who had guns. The guns Vinnie and Gareth had collected were lying on a bed in the second bedroom. They decided to hide them as a precaution.

About two days after Vinnie's van had been hijacked, he woke up about 2 A.M. in a panic. He realized that he had left two debit cards in the van. One was a personal debit card; the other was for his business account.

The day before the storm he was getting gasoline at a self-service station. The store was closed, but it was still dispensing gas to customers using credit or debit cards. A woman who was also trying to get gas asked him to pump $25-worth of gas into her vehicle on his card in exchange for $25 cash. Vinnie obliged. When he drove off he put his debit cards in the console between the front seats and forgot to return them to his wallet. "It was the first time I did that, and it'll be the last time."

It was a case of no good turn going unpunished.

He had been unable to get through to the police to report the robbery, and now it took him several days before he could get through to the card company to report the loss of the cards. One of the problems was that his telephone service was sporadic. Most of the time he could receive calls, but only occasionally could he call out.

Daryl recorded on her blog on Sunday, September 4, that Vinnie had been able to contact the card issuer that morning. She wrote: "Seems that credit card has been making charges all over Fort Bend County, Texas, the last few days. And guess where I'm writing from right now.....? Too funny."

Katy, where Daryl lives, is in Fort Bend County. Debit cards, which are what Vinnie lost, allow the possessor to pay for merchandize by taking money directly from a bank account. Use of a debit card requires a personal identification number or PIN. Vinnie had no idea how the robbers got these numbers. He couldn't even remember the PIN for his business card, so he had to use his personal card to pump gas for the woman. That was why he had taken both cards out of his wallet.

The card company stopped his personal card but apparently not his business card. By then the robbers had already used the card to pay for about a-thousand-dollars-worth of gas, fast food, and other merchandize. Finally, his local bank reopened and the manager, who was a good friend, called to tell him he had more problems. "They've drawn $20,000 out of your business account."

She said they had gone to Wal-Mart four or five times on the same day. They went to a Diamond Shamrock gas station repeatedly, and to McDonald's restaurants, Burlington Coat Factory, a beauty-supply house, and other retailers.

"It freaked me out. There was $21,000 out of my accounts gone."

It took the robbers a week to ten days to go through $21,000. The manager told him the bank would replace the money, but it took about six weeks before the bank credited his accounts, Vinnie said.

"I was willing to do anything I could. I even called the Fort Bend sheriff's office." That was the first night he knew his debit card was being used there. He gave them a description of the van and told them what had happened. They told him they could not do anything because he had not reported the van stolen to his local police department. He said he was in a disaster area, and there was no one to report the robbery to.

"They would not help me."

He said he was not worried about the van or the tools, because he had insurance to cover them. He was concerned that there were three criminals, two of them violent, who were roaming around Fort Bend County, and he didn't want anyone else to get hurt. They had gone to the same gas station several days in a row. All they had to do was look for a white van with a broken window in the back.

"They wouldn't do it. They said it was illegal."

He never got his van back. He got a used truck to replace the van, and about a month later he got a letter from the City of Houston saying his van had run up almost a thousand dollars in towing fees and storage charges. He called Houston and was told his van had been there forty-five days. He said he had been calling Houston and the Fort Bend sheriff's office. He assumes that his insurance company picked up the van. Apparently the bad guys were never caught.

"It's definitely changed my perception of how I look at young black men now. One day I was going up the road to Home Depot, and I was at a stop light right in front of the housing project here. I'm 99.9 percent sure that the young man who assaulted me was walking right in front of my van. I just froze. At one second I thought how I wanted to just ram him with my new truck. I thought, No, he might not be the right one."

He froze until the light changed and a woman behind him started blowing her horn for him to move on.

One couple who had stayed on the Point lived right behind Vinnie's and Gregg's house—between it and the river. Across the street from these neighbors was a barn where school buses were kept. The same young men who were looting in the neighborhood were stealing the buses at night, stealing the gasoline from them. One of them stole a bus, drove it to the projects, loaded it up with refugees, and drove it to Houston.

Vinnie's neighbor cut a gun port in the plywood covering the front of his house so he could see what was happening and, if necessary, shoot through the hole. About the fourth day after the storm, the man came over and, according to Vinnie, said, "I'd love to be able to stay and help you guys, but my wife is scared to death here. These people, these thugs, come closer and closer every night. We're the only ones in our street; we've got to go."

When the couple left, Vinnie worried that there was no one protecting the back of their house on the north side of Pelican Street. There were no residents between them and the river two blocks away. He decided they needed an escape route in case a gang tried to rush the house. He put one-half of an extension ladder against the seven-foot fence that surrounded their back yard. He put the other half of the ladder against the fence in a neighbor's back yard. They could escape by climbing up one ladder and down the other.

"Gregg is very meticulous with our home, and we have eight-foot shutters on our front porch that close three windows and our door. We had those open, and I just could not get over to Gregg that, 'Gregg we need to close those because those are protection.' Because anybody running up our porch has just got to run through that glass into our home. Once we put those ladders up, then he realized that we didn't have people behind us. He said, 'I guess you're right Vinnie.' So we closed those shutters up."

Vinnie figured they would have enough time to escape as any attackers were breaking through the shutters. He explained the escape route to the others, and they all went upstairs and made contingency plans for getting out. Miss P expressed doubt that she could make the climb.

"My mom, 75-years-old—she had never touched a gun in her life. And for the first time that night, I handed her a gun. I handed her a pistol." Vinnie told her she had to be able to protect herself.

"She slept at nighttime with her rosary in her hand and her .38 on her night stand."

Word got around the neighborhood about "Miss P, her rosary, and her .38."

That morning about 4:30 they were wakened by a popping sound like gunfire. Miss P and Gregg came running out from the bedrooms. They thought they were under attack. From the upstairs balconies on the sides of the house they looked north towards the river. They could see flames. At first they thought the bus barn was burning and perhaps the thugs were trying to burn them out.

Daryl D'Angelo in Katy said she got a call about 4:30, but she was in bed and did not get to the phone in time to answer. She saw it was Vinnie from the Caller ID. She repeatedly tried to call him back but could not get through. Her husband suggested she check the messages.

"I checked the messages, and it was Vinnie, and he was crying. 'There's been an explosion. We don't know what's happening. It's blowing up around us. God help us all.'" Now Daryl was really panicked.

Back at Fort Pelican, Miss P thought she heard attackers coming up the ladders they had placed against the fence. But she was mistaken. They opened the shutters and looked out the back windows that faced north. They realized the fire they were seeing was a warehouse on the East Bank that had exploded and was on fire. It contained something very flammable—chemicals or petroleum. "It was humungous. That thing burned for three or four days," Vinnie said.

That night Vinnie had trouble getting back to sleep. He was faced by a troubling question: what would he do if a gang of thugs rushed the house?

"The most significant part about that night was a lesson for me. Because after we had settled back down to sleep, it became a very hard time. I realized that if my mom can't shoot somebody attacking her, and there's just too many that rush us, I cannot let my mom. . . ." Vinnie was thinking the unthinkable: if there were too many attackers, he was going to have to kill his mother rather than let her fall into the hands of a gang of thugs.

He choked on the thought, then continued. "And the thought that you had to take your mother's life to save her, that has haunted me since that day. And I vowed that my mom would never stay with us for another storm. We're going to have her evacuated."

"Then laying on the balcony that morning, thinking about it, just looking up at the stars—you really couldn't see much other than a few stars—I got thinking: we're here fighting the storm, fighting for our home, fighting for our lives, for what? The city is in ruins. This city will never be the same. And it isn't. It completely changed my thought about gun control, and I've got to get a gun and a license to carry one."

Later that morning, Vinnie talked to Gareth about what was bothering him. "I told him what I was going through because he noticed something had changed me that night. I said, 'For the first time, I really began thinking about what if that many came, what would I have to do?'

"He said, 'Well, what were you thinking?'

"I said, 'My mom would go first, then Gregg, and then you Gareth.'

"He said, 'You'd make me suffer that long, eh?'"

Gareth tried to lighten the mood, but for Vinnie, his decision weighed heavily on him. It was a real-life version of an incident in the classic Western film *Stagecoach*, where a former Southern gentleman and gambler is killed, just as he is about to put his last bullet into the head of an Army officer's wife rather than let her fall alive into the hands of the Apaches.

At night the seven-hundred block of Pelican Street was dark except for the three gas lamps on Vinnie's and Gregg's porch. The occupants of Fort Pelican stood guard on the balcony above the lights and so were effectively hidden from anyone on the street.

Just west of the house a huge Arizona ash tree had fallen across the street blocking it to vehicle traffic. However, there was one spot where people could get through the tree, even though a pedestrian had to stoop to do it. So they got a bunch of empty soft-drink cans somebody had saved for recycling and laid them across the street where the gap was. Anybody trying to go through there at night would stumble on the cans, and the noise would provide the watchers with a warning.

Daryl D'Angelo reported on Saturday, September 3, on her Polimom blog that overnight the people on Pelican Street heard someone prowling around in their block.

"They know because they've scattered some aluminum cans about as an alert system," she wrote.

Vinnie said they heard the crash as someone kicked the cans. "Who is it?" he called out from the balcony.

Nobody replied.

"I'm going to count to three and after three, I'm just going to fire," he warned. He counted to three. When he shouted "three," somebody cried, "Don't, don't, don't shoot." This was followed by the sound of running footsteps.

They didn't think the cans would work as well after word got around, so they took other precautions. They took the headlights from a car that had been wrecked by a falling tree. Vinnie put the headlights on his upstairs balcony, one pointing left and one pointing right towards the street. He hooked them up with a battery he had in his shop. When he heard the cans rattling or any other noise from the street, he could touch the headlight wires to the battery and light up the street. "Those lights would blind anybody with the high-beam lights on."

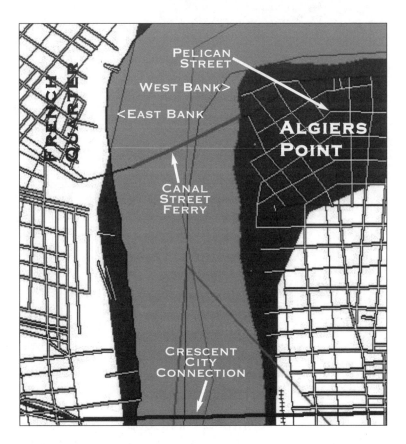

Some days after the storm the people at Fort Pelican had a visit from the head of the local neighborhood watch, who is also an attorney. He told Vinnie that police on the Crescent City Connection bridge that joins the West Bank to the East Bank had stopped him, frisked him, and taken a handgun he had borrowed for protection.

The West Bank end of the bridge is in Jefferson Parish, and apparently the sheriff had stationed officers on the ramps leading from the bridge to stop people evacuating from the East Bank. It was these officers that had taken the lawyer's gun. He was distraught at having his only means of protection confiscated, so Vinnie gave him one of the revolvers he had collected.

"That's when we really became fearful, because he heard that the military here and the Texas rangers were knocking on people's doors and were taking their guns away—going into people's homes and taking their guns away," Vinnie said

A spokeswoman for the Texas Department of Public Safety said no Texas rangers were in Louisiana in an official capacity after Hurricane Katrina.

The residents of Fort Pelican were concerned when they heard about the confiscations. They had been hearing frequent gunfire each night since the storm, and it seemed to be getting closer and closer to Algiers Point. "We thought, God, what do we do? It was unbelievable."

These shots were coming from the West Bank. They sounded about ten blocks away but always getting closer. More and more residents left, afraid for their lives.

They were getting their information about what was happening in the city from the radio, later a television, word-of-mouth, and by telephone. They heard that they couldn't trust the police because thugs had stolen police cars. They also heard that a policeman was shot in the head about a mile from Pelican Street when he tried to stop looting. He survived.

"So then you hear that story; then you hear that the police that are here are taking away guns; and the ones that are driving police cars may not actually be police; and then you've got the story of the National Guard going around knocking on doors and telling people they can't have guns and now you have to evacuate. You have to leave the city; the city's dead."

All these rumors and reports created extensive anxiety and paranoia. It was like a badly kept bookstore: the fact and the fiction were all mixed together, and people didn't know what to believe.

Nobody ever did disarm the residents of Pelican Street, their house was not attacked, and they were not forced to evacuate.

About ten days after the hurricane the National Guard arrived and things began to return to normal. About 11:30 at night they heard a big helicopter getting louder and louder, nearer and nearer. "It looked like it was about twenty feet above our house, flying up and down the street ve ry slowly, with these big huge spotlights and like they were checking every block."

About ten minutes later they heard heavy vehicles arriving, just rolling over tree branches. They sounded like tanks, but they were two military transport vehicles.

"We felt a little more relief then."

The siege of Algiers Point was over.

Gareth, Miss P, Vinnie, and Gregg at Fort Pelican.

Reflections

When somebody like Vinnie Pervel, who yesterday didn't like guns and supported gun control, is asked today what he needs and he answers, "guns," it doesn't take an MBA to figure that something major has happened.

"I guess the biggest lesson I've learned is the hurricane is not the one that is going to do damage. It's the thugs in the neighborhood who would do more damage. I can't put up any more plywood around my windows; I can't close any more shutters than I already have; but one thing I will do is make sure I have more protection, armor-wise. I'll have my gun this year. Gregg bought me for Christmas night-vision goggles to see at night-time. Gareth has already bought his shotgun. I'm going to get my gun."

He also plans to get a piece of sheet steel to put across the front of the balcony for cover. At present there are only wooden spindles to protect anyone on the second-floor balcony.

What would have happened if the residents of Fort Pelican had not been armed? "I think we could've easily been taken over. I think that the word got out that the people in Algiers Point were protecting themselves and they had their own little militia. Like we were called the Algiers Point Militia. People from the other side of the tracks, more or less, the low-income neighborhood, they classified us as the Algiers Point Militia."

Only a couple of houses on the Point were looted, Vinnie said, and he credited word of their unofficial militia acting to deter would-be looters. Fortunately, none of the residents of Fort Pelican had to shoot a gun. Possession of the guns was enough to deter violence.

Vinnie is no longer afraid of guns. He had forty in the house, and he looked on them as lifesavers, not liabilities. What did scare him was the threat that government minions might confiscate his guns.

Which did he fear more, the looters or the possibility of government seizure of the guns? "It would have to be the guns confiscated, because without the guns, I couldn't protect my home."

He is now convinced that every law-abiding citizen should have the option of having and carrying a gun for protection. He intends to buy a gun, get training in its use, and get a concealed-carry license.

Vinnie's mother, Miss P, is also interested in learning to shoot and defend herself, he said.

In February 2005 Fox News ran a story about how gun sales in New Orleans were still way ahead of normal. Along with the rest of the people of New Orleans, the residents of Algiers Point have become more interested in owning and using guns for protection. Last March Vinnie organized a meeting of the neighborhood association with an elderly lady who owns a gun shop in Gretna, a small city just south of Algiers.

"She's 75-years-old, but she's going to come and talk to us about guns, and the membership is all excited. They want to hear what she's got to say."

He is also hoping that an NRA vice president will be coming down to talk to them about the Second Amendment and the right to carry a gun.

Anarchy and the law of survival take over when law and order break down, whether it is caused by a terrorist attack or a natural disaster like Hurricane Katrina. The people who are most likely to survive are those who can defend themselves. The best tools for average citizens to defend themselves with are firearms.

As I pointed out in my earlier book, *The Concealed Handgun Manual*, the federal government is remiss in its advice to ordinary citizens when it omits any mention of firearms as essential supplies for terror attacks. Duct tape just isn't going to cut it. I suspect there are two reasons the federal bureaucrats made such an omission. They don't want to stir up the anti-self-defense crowd, and they don't want to admit that there will be times when law and order will break down. They want the average citizen to believe that the government will protect them—this, even in the face of massive evidence to the contrary.

Law enforcement officers confiscating lawfully owned firearms from New Orleans residents in the aftermath of Hurricane Katrina prompted pro-gun-rights organizations to ensure such a thing never happens again. Several bills are wending their ways through state legislatures to prevent gun confiscation from law-abiding citizens in times of emergency. During the spring of 2006, NRA Executive Vice President Wayne LaPierre gave speeches to groups across the country promoting the battle cry, "Remember New Orleans."

In February LaPierre told the Conservative Political Action Conference in Washington, D.C., "Never again can the anti-gunners claim that honest citizens don't need firearms because the police or the government will be there to protect you. We're gonna' make sure that New Orleans sets the anti-gunners back twenty-five years. And maybe we'll make it a new slogan.

"Why do you need to own a gun? Remember New Orleans.

"Aren't you just being paranoid and afraid? Remember New Orleans.

"Why does anyone need right to carry? Remember New Orleans.

"Why does anyone need a high-capacity magazine? Remember New Orleans.

"What's wrong with a fifteen-day waiting period? Remember New Orleans.

"What makes you think our government would ever confiscate your guns? Remember New Orleans.

"Is the Second Amendment really relevant in the twenty-first century? Remember New Orleans. And never, never, never forget."

Vinnie Pervel has rejoined the NRA, this time knowing full well what it stands for.

Chapter 2

Learning Curve:
Ray Messick

They say the difference between a liberal and a conservative is one mugging. The implication is that there is nothing quite like facing the wrong end of a gun held by a bad guy to get a person's mind focused on self-defense. And self-defense—taking responsibility for your own safety—tends to be something that conservatives are more likely than liberals to embrace in this era of zero tolerance and political correctness.

Liberals have vilified guns, so shooting teams are disappearing from high schools and students get suspended for drawing pictures of guns. While not without exceptions, liberals tend to abhor guns and look to the government for their safety, while conservatives view their safety as a personal responsibility.

However, a person does not have to be a liberal to learn from experience. In October 1991 Suzanna Gratia saw her parents, along with many others, gunned down in a Luby's cafeteria in Killeen, Texas. Her gun was out-of-reach in her car, because Texas did not have a concealed-carry law. As a result, Suzanna Gratia, now Gratia-Hupp, became one of the best witnesses in state legislatures across the country for promoting concealed-carry laws. These laws, which have swept the states like wildfire in the last twenty years, allow ordinary citizens to carry handguns concealed in public for self-defense.

There is no more effective tool for self-defense than a gun. Professor John Lott of the American Enterprise Institute states in his excellent book, *The Bias Against Guns*, that people who defend themselves against a criminal threat or attack are much more likely to survive unscathed than are those who passively submit or those who fight back without a gun. One survey he conducted found that 30 percent of those who were threatened with violence, but did not have a gun, were injured in the incident. None of those who resisted with a gun were harmed.

However, carrying a gun is only part of the preparation for self-defense. An equally important part is always being aware of what is going on around you. Because people in the United States are relatively safe from criminal threat or attack, they are lulled into a false sense of security. When they are attacked, they are surprised. They miss all the warning signs leading up to the attack. Carrying a gun for protection requires a permanent state of alertness. It is essential to keep your eyes and ears open and to interpret what you see and hear.

If, for example, you see several people hanging around your car in a parking lot, instead of blundering up to them, it might be better to wait until they have moved on. Above all, trust your instincts. We still have instincts that warn us of danger. They are not as well honed as they were when human life was short and violent, but they are still there.

While it took Raymond Messick of Atlanta two experiences at the wrong end of a gun to get the message, he did learn the lessons.

Ray Messick

In 1996 Ray Messick went to the Smith & Wesson Academy to take a three-day course in self-defense with a handgun, entitled "Dynamics of Personal Protection." On the first day of class the two instructors asked if anyone had ever been in a deadly-force incident. Ray was the only one who raised his hand.

At that point in his life—he was 42—he had been involved in three episodes of criminal activity more intimately than he would have liked. In the first incident, he was an unarmed witness who could easily have become a victim in the armed robbery of a store. The second time, he was an unarmed employee of a store that was also robbed at gunpoint. But he learned from his experiences. He had a gun on the third occasion, preventing a robbery or carjacking on the highway. This may even have saved his life.

After Ray told the class what had happened during the three incidents, there was a serious discussion of each. The instructors laughed and said, "You know Ray, we don't want to go anywhere with you. Bad things happen to you. We don't even want to go to lunch with you," Messick recalled.

The Stereo Village Holdup

The first incident happened just before Christmas in 1984. Ray walked into an electronics store in Atlanta called Stereo Village. He wanted to buy a Technics record turntable as a Christmas present for his parents.

It was right at 9 P.M.—closing time. He had picked out the turntable he wanted and was standing at the counter waiting to have the sale rung up. Ray was looking at the literature about the turntable, not paying particular attention to what was going on around him.

"It was just me and a 19-year-old kid working at Christmas time," Ray recalled. "So, this young black male walked in with a green Army jacket on and pulled a .357 out of his jacket. He put the end of the barrel right on the kid's chest and said: 'Gimme the cash.'"

The counter was a rectangular glass display case; the robber was standing in the center of the long side. Messick was about six feet away at the end of the counter on the short side.

"So I'm standing there thinking: Okay, robbery in progress. I've got no gun. I'm standing in front of a glass display case. If I duck down I can still be seen, and obviously shot, through the glass. There's nowhere to go. I've got nothing I can do, so I'm just going to read my literature and ignore this guy and not give him any reason to shoot me. And maybe I'll scrape through this."

Acting as though the robber had asked politely for change for a twenty, Ray pretended to read the turntable literature. In his peripheral vision he saw the clerk pull the drawer from the cash register and put it on the counter in front of the robber. The holdup man flipped up the clips holding the bills and scooped out the greenbacks. He stuffed the money into his pockets, paused, and for a couple of long seconds he looked back and forth at Ray and the clerk.

"He looked at both of us like he was trying to decide whether he was going to shoot us or not, because we were the only two standing there and the only two who could identify him," Ray recalled.

The robber turned and ran out of the front door.

Immediately the clerk started yelling for the manager, who appeared from the back of the store. "He was obviously very angry. I said, 'Well, I still want my turntable.' And the manager said, 'Get the hell out of my store.' He threw me out."

The police arrived as Ray was leaving the store, but he didn't stop to talk to them.

"I made a mental note that night never to shop at closing [time] again," he said.

Ray called the manager the next day and said he still wanted the turntable. Stereo Village was the only place he could find the particular model he wanted in stock.

He got his turntable. And the manager gave him a record cleaning kit and an extra bottle of record cleaner as compensation for being thrown out the night before.

In those days Ray had no interest in guns or self-defense. "I was young and out of college, and I was interested in stereos and women," he said.

The Toys"R"Us Robbery

The next incident happened at a Toys"R"Us store where Ray was working part time. The store was on Cobb Parkway, in Akers Mill Square, a big retail area on the northwest side of Atlanta. It was July 1990 and his situation had changed. He was married and living with his wife in an apartment complex nearby. He had completed his BBA degree in management and finance and was now taking additional courses in commercial insurance underwriting. He was more interested in guns and had been reading gun magazines occasionally, though he did not subscribe to any. He did not own a gun at the time.

Ray was in Toys"R"Us at the back of the store in the stockroom doing inventory reports on damaged merchandise. They were called RTV reports for "Return To Vendor." The merchandise had to be accounted for and then packed in boxes, prior to being sent back to the warehouse. He was working on a computer, generating these reports and packing the damaged items in boxes. The time was about 9 P.M.

"I did everything wrong that night. I did all the things that the [gun] magazines said that I would do. I ignored all the warning signs," Ray recalled.

The first indication that anything was wrong was when the manager, Ray Carper, came on the intercom and said that whoever took the phone cords off the phones should put them back immediately.

Someone had gone around the store to every telephone and removed the cords that run from base to handset. Although the handsets were still in place, the telephones were useless. Many were wall phones located just inside the doorways between the sales floor and the stockroom area.

The manager emphasized that it was not funny and said no one was going home until all the cords had been replaced. Carper obviously thought an employee had removed the cords as a joke. They hadn't.

Ray noted the manager's announcement, but took no action. "I thought it was just one of the employees pulling a prank," he said.

He finished his reports and, carrying the printouts in both hands, started walking down a side aisle of the store toward the front. He noticed empty places on the shelves that needed filling with merchandise and intended to mention the gaps to a floor manager.

The second thing he heard that should have warned him something was wrong was the clatter of change dropping on the floor. It sounded like someone had hit the jackpot on a slot machine—several times. "I thought, somebody's really being sloppy. They're going to get in trouble for doing all of that. But alarm bells should have been going off in my head."

It was a big store with employees straightening up the shelves in the many aisles after closing. They were pulling the toys to the front of the shelves, stacking boxes, and restocking. The employees were working quietly as usual without talking. The only sound was the music coming over the intercom.

Ray, his hands still full, reached the end of the aisle on the extreme left side of the store, as viewed from the front. He turned the corner and walked into the area between the aisles and the line of cash registers.

He saw an older employee lying on the floor near the first cash register. His face was turned away from Ray, and his head was against the base of an endcap, where merchandise is featured on the end of an aisle.

Ray's immediate reaction was that the guy had suffered a heart attack, had fallen down, and hit his head. It was quite a distance from where he was at the side of the store to where the employee was lying in front of the customer service area.

"I was quickly walking over to him to see what was wrong. Next to the fifth cash register this guy pops up like a jack-in-the-box, points a 9 mm pistol at me, and yells: 'Get on the floor!'"

The man was wearing a light blue jump suit, a black ski mask, and black leather gloves. The skin around the man's eyes and on his neck was visible, so Ray saw that the man was black. But what captured his attention was the gun.

"I experienced visual exclusion. It's like I turned a zoom lens on in my mind, and I just zoomed all the way. The end of that barrel looked as big as the end of a roll of paper towels."

Ray dropped the reports and got down on the floor. The robber walked up and stood over him.

"I thought he was going to blow my head off right there. So, I'm on the floor and looking at this piece of floor tile, a one-square-foot piece of floor tile, and I'm looking at it, and it's dirty. And I'm lying there thinking that this one square of dirty floor tile is the last thing I'm ever going to see. I'll never see my wife, my family, and my friends again. I was lying there literally waiting for the bullet."

After what seemed like three days, the robber stepped away from Messick and started walking over to the front of the store where the two safes were located. Using his feet and pivoting on his chest, Ray turned himself about ninety degrees, so he was facing the front of the store and could see what was happening. That was when he saw the second robber, dressed like the first in a similar light-blue jump suit and wearing a black ski mask and gloves.

"I saw that he had a revolver and that the hammer was back. I thought, these guys are either really serious or they're really stupid. One or the other, but somebody's going to get hurt."

The robbers had already roughed up the manager and sprayed him with Mace until he had opened the safes. Messick was still lying out in the open in the main aisle where the cash registers were located, so the robbers obviously thought he was under control and would not cause any problems.

"Both safes were open, and no alarms were going off. I didn't know if there was a silent alarm or if it had been activated. I quickly decided that alarm systems were expensive—and that Toys"R"Us probably had not spent the money to buy one. I knew that I had to do something, so I got this mental picture of one of those red fire-alarm pulls that you see on the wall of a building."

As a part-timer Ray had little idea of the store's security systems. He intended to set off the fire alarm, but couldn't remember the location of the alarm pulls. He decided to find a floor manager who would know about the alarm system. He found out later that there were no fire-alarm pulls—only a heat-sensitive sprinkler system.

He jumped to his feet and sprinted all the way to the back of the store, looking for a floor manager he had seen a few minutes before, near the diapers. He couldn't find her, so he ran back inside the stockroom. He ran down the aisle inside the stockroom, checking all the wall phones to see if there was one with its cord still in place. But the robbers had been thorough—all the cords had been taken.

Ray decided to open a couple of the doors that led from the stockroom to the outside of the building. These doors had local alarms that would ring and might scare off the robbers. He escaped out of the second door he opened, because he heard the robbers yelling something to each other, and then he heard someone running down the aisle. He wasn't going to wait and find out if it was an employee or one of the robbers. He left the store with the alarms ringing. He found out later that the robbers had heard the alarms, and they left the store a few minutes later—but they already had all the money.

"As I left the store I knew that all of the other stores were closed; I didn't have a cell phone; and I didn't know where the nearest pay phone was located."

Ray waited outside the store until the police arrived. By the time they arrived, the robbers had escaped. They had a driver in a getaway car parked near a little-used exit on the side of the store. They escaped with between $40,000 and $50,000, Ray recalled.

The robbery had been well-planned and carried out professionally. The two robbers had come in wearing ordinary clothes, carrying their jump suits, ski masks, and gloves in small bags. They changed in the stockroom where there were many aisles with floor-to-ceiling racks of merchandise, which provided plenty of places to hide. One employee saw one of the robbers in the stockroom and told him to get out, but the robber just moved to another part of the stockroom. The employee did not report this to a manager because customers walked into the stockrooms every day, Ray said.

The Toys"R"Us store was an easy target. The store managers had never heard of a Toys"R"Us store being robbed. The worst that had happened up to that time was that a few female customers had had their purses snatched in the parking lot, Messick said.

When the police arrived Ray went back into the store and called his wife, Susan. He told her they had been "held up" and that he wouldn't be home until later. She misinterpreted his statement, thinking that he was just delayed at work and made a comment to that effect.

Ray snapped at her: "No, we've been held up, do you understand? We've been robbed."

Susan became upset, but Ray told her the police were there; he was uninjured and would be home eventually.

He snapped at her because, although the danger was past, he was experiencing a reaction to the adrenaline still in his system. "It's a delayed reaction. You're presented with a problem, and you have to decide what you can do—to see if there's a way out of it. I was surprised, after thinking about everything, how little fear I felt while it was going on, simply because I was busy doing other things, trying to figure a way out of the situation."

Messick told a uniformed officer what had happened, and then he wrote a statement describing his view of the incident. "I handed him my written statement, and I was standing about three feet away from him. I looked down at his gun, and I looked him straight in the eye and said, 'If I'd had that gun, I would have killed them all.'

"The cop looked at me, and he took a step back, and he put his hand on his gun. He obviously thought I was going to freak out and try to grab the gun away from him. It was the way I said it that scared the crap out of him. In retrospect, probably not a wise thing to say, but I was so angry. I've never been that angry in my life."

Ray was still seething when he returned home. He didn't go to bed, but spent the whole night reading his gun magazines, trying to calm down and trying to determine what he should have done differently. The next day Ray went to work one hour early. He walked around Akers Mill Square until he found the pay phone nearest to Toys"R"Us store. "The phone was on the other side of the big parking lot, in front of the movie theater. I wanted to make sure that I knew where to go if I needed to call for help again."

The following week he bought a stainless SIG Sauer P230 pistol in .380 caliber. The gun was smaller and not as powerful as a 9 mm, but it would not recoil as much and was easy to carry in a holster or a purse. He wanted his wife to be able to shoot it.

"I said, the next time I will not be caught with nothing."

Attempted Carjacking

The next time, he wasn't. It happened on Sunday, July 31, 1994. Ray and his wife, Susan, were moving back to Atlanta from Charlotte, North Carolina. Ten months before, Susan had been transferred temporarily to her company's office in Charlotte. Her job there had been completed, and Ray was moving their belongings back to Atlanta. He had already taken several loads towing a U-Haul trailer. He was taking the last load of a few remaining items back to Atlanta without the trailer. The trunk was full, and the back seat was piled high with boxes, so he couldn't see out of the rear window.

His Smith & Wesson Model 3953 was tucked behind a box on the passenger seat. It was fully loaded and easily accessible. The handgun was a semi-automatic pistol in 9 mm caliber. It was a compact model with eight rounds in the magazine and one in the chamber. He had bought the gun about two years after buying the SIG P230, because he wanted a gun with more stopping power. He also didn't like the heavy trigger pull needed to fire the first shot of the SIG P230. It contrasted with the much lighter pull required to fire subsequent shots. The Smith & Wesson had the heavier, long pull for all shots, not just the first one. Ray had replaced the recoil spring and mainspring with Wolff-brand springs. Using a trigger-pull gauge, he had trimmed the new mainspring until the trigger-pull weight was eight pounds. He had installed a set of Hogue rubber grips and had fired two hundred rounds at the range with no misfires. Trimming the mainspring is not recommended unless you know what you are doing, because it may lighten the hammer blow to the extent that the gun will not fire every time.

Ray was driving his Oldsmobile Cutlass Ciera 3.8L southwest on Interstate 85 approaching Spartanburg, South Carolina. He was focused on reaching a Wendy's restaurant about halfway between Charlotte and Atlanta. He and his wife had stopped there on previous trips. It was about 2 P.M., a beautiful day with no clouds in a bright blue sky, and there was very little traffic. The temperature was about ninety degrees, so he had the windows rolled up and the air-conditioning on. The interstate had two lanes in each direction, and Ray was traveling at about seventy miles an hour in the right lane.

"Because I could not see out of the back window, I wasn't really paying attention to traffic behind me like I usually would have," he said.

So he was surprised when suddenly a canary yellow Oldsmobile '98, containing three black men, pulled alongside him. The car was an old four-door sedan, bigger and more powerful than his Ciera. Two of the men, who appeared to be in their mid-to-late twenties, were in the front and one in the back. All their windows were rolled down.

Instead of passing him, the car stayed beside him, while its occupants looked over his car. They could see the boxes piled to the roof in the back seat. "So they were pacing me, looking me over, looking at all the stuff in the car, and making a decision about what they were going to do."

Suddenly, the driver swerved the big car into Ray's lane to cut him off and slowed down trying to force him to stop. Ray swerved onto the shoulder of the highway and floored the accelerator. The Ciera surged past the bigger car, swerved back into the right-hand lane, and went speeding down the highway. The speedometer dial went up only to eighty-five miles per hour, but Ray figured he must have been going at least a hundred. The accelerator was floored, and the transmission had shifted into fourth gear. The Olds '98 careered after him, but stayed behind him.

Ray saw an exit sign for State Highway 9 and took it at speed. At the end of the exit ramp was a stop sign where the highway crossed over the interstate. Ray intended to shoot through the stop sign, turn onto the highway, and find a store or a restaurant—anywhere there were other people, which would help to discourage an attack. But there was considerable traffic, and he could not turn onto Highway 9.

"There were three of them and only one of me. So I needed to take some specific action to let them know that this was not going to be easy if they were going to proceed." He stomped on the brakes and screamed to a stop in the left-hand lane. He grabbed his gun, got out of the car, and took up a kneeling position behind the driver's-side front wheel. This put the engine block between him and the guys in the yellow car.

"I did not point the pistol at them. The thought came to mind: I really want them to see that I have a gun. Part of the problem is that when you actually have a gun pointed at you, all you can see is the muzzle. I wanted these people to see that I was armed before they got out of their car and started toward me. So I held the pistol in front of me at chest level, pointing it to my left, so that they could see the full profile of the pistol and it would be unmistakable."

The yellow Olds '98 pulled alongside Ray's car. The driver was leaning out of the window.

"He looked like a fairly normal guy. He didn't have long hair, no dreadlocks, and no afro." He was wearing a blue shirt and was holding the wheel in his left hand with his left elbow on the windowsill. Police are taught, in a stress situation, to watch the hands. Hand movement is almost always the start of aggressive action. Ray could not see the driver's right hand, and that concerned him. Was he holding a gun or not? Messick was aware of the two passengers, but his focus was on the driver.

The big car had slowed right down when the driver saw Ray's gun. He said the driver's jaw dropped, and the expression on his face was a mixture of frustration and anger, as though Ray had spoiled his fun. "His expression was absolutely pure predator."

The Olds '98 didn't stop but sped up a little, cruising past a yield sign, and turning north on Highway 9. Ray watched it until it was obvious that it was not going to turn around and come after him again. A little shaken, he got back in his car, crossed the highway reaching the on ramp, and drove back onto Interstate 85.

When Ray Messick got out of his car left of the stop sign, the yellow Olds '98 turned right.

"The only thing that really surprised me about the whole incident was the fact that the guy didn't floor the gas pedal and get out of there. In retrospect, the only thing I can think of is: I wasn't pointing the gun at him; I was just profiling it, and so he just cruised on through. I got the distinct impression that these guys really were not afraid of guns, and they weren't afraid of me. I had simply deselected myself from being robbed that day."

Ray did not experience the anger he had during the Toys"R"Us robbery. He had a gun, so he felt more in control of the situation. It wasn't the first time he had been in a dangerous situation, and he saw no evidence that any one of the three was armed. He felt that he had been perceived as a target of opportunity for the men.

He was still hungry, so he pulled off at the exit leading to the Wendy's restaurant that he was looking for, when the yellow Olds first tried to run him off the road. He didn't have a cell phone at the time, so he called his wife collect from a pay phone at the restaurant.

When Susan picked up the phone in Atlanta, she asked him if he was all right—several times, quickly. He said he was fine; told her he was at the Wendy's and would be home in a couple of hours. He did not tell her what had happened, because he didn't want to worry her.

Whenever Ray takes off on any long trips, Susan says a little prayer for him that everything will be fine on his trip. She had said the prayer when he left to drive to Charlotte to collect the last of their belongings. On that afternoon, she felt he needed another prayer.

"I just had this thought pop into my head that I needed to say a prayer for him. And I thought it was kind of unusual, because I had already done that. And so I said a prayer that everything would be all right and that he would come home safely. I didn't think about it until ten minutes later when he called me. And that's when I thought, something must be wrong; maybe that's why I said a prayer; now he's calling me. And it turned out that's exactly what happened. The time that I was praying was during the time that he was being chased."

Reflections

Like the majority of people who defend themselves with guns but don't fire a shot, Ray did not report the attempted carjacking to the police. He had solved the problem and, as he put it, didn't want to get into playing twenty questions with the police. In many cases, law-abiding citizens have been charged with infractions of the law after they have pulled a gun in self-defense, because they didn't know the laws of the state where it happened.

"You never know what kind of reception you're going to have," Ray said.

He also mentioned that the experts writing in gun magazines advised against talking to police about the details of an incident until after a cooling-off period and getting advice from an attorney. The lawyer should be present during the police questioning.

Messick referred to the incident as an attempted carjacking, though it is impossible to know what the trio intended. The most likely scenario is that one of the three would have driven the Ciera to another location where they could unload it at their leisure, leaving Ray, at best stranded, at worst murdered, on side of the interstate.

Was there anything Ray would have done differently during the attempted carjacking? "No, I just had the idea that I had to make a quick move and demonstrate action quickly," he said. "I took a defensive position behind cover and did not over-react. The articles in the gun magazines and the books that I had read during the eight years before this incident gave me the basic knowledge that I needed to manage the situation."

After the attempted carjacking incident was thoroughly discussed in the classroom during the "Dynamics of Personal Protection" course at the Smith & Wesson Academy, Ray said, "The instructors said that I did everything reasonably well. There was some discussion about whether or not I should have stopped on the side of the interstate, instead of taking the next exit, which turned out to be somewhat more isolated. The other side of that discussion said that the idea of moving off the interstate to find a more public place was good strategy. The instructors also asked me where I got the idea to profile my pistol so that it could be seen at a greater distance. I told them that I just made it up at that moment, and that I knew it would take only half a second more to aim and fire my pistol from that position. The instructors were satisfied with my answers."

Ray has maintained his interest in firearms and self-defense. Typically, he carries a Kahr P9 Covert in a Mitch Rosen holster. The P9 Covert is a 9 mm semi-automatic pistol with a polymer frame. He has equipped it with XS 24/7 Big Dot Tritium sights, which are easier to see. He also carries three spare magazines in a small camera bag that fits on his belt next to his cell phone. He favors Glaser Silver safety rounds, which are designed not to over-penetrate. He has a Georgia concealed-handgun permit and carries his gun most of the time.

Chapter 3

Her Home Is Her Castle: Deanna Eggleston

An Englishman's home used to be his castle. He could defend it with deadly force against criminal intruders, and he possessed the arms that were the most effective tools to accomplish this. In the late 1700s the great British jurist William Blackstone identified the possession of arms as a fundamental right of Englishmen. Since 1920 however, successive governments have systematically eroded this right. At the beginning of the twenty-first century, it is virtually against the law in Britain to use force, let alone deadly force, to protect one's person or property, and the government has confiscated most privately owned firearms, which are the most effective means of self-defense.

For decades British governments have not considered self-defense to be a legitimate reason for possessing a firearm. As a result violent crime in England has surpassed that in the United States. According to author Joyce Lee Malcolm, in her excellent book *Guns & Violence: The English Experience*, almost half of all burglaries in Britain take place when a resident is home. In the United States it is only 13 percent. The obvious conclusion, supported by research, is that criminals in the U.S. are afraid of confronting an armed homeowner. In Britain burglars do not care because they are confident they will meet no resistance.

Fortunately, in most of the U.S., an American's home is still her castle, and she is as likely as not to have a firearm in it to protect herself. Nevertheless, the majority of people who defend themselves with guns in the U.S. never fire a shot. Production of the gun is usually enough to remind the bad guy, and it usually is a guy, that he has urgent business in the next county.

Gary Kleck, a criminology professor at Florida State University, has conducted extensive research on the defensive use of guns in the United States. He estimates ordinary citizens use guns about 2.5 million times a year to defend themselves or others against criminal threat or attack. More than two-thirds of these cases involve use of a handgun. In the book *Armed: New Perspectives on Gun Control*, which he co-authored with Don Kates, Kleck states: "Only a tiny fraction of criminal gun assaults involve anyone actually being wounded, even non-fatally, and the same is true of defensive gun uses. Neither victim nor offender is hurt in the vast majority of cases."

The Incident

After I pressed the bell beside the front door of Deanna Eggleston's smart brick home in a residential subdivision of Arlington, Texas, there was a long pause. I did not hear the ring of the bell inside the house. Initially I heard no noise at all. I was beginning to wonder whether the bell worked. Then I heard the noise of some movement inside the house and a female voice, but I could not hear what she said. There was a very long pause while Deanna checked me out through the peephole in the door. Eventually, the door opened a little, and an anxious face appeared.

"Chris?" Deanna asked tentatively. Even though she was expecting me, Deanna was leery about answering the door in the middle of the day, because that was where it all started thirteen days before.

She was supposed to be out of town on July 23, 2003. If her 6-year-old son, Austin, had made it to the state T-ball tournament, she would have been at the championship game. T-ball is a baseball-like game for young children. When she wasn't supervising Austin, she worked part-time as a reservations agent for American Airlines at Dallas/Fort Worth International Airport.

That July morning Deanna was home alone. She was asleep after taking medication for a migraine headache. She awoke shortly before 11 A.M. to the noise of someone at her front door.

"Somebody came banging on the door and ringing the doorbell, just constantly, like they wanted me to get out of bed. And so finally I got up," she said.

Wearing her pajamas, she padded quietly to the front door, where she looked through the peephole. She noticed the man at the door was wearing a blue shirt and had a white rag in his hand.

"It was a black guy. I didn't recognize him, so I just thought, I'm just going to ignore him, forget it," she said.

She went back to her bedroom at the back of the two-story house and got back into bed. A few moments later Deanna heard the gate leading to the backyard open. The gate was at the side of the house right next to the bedroom. It was a noisy gate to open and close.

"About that time, I realized something's wrong," she said. She got back up, picked up her cordless phone, and dialed 9-1-1.

Operator: "Arlington nine-one-one."

Arlington, Texas, is a bedroom community of about 350,000 residents located between Dallas to the east and Fort Worth to the west. It is home to the Texas Rangers baseball team and Six Flags Over Texas amusement park. It has a police department of about five hundred officers and a relatively low crime rate. In 2003 the police department reported nine homicides and 3,606 burglaries. Like most residential cities, Arlington has a much lower crime rate than its larger neighbors.

Deanna Eggleston, 33, and her husband, Lee, have lived in their house for seven years. Lee works for a food company located about twenty minutes' drive away. When she first started dating Lee, Deanna hated guns because she was afraid of them. After he had been shooting with friends, Lee would clean his gun. She would tell him to keep it away from her. "I was freaked out by it," she said. "I wasn't ever anti-gun *per se*, like people shouldn't have them in their house; I was just so afraid of them that I didn't want to have anything to do with them."

Lee was adamant, though. He told her he would not live in a house without a gun. Eventually, when she was about 20, she let Lee take her to the shooting range. He started her off with a .22-caliber handgun. At first, it scared her because of the loud noise, but she actually enjoyed the experience. Soon they were going to the range twice a month, and Deanna learned to shoot Lee's .357 Magnum revolver.

"I realized as long as you're safe with guns, as long as you know how to use them, it's better to have one than not have one. And we weren't going to have one in the house unless I knew how to shoot it," she said. "So he taught me to shoot it and clean it. He showed me how to check it to see if there's a bullet in the barrel. He taught me to be safe with it and not to be afraid of it anymore."

They bought Deanna her own .38-Special-caliber, five-shot Taurus revolver with a two-inch barrel. However, Lee, who has a concealed-handgun license, used to borrow it when he wanted to carry concealed because it was easier to conceal and carry than his larger, heavier .357 Magnum. In 2003 Deanna said she felt very comfortable with the .38, though she confessed she had not shot it in about ten years.

D eanna felt a slight sense of relief when she heard a woman operator answer her call.

Deanna: "Someone's trying to break into my house."

The operator asked her for her address, and Deanna gave it.

Operator: "Okay, tell me what's going on."

Deanna: "Someone just rang my doorbell, banged on my door, and I went up there and didn't answer it, and now they're coming and trying to come through my back door."

The operator asked Deanna for a description of the man. She said he was dark and had very curly hair. She didn't remember much of anything else, since the peephole had restricted her vision.

Operator: "I've got officers on the way. Stay on the line with me."

Deanna: "Thank you."

There was a pause while the operator typed the information into her computer terminal. Meanwhile Deanna was arming herself. She and Lee kept three handguns in a GunVault cabinet with a combination lock. There are four finger grooves in the top of the cabinet with buttons where the fingertips lie when a hand is placed on the box. The buttons can be set to a combination that is required to open the safe. The GunVault was on a shelf in the bedroom closet.

The stress of the situation was increased when Deanna wasn't sure she could remember the combination. She sighed with relief when the safe opened and she saw the guns inside. She first grabbed the short-barreled, five-shot Taurus—her gun.

"I thought: no, the.357. I'm going to take the .357. I know how to shoot it, too." Deanna picked up the stainless-steel Smith & Wesson Model 66-2 revolver with a four-inch barrel. She felt the comforting weight of it in her hand. She snapped the gun safe closed in case the burglar got past her and found it.

Operator: "Are you there by yourself?"

Deanna: "Yes, I am."

Operator: "What kind of gun do you have?"

No preliminary: "Have you got a gun?" Just: "What kind of gun do you have?" This might be described as the American assumption—the confidence that the average middle-class homeowner will have at least one gun in the house—particularly in Texas.

Deanna told the operator she had a .38 Special, then added that she also had a .357 Magnum. The operator asked which revolver she had with her. She said she had the .357 Magnum.

Operator: "Do you still hear him or see him at the back door?"

Deanna: "I have to go back out into the other room."

She followed the gun from the bedroom to the living room where she could hear someone trying to open the back door. It sounded as though he was trying to jimmy the lock.

Deanna: "Yes, I can still hear him."

Operator: "What does it sound like? Describe what you are hearing."

Deanna: "Sounds like somebody is messing with the door knob."

All she could hear was the man trying to open the door. She backed up towards her bedroom.

"I heard the back door open. That's when my heart just dropped. I said, 'Oh my God, he's in my house,'" Deanna recalled.

Operator: "Do you have any cars parked in front of your house?"

Deanna didn't answer. She was watching the living room from the hallway that led to the bedroom.

Operator: "So there shouldn't be any cars parked in front, right?"

Deanna was not concerned with whether or not there were cars parked in her driveway or on the street. She had more immediate things to worry about. There was a strange man in her house, and she didn't know what he might do.

Deanna: "Should I tell him I have a gun?"

Operator: "I'm sorry."

Deanna: "Should I tell him I have a gun?"

Operator: "I wouldn't say anything. It's your call because you're there. I can't . . . I don't know that particular situation. If you don't think he knows you're there. . . . Tell me where in the house you are."

Deanna was at the entrance to the hallway leading sideways to the bedroom. She could see into the living room while exposing very little of herself. The hallway was dark, making her hard to see. She watched the man she had seen at the front door only moments before, though it seemed like a lifetime. He came into the living room where there was a pool table covered with her son's T-ball equipment.

"So I was watching him, and as he got to the pool table, which is getting closer to my bedroom, I backed up more into my bedroom. I was just shaking because at that point I knew that there was going to be a confrontation," Deanna later recalled.

"But I felt confident because I had the gun, and I was pretty sure that he didn't have one. I knew he didn't have a gun in his hands, because I had been watching him. He could have had something concealed but he had a rag. He still had that rag in his hand. I heard him jingle something, maybe change, something like that."

Operator: "He's at the back of the house? You think he's inside now? Okay."

Deanna didn't reply as the man was close enough to hear her if she said anything.

Operator: "Are you at the back of the house? Is he at the back of the house?"

The operator realized that Deanna couldn't talk.

Operator: "Tap once on the phone if it's yes."

Her hand was shaking so badly, Deanna didn't know whether she tapped once or five times. She was also thinking about the operator's question. Was it the back of the house or not?

"And I thought, well this is kinda' the back of the house. There really isn't a yes or a no, so I just kinda' kept tapping."

Operator: "Is he at the front of the house?"

Before she could tap an answer the man rounded the corner and advanced towards the bedroom. She had the gun in both hands, aiming at him, and the phone cradled between her shoulder and her ear.

Deanna: "What do you need?

She was speaking to the man who had just broken into her house. His answer cannot be heard on the 9-1-1 tape, but Deanna vividly remembered his reply. "I'm looking for you," he said.

His reply was matter-of-fact and unsettled her. He appeared so casual that Deanna felt he didn't realize the danger he was in and that she might have to shoot him.

Deanna: "Why are you looking for somebody? Why are you in my house?"

Her voice was strong and angry. She later found out from the police that the burglar was high on drugs, and she believes he did not see the gun in her hand initially.

Suddenly he seemed to realize he was within a half-inch trigger squeeze and a quarter of a second of entering the great penitentiary in the sky. He threw his arms up to shoulder level, palms towards her, as if giving up. He turned around and walked back the way he had come until he got to the kitchen, when he broke into a run and disappeared through the back door.

Operator: "Out the back door?"

Deanna: "Yes."

Operator: "Let me know which way he goes. Can you find out for me?"

Deanna: "He's going out the gate of my house. Shall I open the front door and see where he goes?"

Operator: "Can you look out a window?"

Deanna: "I can try."

She went into her son's bedroom and looked out of the window.

Deanna: "He just laughed at me. You heard him?"

Operator: "I heard something. I couldn't tell what it was."

Deanna: "Yeah. He just laughed at me and said, 'I was just looking for somebody, something, in our living room.'"

He walked around. . . . He's leaving. He's running towards the Texaco, and he's running very quickly."

Operator: "Okay, now you've got a handgun?"

Deanna: "Yes."

Operator: "Okay. Are you okay?"

Deanna: "I'm okay."

Operator: "You stayed so calm."

Deanna: "He left. He saw a gun in his face, and he left."

Operator: "I'd be a complete basket case."

Deanna: Laughs. "The fact that I caught him doing it."

Operator: "Yeah."

Deanna: "I was in bed."

Operator: "Bless your heart."

Deanna: "I can't see him anymore."

Operator: "Okay."

Deanna: "He had on jeans, a T-shirt."

Operator: "What kind of T-shirt?"

Deanna: "It was like dark, like a blue, and he had a rag in his hand."

Operator: "What color was the rag?"

Deanna: "White. And when I walked in, when he walked up to me, 'cause he came around the corner into my bedroom."

Operator: "Goll-ee."

Deanna: Laughs. "He saw me. . . ."

Operator: "Okay, I hear you. We have officers in that area. Can you go ahead and put the gun away?"

Deanna: "Yes."

Operator: "Because when the officers get there, I don't want them. . . ."

Deanna: "Yes, I understand. Let me lock my backdoor."

Operator: "Yes, that's fine."

She put the gun away and told the operator she had done so. She said she heard the suspect handling what might have been change, but she couldn't see him as she was hiding in the bedroom at the time. The operator told her not to touch anything the burglar might have touched, in case he left any fingerprints. The operator asked if she was dressed. Deanna said she nearly was. The operator said there was an officer in front of the house and said goodbye.

The 9-1-1 call lasted seven-and-a-half minutes—the longest seven-and-a-half minutes of Deanna's life.

The Aftermath

The first officer to arrive asked her what had happened. Deanna explained and led him to the back door. There was no damage to the lock, and the window in the

upper part of the door was intact. She told him she had touched the door handle when she locked it. The officer said the burglar probably used the rag he was carrying to wipe off any fingerprints.

In his report Officer Chuck Johnson stated the suspect "was able to make entry by reaching through a doggie door at the bottom of the door unlocking the deadbolt and the spring latch lock."

By then several more officers had

arrived. Johnson said he advised the Egglestons to replace the door with a solid door without a window in it. One officer said they should at least get a lock that has a key on the inside, so it can be locked and the key hidden. However, another officer said that was not a good idea because it was a fire hazard. If the occupants needed to leave in a hurry because of a fire and they mislaid the key, they could be trapped inside.

Deanna said her husband, Lee, would call her from time to time during the day to check that she was fine. He called while the police were still in the house, and Deanna told him what happened. She assured him that she was all right. Lee still made it home driving as though he was competing in the Indianapolis 500.

Lee said if he'd been stopped for speeding he would have told the officer to follow him to his house.

"My husband is wonderful," Deanna added.

In his report Officer Johnson stated, "I also advised the victim that if she heard someone knocking on her front door that [she] should answer the door vocally by asking what they wanted. I advised that most burglars will ring the door bell in attempts to see if someone is home. If they don't get an answer, then they'll break in."

Johnson finished gathering all the information he needed for his report and left. He and several other officers spent about thirty minutes searching the area for the suspect without success.

At 12:16 P.M. the dispatcher advised Officer Ted Eby of a suspicious person in the area of the westbound access road to Interstate 20 near the south end of Lake Arlington. Ms. Ila Johnson reported seeing a man "carrying unusual items" as she was driving west on the access road. She described him as a black male wearing a dark blue T-shirt and blue jeans. She said he was carrying a purple backpack and two rifles, one in a black carrying case and the other wrapped in a Mexican blanket.

Eby and another officer arrived at Applejack's Liquor Store just over the Arlington border in Fort Worth. In a grassy, wooded area on the west side of the store they spotted the suspect crouching in the shadows about twenty-five feet from the road. He had a purple and gray back-pack with him.

"The suspect looked up and saw Officer Witt and I and began throwing items from the backpack toward the field between himself and Applejack's Liquor Store," Eby said in his report.

The two officers arrested Joe N. Haywood, 51-years-old. About six feet from where he had been crouching they found a gun case containing a Remington 12-gauge shotgun and a 20-gauge shotgun barrel. They found a video-cassette recorder in the backpack along with items of jewelry. Joe Haywood had been a busy lad. He was on parole for convictions including burglary of a building, possession of drugs, and possession of a firearm by a felon.

When questioned by Officer Eby Haywood said all the items including the shotgun were his. Eby asked him about the burglary of Deanna's house. "Mr. Haywood would not look at me when answering and appeared to be intentionally refusing to answer my questions on that topic. He was vague, only saying that he did not do it," Eby's report stated.

Eby contacted Officer Johnson who called Deanna. He told her they had caught a suspect who fit the description she had given and asked her if she would try to identify him. He said he would fetch her and assured her that the man would not see her. She agreed. The police drove her to Applejack's Liquor Store.

"We pulled up and we were a good distance from each other. They pulled him out of the police car and stood him up. As soon as they did, I said that was him, no doubt in my mind, that was him."

Deanna said the police searched the suspect and read him his rights in front of her. "That was really satisfying," she said.

An officer told Deanna that the burglary of her house would put Haywood back in the penitentiary. She was told there would probably be no trial.

Ila Johnson also identified Haywood as the man she had seen when driving on the access road near the liquor store. The items seized when Haywood was arrested were loot from a burglary more successful than his attempt at Deanna's. The officer who drove her back home reassured Deanna that Haywood was on drugs and probably would not remember her or her house. That made her feel better.

In the days that followed, Deanna told the story of what happened over and over again. "I'm everybody's hero now," she said shortly afterwards.

A few days after the burglary a detective called to ask if anything else had been stolen from her house. She thought the only thing the intruder stole was some metal tokens.

Some days later Deanna received what appeared to be a form letter sent to victims of residential burglaries. The two-page letter from the Arlington Police Department Victim Assistance Program outlined the reactions and feelings people have after a break-in. It was helpful and made Deanna feel she was not the only person to go through a traumatic incident.

"Burglary is a violation of the extension of the self. Most people feel their home is a place of refuge and safety, a shelter from the dangers of the outside world. It is often the intrusion of their safety and privacy that is felt more deeply than the loss of property," the letter stated.

Some years before, when she lived in an apartment, Deanna had been the victim of a burglary. She was not home at the time, but the feeling of violation was stronger than on the occasion she confronted Haywood.

"I felt very violated. They went through my underwear drawers. They took all the CDs and the VCR," Deanna recalled.

"When it happened at my apartment, I had a hard time going home for quite a while. And I had a hard time even wanting to be there, because it just felt different. It's like I said, I felt very violated. I felt like somebody had been through my personal things. But this time, he didn't get that chance, and I was the one that kept him from doing it, and I stood up to him, and he wasn't going to take anything from my house. And that's the way I felt and I still feel."

In an interview two weeks after she confronted the burglar Deanna felt a sense of unreality about the whole episode. "I still feel it didn't happen. It still feels like it was a dream or like I was on the outside looking in. Once in a while something will happen that'll put me right back in it. But most of the time it's like it didn't happen. And I see his face, see his face a lot in my dreams. And when I walked around the day after it happened, I walked around with the .38 in my hand all day. It took me a while to get past it. The first time I walked around that corner into the living room, my heart dropped again, just like that feeling."

In the days immediately after the incident other routine things triggered a reaction in Deanna. Her mother was in the habit of bringing Deanna's niece over to visit every Saturday. On the Saturday after the burglary, she was still in bed about 11 A.M. when her niece rang the doorbell. "It was kind of the same sound, and I froze. I couldn't move. My husband said: 'Deanna, Deanna, did you hear the door, Deanna?' And finally I snapped out of it, and he said, 'Were you asleep?' I said, 'No, I wasn't asleep; I just froze, couldn't move.' It was the exact same sound, so that really freaked me out and kind of brought me back."

Another time she was asleep when the neighbor boys came through the side gate into the backyard to mow the Eggleston's lawn as they usually did. Deanna freaked out again. She looked out of the window and saw who it was. "So I knew then that it was okay, but it's never going to be the same. I've always been the type of person who was afraid of noises, and afraid of break-ins, afraid of all that kind of thing."

Interviewed two years after the incident Lee Eggleston said that if he comes home unexpectedly during the day, he makes sure Deanna knows it's him. "I make sure I announce who the heck I am before I walk around the corner: 'Honey, I'm back!'" he said. "It makes me feel good that she can handle herself, and I feel confident when I leave that she's going to be okay."

Reflections

When I interviewed Deanna two weeks after the burglary I asked her to show me the gun she used. She went into the bedroom closet where the GunVault cabinet was on a shelf. I noticed that it took several tries before she got the combination right and managed to open the box.

She said two weeks before the burglary she had tried to open the safe but initially could not remember the combination. She and Lee finally did remember it and opened the safe. If that incident had not reminded her of the combination, she would not have been able to open the cabinet when she desperately needed to.

Deanna said she and Lee had bought the GunVault about a year before, when their son, Austin, was going through a curiosity stage and was climbing on furniture to reach things. They had kept the guns on the top shelf of the closet, but decided that was no longer inaccessible to an active 5-year-old.

Obviously, if you are going to keep your self-defense weapon locked up, it is essential to remember where the key is or remember the combination.

Before the burglary Austin was not aware that his parents had guns in the house. However, since then he has shown an interest in guns.

"We decided we had to tell him the story. We had to tell him basically what happened: that I used a gun and scared the guy away. He asked me, 'Where is the gun? Well, I want to see the gun.' We might show him the gun, but he's not going to know where the gun is. We told him as soon as he's old enough we'll take him out and teach him how to shoot.

Deanna said she expected the 9-1-1 operator to tell her what to do. It is an unrealistic expectation, because she was there and the operator was not. Besides, in this era of win-the-lottery litigation, police departments shy away from giving advice for which they could be held liable. The duty of a 9-1-1 operator is to discover as much as she can about the emergency and the people involved. Deanna essentially made the right decisions on her own, though reflecting later there was one option that never occurred to her. She said she could have run out of the front door as the burglar came in the back.

"It never even dawned on me. My thought was to get my gun and protect my house. I knew that he didn't have a weapon, and since I knew that I felt safer. If I had seen he had a weapon I might have started running out the front door."

Despite the advice of the police to replace the back door with one that had no window, the old door was still in place, though Lee had installed a bolt high up so it couldn't be reached through the pet door.

Two-and-a-half years after the burglary, Deanna said Lee renewed his concealed-handgun license, and she has applied for hers.

The incident still affects Deanna. Her heart rate still cranks up when she hears the side gate open. "I still have nightmares—not real bad; not real often. Sometimes I'll wake up in the middle of the night and think I hear something. I've always been real cautious about who's at the front door and things like that, but I'm even more cautious now about who's at the front door and not opening it. I'm real cautious about my 8-year-old. He's gotten to where he hears the door bell and runs to answer the door." She has had to sit him down and explain that it's not always going to be his friend from across the street. She feels she has to be really careful when she lets him play outside.

"It's sad that when I walk outside I'm looking around to see who's outside and who's walking around." She admits to some racial profiling because the man who broke into her house was black.

Lessons Learned

After the incident Lee put together a two-page e-mail letter that he and Deanna sent to all their friends and relatives. They wanted them to benefit from Deanna's experience. Deanna particularly felt that others should not make the mistake she did in not letting the burglar know that someone was home. "This is something that I think is very important. I've been telling everybody. My biggest mistake was not answering the door; not saying, 'who is it?'"

Deanna has talked to her women friends, and most of them say they do what she did and just do not answer the door.

The burglar broke in because he thought the house was empty. If she had let him know that someone was home he would have gone elsewhere. The police told her that usually a burglar will ask if a particular person, for example "John," is there. When the person who answers the door says no one named John lives there, the burglar will try the same approach at other houses until he finds an empty one. Then he will break in. Police suggested when a potential burglar makes that approach, the occupant should call 9-1-1 and report a suspicious person in the area.

She has talked to many people about the incident, and some have said what happened to her made them consider getting a gun. Deanna's sister and her husband got rid of their gun when they had a child, but considered replacing it and getting a gun safe to keep it in.

Deanna said she was very relieved when the suspect was caught and taken off the street. But she was also glad she had gotten over her fear of guns. She has become a hero to many of her friends, because of the cool way she stood her ground and handled the situation. "For those people who are totally against guns, maybe they should think about it, because it gave me complete confidence. I felt utter confidence," Deanna said.

As Lee put it at the end of his e-mail: "And the potential victim became a survivor thanks to her willingness to step outside her comfort zone, learn self-defense, and stand up for what is right."

Chapter 4

Death of a Police Officer: Rory Vertigan

When I teach civilians the course to qualify for the Texas concealed-handgun license, I advise them to use their guns only to defend themselves, their family members, or very close friends. I advise them not to get involved in third-party disputes. The average civilian is usually better advised to accurately observe the action, get good descriptions of the participants, and call the police.

A danger is that the concealed-handgun license-holder is not fully aware of what is happening. Suppose, for instance, a license-holder sees a scruffily dressed man with long hair running out of a bank with a gun in his hand. Is the man a bank robber, or is he an undercover police officer chasing a bank robber? Taking action based on a mistaken apprehension can be serious for the citizen's wallet, his freedom, and his life.

However, there are circumstances when a civilian, particularly if he or she is well trained, chooses to become involved and makes the right decisions. Helping or backing up a police officer who obviously needs assistance can be one of those occasions.

Rory Vertigan

When Rory Vertigan was about to leave his office March 26, 1999, he picked up his Beretta Bobcat and stuck it in his front pants' pocket. The Bobcat is a .25-caliber, semi-automatic handgun good for exterminating small vermin or as a backup gun. It is not a first choice for self-defense. Vertigan, 27, stepped outside and was walking to where his car was parked when he stopped, paused a moment, then retraced his steps.

Back in his office he put the Bobcat back in the drawer and took out his Glock Model 31, a full-size semi-automatic which can hold sixteen rounds in .357 SIG caliber. The .357 SIG round is used by Texas state troopers, among others, and the Glock is the most popular handgun among law-enforcement agencies in the United States. Carrying the Glock, Rory went back to his car. He had no idea why he decided to exchange the "poodle shooter" for the bigger handgun.

Rory Shawn Vertigan was born in Arizona in 1971 and lived all his life in Arizona. He referred to himself as an Irishman because his great-grandparents on both sides of his family had migrated from Ireland. His parents had moved to Arizona from the Buffalo area in New York. Rory grew up on the south side of Tucson, where most of his friends were Hispanic. He and his family moved to Phoenix when he was twelve.

His father and grandfather owned guns and were members of the National Rifle Association. Rory had hunted and owned firearms for most of his life. He did a lot of target shooting as a kid. He owned his own shotgun, handgun, and rifle before he was 18 years old.

Rory was in the Reserve Officers Training Corps in high school. He had always had knee problems because of his weight; they kept him out of the military and over the years they deteriorated to the point that he had to have surgery. He had considered becoming a police officer, but decided against it mainly because he was concerned that it would worry his mother. Instead, he has worked as a private investigator and security officer in Phoenix since he was a teenager. He became an unarmed security officer at age 18. When he turned 21 he became an armed security officer.

In the spring of 1999 Rory Vertigan was tenant-relations director for a large real-estate-management company in Phoenix. He ran the security department for the company and took care of disputes between tenants and management. The company had five properties comprising about seven hundred apartments. Most of the properties were in the Twenty-seventh Avenue corridor, a high-crime area on the west side of Phoenix and a hot bed of drug trafficking. Rory and his partner, Lonnie Bellamy, patrolled the properties at night in uniform. They had had frequent confrontations with undesirables in the area and seldom went anywhere unarmed.

Rory had had to pull his gun on suspects a few times and in 1991 had been involved in a shooting incident. He and his partner were on their way home from work, when a guy in a vehicle pulled up alongside their unmarked white patrol car. The man started yelling at them in Spanish then fired a shot at them from a sawed-off, 12-gauge shotgun. The birdshot hit the vehicle, but missed Rory and his partner. Rory pulled the .357 Magnum revolver he carried at the time. "I returned fire, and I fired five rounds into his vehicle," he said.

The vehicle took off. Vertigan and his partner were in uniforms that looked very much like Phoenix police uniforms. Rory believes the man involved was an illegal alien and feels sure he mistook them for police officers.

The police found the vehicle a few days later with the bullet holes in it. It appeared that Rory didn't hit the shooter as there was no blood in the vehicle. The suspect matched the description of a man who had robbed two liquor stores and shot at a couple of people a few hours before shooting at Rory. Phoenix can be a rough town.

The Prelude

In the late afternoon of March 26, 1999, Rory was driving Lonnie to pick up their patrol car, which was being serviced at B&B Auto, a repair shop owned by a former police officer. Vertigan dropped Lonnie off at the shop at 5:24 P.M. then turned eastbound on Thomas Road.

Rory Vertigan is a big man. The red-haired Irish-American is six feet five inches tall and weighs just over three hundred pounds. He was squeezed into a very small car—a green Kia Sephia. He had bought the car because it got great gas mileage, and he had been putting on a lot of miles at the time doing private investigation work around the city. He was in plain clothes and, except for a small beard, he looked and even sounded like a cop. He was wearing Levi's, his cowboy boots, and a T-shirt. He was smoking a cigarette, and his window was rolled down to let the smoke escape. His Glock 31 was lying on the passenger seat in a bikini of a belt holster that covered only the trigger guard and part of the slide. He had no spare magazines and no backup gun.

He was not much more than a block from the auto-repair shop when he turned north on Thirtieth Avenue, taking a shortcut because of rush-hour traffic. The area was light industrial, with small single-story factories and warehouses clustered around streets that mostly lacked painted lane lines. Rory was about three hundred feet short of the intersection when a white Lincoln Town Car came careering out of Catalina Drive, running the stop sign and burning rubber as it swung north in front of Vertigan.

What a jerk, Rory thought as he continued towards the intersection. He was only about twenty-five feet from Catalina when movement caught his eye. He turned his head and saw a marked Phoenix police car speeding towards him along Catalina Drive with lights flashing and siren wailing. The police officer, apparently chasing the white Lincoln, also blew through the stop sign and swung north on Thirtieth Avenue right in front of Rory.

As his eyes followed the squad car, he realized the Lincoln had stopped in the middle of the street a couple of hundred feet ahead of him. He saw a man running across the street in the direction of the Bristow Optical Company. Another man, who had just exited the Lincoln, was standing beside the driver's door. He had a Smith & Wesson .357 Magnum revolver in his hand.

As the squad car approached the Lincoln, the man raised the revolver and took up a two-handed Weaver-style stance. He opened fire at the police car as it approached him, then he tracked it, still firing as it went past him.

Rory reached for the Glock on the passenger seat of his car.

Officer Marc Atkinson

Phoenix police officer Marc Atkinson was not afraid of trouble. A former U.S. Marine and veteran of Operation Desert Storm in Iraq. The 28-year-old officer had joined the Phoenix Police Department in 1994. Initially assigned to patrol the neat and well-tended

suburbs of north Phoenix, he found that area too quiet and law-abiding. He requested a transfer to Maryvale, a poor, mostly Hispanic area with a high rate of violent crime and drug trafficking, where he had been for three years.

In his time at Maryvale Marc had earned a reputation as a conscientious officer who was a self-starter. He did not wait around to be dispatched by radio, but sought out crime and criminals on his own initiative. He had been commended in his performance reviews for good police work and a good attitude. He often arrived early for his shift and was described as being a valuable resource to his colleagues. If he had a fault as a police officer, it was that he was perhaps too enthusiastic and gung-ho, taking more calls than his share.

Like many Phoenix police officers, Marc was not a native of the city or even of Arizona. He was born in Pocatello, Idaho, and grew up in West Valley City, Utah. The blond-haired, blue-eyed officer was happily married to a nurse and was the father of a six-month-old son.

On March 26, 1999, Marc Atkinson asked his sergeant to keep him free of regular radio calls so he could follow up on a tip. He had heard that someone was dealing drugs out of a white Lincoln in the parking lot of the Scoreboard Tavern at Thomas Road and Thirty-fifth Avenue. About 5 P.M. he drove past the Scoreboard and noticed a 1988 white Lincoln Town Car in the parking lot. He checked the license plate and found it was suspended. He called for backup and returned to the tavern with two other officers. As they pulled up in their three squad cars, three young Hispanic men ran from the Lincoln into the bar. The officers followed them in and questioned them and the bartender. The three were later identified as 17-year-old Felipe Petrona-Cabanas, a slightly-built young man of 140 pounds, wearing a white T-shirt and black jeans; Orberlin Cabana-Salgado, 18, also slightly built at 135 pounds and five feet six inches tall, clad in a brown jacket and dark red pants; and Fredi Bladimir Flores-Zevada, 22, almost six feet tall and 170 pounds. All were Mexican nationals in the United States illegally. Without enough evidence to make arrests, the three officers left the bar and drove off. The other two officers were called away, so Marc kept watch on the white Lincoln from a distance.

Just before 5:30 P.M. the three Hispanics emerged from the Scoreboard and piled into the Lincoln. As it pulled out of the parking lot and turned east on Thomas Road, Marc Atkinson reported on his radio that he was following the car and intended to pull it over. The Lincoln increased speed, the occupants apparently aware the police car was following them. The suspect vehicle zigged north on Thirty-first and zagged east on Catalina. Atkinson flicked on his bar lights and siren. As he turned the corner at Catalina and Thirtieth he apparently saw the Lincoln stopped in the middle of the street as two of the suspects ran from the car. He yelled "Bailout" into his radio. Marc closed on the Lincoln, but Felipe Petrona-Cabanas opened fire with a .357 Magnum revolver, tracking the police car as a shotgunner would track a pheasant.

The Incident

Rory Vertigan rolled to a stop about fifty feet behind the white Lincoln Town Car. He watched horrified as Petrona fired at the police car. His window was down but he didn't hear the sound of the shots or the wail of the police siren. He did see the revolver bucking in Petrona's hands. He saw the officer slump down in the squad car. The police car slowed, veered off the street to the left, and smashed into a utility pole, snapping it in two.

Petrona, still holding the Smith & Wesson revolver in both hands, then turned towards Rory. The big Irishman thinks the young man fired a shot at him. "I'm not sure if he actually fired a round at me or not, but I know the gun was pointed at me after he fired on the officer," Vertigan said.

Rory passed his Glock from his right hand to his left so he could shoot out of his window. "I just saw the gun coming at me, and I thought I had to lay some rounds down or he was just going to stand there and pluck me off."

Rory pointed his semi-automatic out of the window in the direction of the Mexican youth. He was unable to see the sights on his Glock because his head was inside the car, his gun was outside, and his target was directly in front of his car. "I just pointed the gun in his direction and started firing."

Even while shooting, Rory's training kicked in. He was very conscious of a UPS truck parked facing him beyond the Lincoln and made sure to avoid hitting it.

Petrona jumped back into the white Lincoln to reload his empty revolver as Rory got out of his Kia. There was a pause in the shooting as Vertigan took up a position using the top of his open door as a rest and holding the gun in both hands. He saw the UPS driver leave his van and run for cover.

Petrona's left foot hit the pavement as he turned back towards Rory and raised his revolver. Vertigan let go several more shots at the Mexican.

Petrona retreated back into the car, then Rory saw the Lincoln's reverse lights come on. He got back into his Kia for protection. The bigger car hurtled backwards and smashed into his Kia, knocking it back about five feet. Rory was holding his gun up in his left hand when the Lincoln hit his car. The shattered windshield slammed back into Rory's gun and cut his hand. The cars ended up at an L position to each other.

Rory fired several more rounds and saw Petrona flinch. One round went through the back window of the Lincoln and through the front seat; it hit Petrona in the shoulder.

Vertigan realized his slide was locked back on an empty chamber. He was now in a bad position. He had an empty gun and no more ammunition, and he was facing an armed adversary. It was fight or flight time. Rory could run at his attacker or run away from him. He chose to charge him, "because I'm too fat and too slow to run the other direction."

As he ran at Petrona, he managed to stuff his empty Glock into his waistband at the back. The Lincoln's door was still open and Rory slammed into it. The suspect had his revolver in his left hand and appeared to be groping with his right hand for something on the floorboards of the Lincoln.

As Rory slammed into the car door pushing it forward, Petrona brought up the .357 Magnum revolver, stuck it right in Vertigan's face, and pulled the trigger.

There was a loud click. Police later found three live rounds in the revolver. Petrona had only partly reloaded the gun and had not indexed the cylinder so the hammer would fall on a live round.

"I grabbed the gun out of his hand and yanked him up out of the car and threw him on the ground."

Rory put a large foot on the Mexican youth's back to keep him from getting up. He looked south on Thirtieth and saw two men standing on the southeast corner of the intersection with Catalina. He yelled for them to come and help him. The younger man reached Rory first.

"I handed him the bad guy's gun, and I believe I said something to the effect: 'If he moves, shoot him.'"

Rory ran to the squad car. It was in some bushes, where it stopped when it smashed into the telephone pole, now broken in two. The top half was hanging, suspended by its wires, like a crucifix over the police car.

Rory tried to open the passenger-side door but it was locked. He looked in and saw Officer Marc Atkinson slumped over the car's computer, not moving. There was blood all over the front of the inside of the car. Over the years Rory had seen more than his share of dead people—people who had died violently or of natural causes in and around the apartment buildings he was responsible for. Atkinson appeared to be dead.

"I pretty much realized at that point there wasn't anything I could do."

Rory was concerned that Petrona might get up and start fighting with the young man he had left to guard him, so he ran back to the two cars smashed together almost as though they were engaged in mortal combat.

The guy Rory had given the gun to handed it back and disappeared. The police never did find him.

Rory was worried that the man he had seen fleeing from the Lincoln might come back and attack him, so he returned his foot to Petrona's back to control him and backed against the Lincoln. He held the suspect's revolver in his hand, though he never checked to see if it was loaded. "I figured if nothing else I had the gun in my hand, and I could point it at them if they started coming at me."

Rory quickly realized that within a few seconds a swarm of police cars would be descending on the scene, and there he was standing over the suspect with the Smith & Wesson revolver in his hand. He also had his empty

Glock semi-automatic in his waistband at the back. It was not as bad as facing an armed assailant with an empty gun, but it was not a happy position to be in.

As soon as he saw the flashing bar lights of the first squad car come around the corner from Catalina, Rory placed the suspect's revolver on the roof of the Lincoln. He stepped away from the car and raised his hands to shoulder level, palms towards the police car.

The Aftermath

The squad car pulled up well behind Rory's Kia. Two officers jumped out and ran towards him.

"The officer's hurt really bad. Someone needs to help him," Rory yelled, pointing towards the smashed patrol car.

The officers ran past him to Marc Atkinson's car. More officers followed. Rory told them that the guy on the ground was the one who had shot the officer and asked if someone would handcuff him. He also told them he had the two guns and asked that they take custody of them. A female police officer handcuffed Petrona and put him in a squad car, while a male officer took the two handguns and put them in the trunk of a police car.

Rory was left standing beside the Lincoln for about ten minutes before an officer approached him and asked what had happened. Officer Stephen Mulligan interviewed Rory and wrote in his report: "Rory was very emotional as I spoke with him. His hands were trembling and his voice wavering. He told me he had shot the suspect who shot a police officer."

Rory remembered his hands starting to shake and his voice wavering in the aftermath of the adrenaline rush he experienced during the shooting. He also started feeling cold, because a light drizzle had begun to fall and

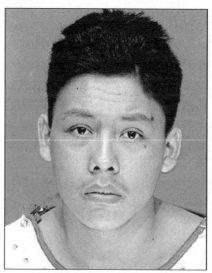

Felipe Petrona-Cabanas

he really needed a cigarette. However, his car, where his jacket and cigarettes were, was now part of the crime scene, and the officers would not let him get them. Officers instructed Rory to move from the two cars in the middle of the street to the northwest corner of the intersection of Thirtieth and Catalina.

Meanwhile officers processed the crime scene, taking photographs and collecting evidence. Emergency medical technicians from the Phoenix Fire Department treated Petrona for a gunshot wound in his shoulder, then transported him to Good Samaritan Hospital. Officer Marc Atkinson was dead, hit in the head by two bullets from Petrona's .357 Magnum revolver.

The police said that Felipe Petrona-Cabanas was the front-seat passenger who slid across when the driver, Fredi Flores-Zevada, fled across the street and into Bristow Optical, where he was later arrested. Rory never saw the third suspect, Obelin Cabanas-Salgado. He ran down the block and hid underneath a vehicle, where a passerby saw him and called police. He too was arrested quickly.

When they searched the Lincoln, police found a loaded Ruger 9 mm semi-automatic pistol on the floorboards of the car. They speculated that when Rory charged him, Petrona was groping for the Ruger. In addition to the pistol officers found a loaded 12-gauge shotgun and a quantity of cocaine packaged for resale. The Lincoln turned out to be stolen.

There was never any suggestion that Rory was a suspect. Later he asked one of the officers why he had not been held at gunpoint and handcuffed. The officer told him that Marc Atkinson had said on the radio he was chasing three Hispanic males. Rory certainly didn't match that description. "I was a large white man standing on a small Hispanic male."

Television news helicopters were circling, filming the scene from above. Rory was supposed to have dinner with his mother that evening, and he hoped she wasn't watching the news. But she was, and she recognized Rory's car in the television news pictures. "The reporter said an officer had been shot, another person had been shot, and somebody was in custody. And she was just freaking out," Rory recalled.

His cell phone was in his Kia and he could hear it ringing. He knew it was his mother trying to reach him, but he was not allowed to answer it because it was in the crime scene.

About the time the police arrived Rory had made two phone calls from his cell phone. He called his secretary and told her he had just seen a police officer shot and he was not coming back to work. He also placed a call to Lonnie Bellamy, his partner, and told him he had just shot a guy who killed a cop. Rory has no memory of making either phone call. After making the calls he must have left the cell phone in his car.

Lonnie was still at the auto-repair shop. Before he could reach Rory, the police sealed off the area. Rory could see Lonnie, but Lonnie was on the other side of the squad cars and the crime scene tape. Finally Rory's mother called

Lonnie, who was able to tell her that he could see Rory and that he was not hurt.

Rory was left shivering in front of the optical store for about an hour, until an officer put him in the back of a squad car. It was warmer in the car.

Later, Harold Hurtt, Phoenix police chief, approached Rory and introduced himself. He asked Rory if he needed anything. Rory expressed an interest in a cigarette, and shortly thereafter an officer gave him a pack and a lighter.

"I don't think I've smoked a pack of cigarettes that fast in my life," Rory said.

The chief said he didn't look very comfortable where he was and invited him into the mobile command center van that was on the scene. While he was sitting there a photographer took shots of his injured left hand where it hit the windshield when the Lincoln smashed into his Kia. The Lincoln hit the smaller car with such force that its license plate was imprinted on the Kia's bumper. Repairs to the Kia, which was about a year old, cost $2,800.

Eventually, Detective Paul Dalton took Rory from the command vehicle to his unmarked car to interview him. Sometime between 10 and 11 P.M. an officer drove him home, because the Kia was too badly damaged to drive.

At the time Rory Vertigan was living part of the time with a girlfriend of eight years, but most of the time in an apartment with his mother, who was handicapped. Though separated from his mother, Rory's father had been living with them while recovering from an illness. Rory's sister lived in the apartment next door. The family has always been close, Rory said.

When he arrived home at the apartment he shared with his mother, it seemed everybody he knew was there. His mother had made phone calls to their friends, who came over to give her moral support. Rory had a few drinks and went to bed sometime after midnight.

He could not sleep. His mind kept replaying the incident. He felt guilty that he had not done more to save Officer Marc Atkinson's life. But he had another more urgent fear. He remembered seeing a bullet hole in the back window of the squad car.

"I laid in bed so sick to my stomach because I was thinking to myself: my God, what if that was one of my rounds. What if it was my round that hit him. I thought: oh my God, I'm going to go to jail."

Rory remembered seeing the clock beside his bed showing 4:15 A.M. At 6 A.M. the phone rang. It was the police wanting him to go to police headquarters downtown on West Washington Street.

It was with more than a little trepidation that he walked through the main door into the lobby at police headquarters that morning. An officer immediately walked up to him and asked, "Are you Rory?"

The man introduced himself as Brian Godbehere, older brother of David Godbehere, who was one of Rory's best friends while he was growing up. Rory and Brian had never met, although Rory knew Brian was a Phoenix police officer. He was relieved that there was someone who knew something about him. "I wanted to hug him because I was so nervous and so scared."

Half a dozen other officers were in the lobby, and when they heard Brian call him Rory they all came over, shook his hand, and thanked him. "It was a really warm welcome. I started calming down at that point."

Paul Dalton, the detective who had interviewed him at the scene, conducted a second interview that was video- and audio-taped. Dalton started by showing Rory a bottlenecked handgun casing that was head stamped .357 on the base. The detective asked him if it was from the type of ammunition he used in his Glock 31. Rory confirmed that it was.

In his report Dalton stated: "I asked Rory if he had sixteen rounds in his magazine. Rory said he believed so, because he usually carries a fully loaded magazine."

Dalton then told him he had only accounted for fourteen rounds. This really panicked Rory. He assumed one of his rounds must have gone through the back window of the squad car and killed Marc Atkinson. "I thought: oh my God, oh my God, I did it, it was me."

Then the light went on. Rory remembered that he had intended to change the springs in all his magazines because he felt they were getting weak from being kept fully compressed all the time. He had been practicing on the range the previous weekend. When he had finished he had loaded only fourteen Federal Hydra-Shok rounds into each magazine. When he racked the slide, one round would have entered the chamber and left thirteen in the magazine. So in fact the Glock contained only fourteen rounds instead of its usual sixteen.

Dalton said that made sense, because police had found fourteen bottlenecked shell casings at the scene and fourteen holes in the Lincoln. All of Rory's rounds had hit the Lincoln. A couple of the first rounds he shot hit the trunk lid. About half a dozen went through the back window, and a few more went into the side of the Lincoln from when the two vehicles were at an L-angle.

"I swear it was like the world had been lifted off my shoulders when they told me every round was accounted for," he said.

After Dalton finished, the police media liaison officer questioned him and wrote a news release that Rory approved. Rory said he didn't want to talk to the media, so the media officer read the release to the assembled reporters. He was irritated when a reporter called him on his cell phone later that day and wanted to interview him. Somehow, he had gotten hold of Rory's cell phone number. Vertigan turned him down.

In the days that followed, members of the news media came to his office and bugged him for an interview. On one occasion he had police officers who were there escort reporters off the property.

On March 30, four days after the shooting, the Phoenix Law Enforcement Association, the police union, held a news conference to honor Rory Vertigan and Francisco Diaz Sedilla, a Mexican national in the country illegally.

The three Mexican drug traffickers responsible for the murder of Officer Atkinson were part of Arizona's crime problem. Unlike them Diaz was part of the solution. He was credited with saving the life a few days before of another Phoenix police officer, Lyn Butcher.

Terry Sills, the association president, announced that the union would replace Rory's Glock, which was impounded for evidence, and gave him a check for $500 in appreciation for going to the assistance of Atkinson. "It is apparent to the officers of the Phoenix Police Department that Mr. Vertigan is one citizen we do not want to see unarmed. We applaud what Mr. Vertigan did," Sills said.

Rory also received a check for $250 from the officers' association of the Arizona Department of Public Safety. He was somewhat taken aback by all the attention and by being branded as a hero. He did not think of himself as a hero. "People said: 'he's a hero, he's a hero,' but in my eyes a hero is somebody who saves somebody. I didn't save anybody but myself that day," Rory said.

In April Rory was honored at the annual meeting in Denver of the National Rifle Association. While he was already a member of the NRA, he was presented with a life membership. The NRA meeting was abbreviated that year, as it immediately followed the tragic incident at Columbine High School. Two students killed twelve of their colleagues and a teacher in a Denver suburb before committing suicide. While the school shooting prompted demands for gun control and was front-page news in the national media for months, Rory Vertigan's responsible use of a gun to assist police was almost ignored by the major networks and big-city newspapers. The exception was that *Time* magazine published a major story about it in June that year.

Consequences

The Phoenix police association paid for and arranged for Rory to get professional counseling by a psychiatrist to help him cope with the stress of the incident. He told the psychiatrist he had experienced an anxiety attack the night of the shooting.

"I told her I was sweating, I was sick, I was freaking out, because all this stuff was playing over and over again in my mind: oh, my God, what if that was my bullet."

Even after he had been assured that none of his bullets had hit Atkinson, Rory still suffered from what the psychiatrist called night terrors. "I'll wake up soaking wet. I'll sit straight up in bed, and there will be a perfect imprint of me in bed from sweat. And I'll wake up with images of that night in my head. It doesn't happen like it used to, but I would say for a good year I probably had a nightmare or night terrors two or three times a week."

In addition to dreaming of that night, he had nightmares of being shot to death. The psychiatrist said he was suffering from Post Traumatic Stress Disorder (PTSD). He laughed at her and said that was something that only people in the military got after intense combat. Not so. She told him that anyone involved in even one shooting can suffer from it.

Later he went to another psychiatrist at his own expense. That doctor wanted to put him on medication, but he refused. He said he would never take medication for that. Six years after the shooting the nightmares occur only about half-a-dozen times a year, he said.

The shooting also likely cost him a relationship. He split up with his girlfriend of more than eight years, because she couldn't handle what he was going through. They had met in 1991, just before Rory's first shooting incident, and broke up in 1999 after the second. "That was one of the biggest strains on my relationship. That's part of why we separated. She said she just couldn't handle the way my emotional mindset was after the shooting."

What troubled Rory the most after the shooting was the feeling that he didn't do enough to save Marc Atkinson's life. Even though investigators, officers, and friends all said he did all he could have, his mind still wouldn't allow him to believe it. "I've played it over in my mind a million times. I was probably the worst Monday morning quarterback there was."

He speculated that he could have warned Atkinson by blowing his horn or that he could have rammed the Lincoln. "Even today it still bothers me. But I know I did everything I could do, but my mind would not let me think that," he said.

After the shooting Rory said he found details of the incident coming back to him over a period of days and even weeks. It was sometimes confusing, because he wasn't sure whether he was remembering something he witnessed or something he had heard subsequently. This initial memory loss happens frequently to people who have experienced high-stress situations.

Shooting fourteen high-velocity .357 SIG rounds without ear protection damaged the hearing in Rory's left ear. He told his doctor he was having ringing in his left ear and was having trouble hearing with that ear. The doctor told him that was normal after what had happened. The ringing went away after a while, but his hearing deteriorated and could have cost him the job he later had with Homeland Security.

For the first couple of court hearings following the shooting Rory had police protection. In Arizona, as in most other states, concealed-weapons permit-holders are not allowed to carry their guns inside courthouses. So a police officer friend got permission to escort Rory to and from the courthouse, because he had to park in a public garage and walk down the street unarmed to attend hearings that had been well publicized. For the first few hearings Rory wore his bullet-resistant vest under his suit. He didn't want to take a chance of getting shot.

The three suspects, Felipe Petrona-Cabanas, Oberlin Cabanas-Salgado, and Fredi Bladimir Flores-Zevada, had all been charged with first-degree murder, aggravated assault, attempted first-degree murder, conspiracy to sell narcotics, and misconduct involving weapons. Rory heard from the police that the three, who were in jail awaiting trial, were associated with, or were members of, a Mexican drug gang. Consequently he was being more careful than usual. He kept a shotgun behind his front door and a Glock pistol in his living room.

On July 31, 1999 four months after the shooting, Rory's mother, Joanne Vertigan, was threatened as she returned to the apartment they shared after shopping. Rory had just woken up prior to going to work.

He was sitting on the sofa when his nephew came running into the apartment screaming that there was a man with a gun in the parking lot with "Grandma." Rory grabbed his cordless phone and his shotgun. As he went running down the sidewalk he heard a car driving away. He saw his mother coming down the sidewalk as fast as she could go, which was not very fast as she had heart problems and diabetes and was overweight. She was screaming that there were three guys in a car and they had pulled a gun on her.

"I put her behind me, and I was walking backwards, on the phone to PD, aiming my shotgun down the sidewalk with my right hand."

When they got to the apartment, Rory told his mother to go into the bedroom and lie down on the floor. Rory stayed by the front door. There was only one way anyone could get to the apartment and that was by coming down the sidewalk. He sat there with his shotgun aimed out of the door, talking to the police on his phone. He told the police who he was, that three Hispanics had pulled guns on his mother, and said he needed an officer out there.

"Within a matter of minutes, there were squad cars from every direction, helicopters overhead, and everything else," he recalled. When he heard the squad cars coming, he put the shotgun down and told the dispatcher he was unarmed.

Joanne Vertigan told police that three young Hispanic men in a white Toyota Camry with a rear license plate from Sonora, Mexico, had followed her into the apartment complex parking lot and pulled up beside her car. She got a good look at the front-seat passenger.

Rory said, "The guy had a gun in his hand, kind of hanging out of the window so she could see it, and said something to the effect of—she doesn't speak Spanish— 'Casa Rory, casa Rory,' something like that, asking like where my house is. She freaked out and sped out of the parking lot."

Instead of stopping at a pay phone and calling the police, she was worried that these guys would go to the apartment, where she thought Rory was asleep, and shoot him. So she circled around and didn't see the car. When they got to the apartment, she told Jeremy, Rory's nephew, to go in and tell Uncle Rory there was someone with a gun out there. Rory said he doesn't know whether they saw him with the shotgun, but they drove off.

The police investigated the incident. Joanne Vertigan had to go down to police headquarters and describe the men to a sketch artist. She described the gun as a large, black semi-automatic. Rory assumed that the guys were colleagues of the three involved in the Marc Atkinson shooting. These guys were never caught.

This was the third time in three months that Joanne Vertigan had faced a man with a gun. Twice the same man had robbed her at gunpoint where she worked as a manager for a storage company. The second time he fired a shot at her and tied her up with duct tape. At the time the Mexicans confronted her in the parking lot, she had been diagnosed with PTSD.

About two weeks after Joanne's encounter with the Mexicans, Terry Sills, president of the police union, organized protection for Rory and his family. He said Rory had stepped in to help a Phoenix police officer and now that his family had been threatened the officers needed to help him. Sills organized a twenty-four-hour-a-day watch on Rory and his family by armed officers in plain clothes and in unmarked vehicles. If his mother went somewhere, two officers followed her; if Rory went somewhere, two officers followed him; if they were home, five or six officers surrounded the apartment.

This went on for about two weeks. Then the police moved the family to an undisclosed location in Phoenix with nothing listed in their names: no utilities, no address. About a month later Rory got a job offer out-of-state and took the family to Memphis, Tennessee.

He had lived all his life in Arizona, in Tucson and Phoenix. After nine months, he moved back to Phoenix. He said the shooting cost him the job he had been doing for ten years because he felt he had to move away.

Felipe Petrona-Cabanas pleaded guilty to first-degree murder of a police officer, conspiracy to transport or sell narcotics, transporting or selling narcotics, aggravated assault, attempted first-degree murder, and misconduct involving weapons.

"He admitted in court that he'd pulled the trigger in my face, and he was trying to kill me. He admitted in court that he tried to run me over, and he admitted in court that he had shot at me," Rory said.

On February 20, 2002, Judge Frank Galati of the Maricopa County Superior Court sentenced Petrona to life in prison without possibility of parole. In rejecting the death penalty Galati took into account that Petrona was seventeen at the time, that he lacked a previous criminal history, and apparently was of good character before coming to Phoenix and becoming involved in the illegal drug trade. The judge also found that Petrona had shown remorse and accepted responsibility for what he had done.

The judge stated: "In the immediate aftermath of Officer Atkinson's murder, defendant was taken to Good Samaritan Hospital where Detective Chavez interviewed him twice on March 26, 1999. Detective Chavez has described defendant as 'cooperative, polite, and apologetic' on March 26, 1999, and further characterized Mr. Petrona's statements to him as a 'full confession.' Also on the night of the murder, and the next day, defendant told Chavez that he knew he did wrong, that he deserved to be punished, and that he wanted to be punished."

So why did Petrona open fire on Officer Marc Atkinson when his two colleagues had fled? Rory could not see any reason why he tried to shoot the officer. It appears from court documents that he was afraid of going to jail if Atkinson caught them. He claimed he was just trying to scare the officer.

Fredi Bladimir Flores-Zevada, the driver of the stolen Lincoln and the oldest of the trio, was found guilty and was sentenced to life in prison with no possibility of parole. Oberlin Cabanas-Salgado was sentenced to twenty-five years to life with no possibility of parole for twenty-five years.

Reflections

Should Rory Vertigan have become involved in the incident? This question can be answered only by Rory Vertigan—the person involved at the time—based on his abilities, weapons, adversaries, and understanding of the situation.

It never occurred to Rory not to get involved. He put himself in harm's way without hesitation. Afterwards he thought occasionally about why he didn't just drive off and call 9-1-1 on his cell phone. But at the time there was no hesitation.

"I thought, that son-of-a-b is shooting at a cop, and he's not getting away with that. That was the first thing that went through my mind. There's no way in hell he's getting away with that as long as I'm standing."

Seeing someone shooting a revolver at a police car leaves little room for doubt about what is happening and who the bad guy is. Rory's understanding of the situation was accurate and comprehensive.

When he grabbed his gun off the passenger seat, Rory went into survival mode. While the action was happening, he said he was not scared or nervous.

"I look back at it now and go: Wow, how did you just not freak out? There was a lot of anger. I remember being angry, and I remember wanting to just pick this guy up off the ground and beat the s--t out of him. And I never did. He was never hurt in any way except for where I shot him."

Rory did experience auditory exclusion. He did not hear the siren on Atkinson's squad car until after it hit the telephone pole, and he said he never heard the shots that were fired. He saw Petrona's revolver bucking as it recoiled, but he never heard the shots.

Rory's previous training served him well. Although security-guard weapon-training requirements in Arizona are fairly minimal, he practiced regularly and had taken defensive-handgun-shooting courses. He was familiar and comfortable with firearms, as he had been shooting since childhood.

Should he have engaged Petrona with his left hand when he couldn't see the sights? Every one of the fourteen shots he fired hit the Lincoln—proof of ability.

"I had practiced point-and-shoot over the years a lot of times during our training. The only reason I felt comfortable firing the way I did was because I had practiced many times with my off [left] hand. I would never have done that if I had not practiced it before."

His training also prompted him to check what was behind his target before he fired and who might be hit if he missed. This is one of the four basic safety rules: be sure of your target and what is beyond it. Rory made a determined effort not to endanger the driver of the UPS truck that was beyond the wrecked police car.

The UPS driver, Steve Bowers, had taken advantage of the best cover available. He hid on the floorboards of his truck, behind the engine block.

In the years after the shooting Rory took more firearms courses and practiced more frequently, shooting two or three times a month. "I'm a lot better shot than I was back then. I guarantee those fourteen rounds would have done a lot more damage now."

Since the shooting, Rory has continued to work in the private-security field. However, he also joined the Arizona Rangers and became captain of the Phoenix Command. The Rangers are an auxiliary law-enforcement-support agency assigned at the discretion of the governor.

Rory Vertigan visits the scene of the incident, where he did everything he could to assist Officer Atkinson, at great personal risk and enduring personal cost.

In 2006 he was a lieutenant in a private security company that is under contract to the Department of Homeland Security. He was stationed at the Bureau of Customs and Immigration Services. He worked with firearms instructors who have made his name into a new word. They instruct their students: "Don't do the Vertigan." This means don't leave home with only your gun. Take at least one spare magazine.

At the risk of being called paranoid, Rory doesn't go anywhere now without extra magazines or a backup gun in an ankle holster. Rory has installed Kydex holsters and extra magazine carriers under the dashboards of his vehicles. "That way I always know I have an extra magazine with me." He normally carries a Colt Detective Special on his ankle. He carries his Glock in an inside-the-waistband holster.

When a white man shoots a black or Hispanic he is almost always accused of racism. While Rory was accused of being a vigilante, he was not accused of racism. It would have been a hard sell. He grew up on the south side of Tucson until he was twelve, and all his friends during that time were Hispanic. He figures that about 70 percent of his current friends are Hispanic.

"It's really sad, because 95 percent of the Hispanics here in Arizona are good people." It's the 5 percent who are bad that give all the others a bad name, he added.

He used to speak Spanish, because his former girlfriend of eight years was from Mexico. When they met, she spoke no English, and he spoke no Spanish. But he learned and used to speak Spanish quite well. Now he has lost some of it, though he can understand Spanish, and that was useful in his work with Immigration.

Coming to the aid of Officer Marc Atkinson cost Rory a lot in terms of post traumatic stress, a relationship, and his job at the time. As he put it, it cost him more than a magazine full of bullets. Would he do the same thing again?

"Absolutely," he says.

Chapter 5

Carryout Shootout:
Habib Howard

Working in a convenience store at night is one of the most dangerous occupations in the United States. This is particularly true if the store is in a high-crime area of a large city. Every year hundreds of convenience store workers are assaulted, raped, robbed, or murdered. Convenience stores are not nicknamed "Stop-N-Robs" for nothing.

Most large corporations that run convenience stores, like 7-Elevens, Diamond Shamrock (now Valero) gas stations, and Stop-N-Gos, forbid their employees to exercise their Second Amendment rights and carry guns to protect themselves at work. A dead convenience store clerk costs a large corporation much less than a customer who was shot accidentally by a clerk trying to defend himself. While state after state has passed concealed-weapons laws that allow law-abiding residents to carry guns for protection, corporate America, ever mindful of liability, has been dragging its feet.

Consequently, those working in convenience stores or carryouts, as they are also known, who do carry guns and fight back against criminals, tend to be owners of independent stores, like the Howard family of Toledo, Ohio.

The Howards

Herbie Howard might be described as an immigrant success story. Born in Lebanon, he arrived with his father in the United States in October 1955 at the age of 10. He was preceded by other family members who Anglicized the family surname. He arrived as Habib Awad, but for most of his life he has been Herbie Howard.

His father returned to Lebanon, and Howard was raised in Toledo by a second cousin, a woman who had never married. As soon as he learned English, he got a job as a paperboy delivering the *Toledo Daily Blade*.

At age 23, after two years of college where he did not excel, Howard bought a bar. The first bar was followed by a second and a third. He was also buying real estate, and in 1970 Herbie bought his first gas station and convenience store.

The family business is American Petroleum, a company that distributes petroleum products to gas stations and convenience stores, including several owned by the family. The Howards build gas stations and carryouts, then sell them with a twenty-year agreement that binds the new owners to stock only American Petroleum products. They have seventeen of these locations, as well as five owned outright.

Howard married his first wife in 1976, and the couple had four sons. The oldest, Michael, is a lawyer, while the others—Thomas, Habib, and John—are employed in the family business. Howard married his second wife—Tammy—in 1993.

The Howards live in Ottawa Hills, a small village of 4,200 residents surrounded by Toledo. He pays four times as much in property taxes as he would if he lived in a similar house in Toledo, just three blocks away. However, the Ottawa Hills school system is excellent, and the higher property taxes are less than he would pay to send four boys to private schools. Per capita, Ottawa Hills is the third richest village in the U.S., Howard said.

"There is some seriously old money in this village," he added.

Habib Howard

Guns were part of the household, and Howard taught his four sons to hunt and shoot. However, his third son, Habib, had a problem with the hunting.

"I've been interested in shooting since I can remember. I've been around guns all my life. My dad brought us up with guns. My dad's taken us hunting. My dad's taken us to gun shows. Ever since I can remember I've had a handgun, had shotguns." Habib said.

However, while he enjoyed shooting, he did not like the killing involved in hunting.

"I could never shoot anything. I really felt bad shooting something. I shot like, I think it was a robin, and I felt bad."

His father confirmed the incident. "He was truly and honestly depressed for two or three days."

Two or three times a year Habib's father bought a lamb or a pig and slaughtered it at the family's summer home in Michigan. The animal was butchered, and the meat went into the family freezer. The hide was sent for tanning. When he was 14 Habib told his father he wanted to kill the lamb Howard had just bought.

"I was trying to be a tough guy," Habib said.

His father handed him the .22-caliber rifle and told him to go ahead.

"When I put the rifle to the sheep's head, I couldn't watch myself shoot it, so I turned my head and I shot it."

The bullet hit the lamb in the jaw. His father told him to give him the gun, but Habib insisted on trying again. Three times he shot the sheep, each time turning his head away as he pressed the trigger, and each time failing to kill the sheep. Eventually his father took the rifle and finished off the unfortunate animal.

At five feet ten inches tall and weighing 160 pounds, Habib is the smallest of Howard's four sons, but he can defend himself quite capably, his father said. When he was 17 he got into a fight with a 21-year-old. After walking away from him for more than an hour and telling the guy repeatedly to leave him alone, the guy finally made a move on Habib's girlfriend, Howard said.

"That's when he crossed the line. The guy needed three surgeries to repair his nose," his father said.

Howard reckoned Habib was the least likely of his four sons to shoot anyone, even in self-defense.

"With a gun, I would think Habib would have been the least likely, simply because of the way killing the bird or shooting the lamb affected him."

Concealed-Carry

On January 8, 2004, Ohio Governor Bob Taft signed into law a bill that would allow law-abiding Buckeye State residents to carry concealed handguns for protection. After a decade-long battle between supporters of gun rights and proponents of gun control, Ohio joined with thirty-seven other states. The law went into effect April 8, ninety days after the governor signed the bill, and county sheriffs started processing concealed-carry applications. Applicants had to complete twelve hours of training by a qualified instructor, and they could take that ahead of time.

Habib Howard was particularly excited. At the time he was working the 4 P.M. to midnight shift at one of the family's gas stations and convenience stores. He didn't need a license to carry a handgun in the store, because he was on his own property. He kept a gun in the store, leaving it there when he closed the store at midnight. After closing he would drive to another of the family's stores in a particularly bad area of the city to collect the day's receipts before driving home. He wanted the concealed-carry license so he could carry a handgun when collecting cash from other stores and taking money to the bank. Habib was so enthused that he paid not only for his own training course, but also for the training for his stepmother Tammy and his three brothers.

The Howards live in Lucas County and took their training at Cleland's Outdoor World on Airport Highway, just east of the Fulton County line in Lucas County. The law states that applicants for concealed-carry licenses can apply to the sheriff of the county in which they live or the sheriff of any adjoining county. So, Habib chose to submit his application in Fulton County: the processing would take less time since substantially fewer people live there, and the sheriff in Lucas County disapproved of concealed-carry.

Cleland's is a large sporting goods store with two archery ranges and a fifty-foot pistol range. Chad Cleland was their instructor. Applicants spend ten hours in the classroom followed by at least two hours on the range. Cleland says he covers the proper mindset for carrying a handgun for self-defense, the use of deadly force, the safe storage of handguns and ammunition, marksmanship, practical tests on loading and unloading, safely decocking the handgun, and how to use holsters safely. At the beginning of the course Cleland goes over the laws and responsibilities of concealed-carry.

"Some people don't realize what the law entails, the responsibilities that they have. Then we go over the proper mindset and the psychological things that can happen to you if you ever have to use that handgun," he said. "Sometimes I lose some folks in the class, and that's why we cover it right off the bat. They realize this isn't for them."

Cleland also covers how to greet police, whether at your home or your business or on the street, after you have been involved in a shooting incident.

On the range Cleland's students shoot at figure targets starting at twenty-one feet. They move back to forty feet and eventually fifty feet, he said. The number of rounds they shoot depends on the skill level of the individual. Everyone shoots at least 110 rounds, but some people may fire three or four hundred. Habib thought he shot about one hundred rounds.

"We work with each individual," Cleland said. "Each individual is different."

Tammy Howard said when she and the boys took their class together, his brothers teased Habib. "I don't know why you're taking these classes, because you can't even shoot a sheep," she quoted.

The Howards took their training on April 4, 2004, four days before the sheriffs were due to start issuing licenses. Habib completed his application forms and took them to the Fulton County Sheriff's Office.

On May 6 in the early afternoon Habib was at Page Distribution getting some cartons of cigarettes for his store. He was in the office waiting to pay for the cigarettes when his cell phone rang. It was a deputy sheriff from Fulton County, who told him his concealed-carry license had been approved.

"It was like, wow. It was very cool," Habib said.

After paying for the cigarettes, Habib drove out to the sheriff's office, where he had his photo taken and received his license. The journey made him late for his 4 P.M. to midnight shift at Howard's Carryout and gas station at 3730 Monroe Street.

The carryout is located in a mostly black, blue-collar, residential neighborhood west of the city center. There is another gas station nearby and a bank. The area comprises mostly single-family homes with one apartment building across the street from Howard's. Toledo Hospital is within sight of the store. Area residents tend to vote Democrat, and many work at the Chrysler factory that makes Jeep Wranglers.

For some local residents who lack a vehicle to get to the nearest Kroger's supermarket, Howard's Carryout is their grocery store. As well as selling gasoline, the store stocks everything from cigarettes to toilet paper.

As one enters the store a counter with the cash register extends to the right along the wall. Parallel to the front of the store four aisles run among shelves crammed with merchandize. The aisles lead to the dozen cooler doors along the left-hand wall where the beer is located.

The Incident

Three days after he received his concealed-carry license, on Sunday, May 9, 2004, Habib was working the 4 P.M. shift. It was Mother's Day. He was still living in the family home in Ottawa Hills, so he went home for dinner to celebrate Mother's Day with his family. He returned to the store about 10:30 P.M. and took over from Amy Smith, the stock clerk, who had been running the store in his absence. Habib helped several customers.

About 10:45 another customer came in—a black man in his early twenties wearing a light-blue shirt. Habib didn't pay much attention as he walked past the counter and down the second aisle to the end where the beer cooler was located. The man opened the cooler and took out a twelve-pack of canned beer. He walked back and put the beer on the counter. Habib was about to ask him for identification as he did with all younger customers.

"Before I could ID him, before I could say anything, he pulled the gun," Habib said.

The young man held a semi-automatic pistol at waist level, pointing it directly at Habib. He demanded the money in the cash register.

"When he pulled the gun, at first it was like it didn't register; like what was happening? I thought it was a joke. And then two seconds later I was going: wow, this is for real."

Once he realized that it wasn't a joke, Habib knew what to do. Although he had never faced an armed robber before, he was prepared. He was wearing a Taurus 9 mm-caliber semi-automatic pistol. The gun was on his right hip, concealed by his shirt, in a Don Hume inside-the-waistband holster. On the advice of his father and others, he didn't keep the ten-round magazine full, because it would weaken the magazine spring and the gun might jam. He usually kept nine in the magazine and one in the chamber. But earlier this day he had been at the range practicing and had only four or five rounds in the gun. They were the jacketed hardball rounds that he used for practice, not the hollow-point self-defense rounds he usually carried in the gun.

In addition to the gun, Habib was prepared because he, his brothers, and his father had anticipated that a

Habib Howard demonstrates a typical transaction at the carryout. (Photos courtesy NRA News)
The store layout includes several aisles and large windows. The office is at left behind the register area.

robbery might occur. They had a plan, and they practiced it again and again until it became a routine.

"I'd walk away, and then I'd pull my gun if I felt threatened. Pull the gun, then shoot. And every time it would
come to pulling out the gun, I would say to myself: I don't
know if I could do it.

"And they'd say: 'You can't shoot a sheep; how
could you shoot a person?'

"And I'd say, 'That sheep never did anything to me;
that sheep never pulled a gun on me.'"

They had decided that they would not draw and shoot
just to protect the money in the cash register. Money is
replaceable. They would shoot only if they felt their lives
were in imminent danger.

When the robber demanded the money in the cash
register, Habib turned the key and the drawer sprang open.
He began to back up behind the counter towards the door
leading into the office.

"I began to walk away just like I had practiced a thousand times before, and as I walked I had my left hand
up in the air, my right hand on my gun."

He was backing up with his body turned to the
right so the robber could not see his right hand or the
gun. The robber was still holding his gun at hip level. Habib
thinks it was a 9 mm or perhaps a .45-caliber semi-automatic. His eyes were riveted on the gun. He didn't
think the robber could see his hand on his own gun.

"The whole [left] hand up in the air, like we'd practiced, was to divert attention away from my other arm.
As I was walking away, I was facing him, sort of."

But the robber had other ideas. He ordered Habib
back to the register and told him to take the money out
of the cash register drawer and put it on the counter. Habib
took his hand off his gun and did as he was told. He put

about $180 in bills on the counter then backed away again with his left hand back in the air and his right on the gun.

The robber picked up the money and the beer while keeping him covered with the gun.

Habib had eyes only for that gun. "I was just looking at that gun," he said. "When a gun is pointed at you in the manner it was pointed at me that night, you don't take your eyes off it."

The robber backed up from the cash register towards the door, clutching his loot and still pointing the pistol at Habib.

"He had it at waist height, and as he was walking out he pushed the door open with his back and lifted up the gun," Habib said. "That was obviously when I felt a hundred percent threatened."

Fearing for his life, Habib drew his gun and opened fire.

He fired two or three shots at the robber from a range of about ten feet. The robber pushed through the door and disappeared outside. He dropped the money and the beer just outside the door, then ran towards his getaway car parked nearby with an accomplice at the wheel.

As the robber fled he passed in front of the large picture window at the front of the store. He still had his gun raised and pointed at Habib, who fired two more shots that went through the window.

Though he didn't know it at the time, Habib hit the robber twice—in the left shoulder and high in the left leg, in the groin area. They were probably the first two shots he fired before the man got out of the door.

The slide on Habib's Taurus 9 mm was locked back, indicating it was empty. He put the gun on the counter, along with his concealed-carry license and his Toledo handgun-owner's card. During the training course, Chad Cleland had instructed him to put the gun down in a place where arriving police could easily see it. It is not good policy to be holding a gun when the police arrive on the scene of a shooting. Habib retreated to the office and picked up the phone to call his family and the police.

The Aftermath

At the Howard house in Ottawa Hills all family members except Habib were in the kitchen. Herbie Howard was at the kitchen table cleaning a lamb prior to freezing it. It was shortly before 11 P.M. when the phone rang. Tammy Howard answered it.

"I'm hearing: 'Oh my God, oh my God, oh my God.' I thought it was a prank caller, because it didn't sound like Habib at all. I hung up," Tammy said.

She told her husband it was a prank caller. The caller ID didn't work in the kitchen, so she didn't see the caller's number.

"Two seconds later, the phone rings again. I answer and he goes: 'Oh my God, I just shot someone; I just shot someone, oh my God."

This time she knew it was Habib. The family members rushed to their cars. In their haste they had a minor accident in the driveway.

Herbie Howard was driving Tammy's car, a Cadillac Seville, barefoot. Running red lights and stop signs, he figured it took him about four minutes driving through mostly residential streets to get to the store. It normally takes about twelve minutes.

Howard and Tammy arrived about thirty seconds after the marked police cars arrived. Howard remembered walking barefoot through the safety glass from the picture window to get into the store. He asked a neighbor at the scene to get him a pair of shoes.

"I walked inside and Habib was sitting in an aisle-way just as stiff as a piece of oak. That's the best way I can explain it. His face was twice as long as it normally is. I can't believe how his eyes were sunk way inside his head and his jaw was locked.

"He was going: 'I don't wanna' go to jail.'

"I'm saying: 'What?'

"He's saying: 'I don't wanna' go to jail.'

"I'm going: 'You don't want to go to jail? What, are you crazy? You aren't going to jail.'

"All I could do was hug him real, real hard. I'm hugging him and trying to scratch his back, trying to rub his neck, and my mind is going a million miles an hour. I'm trying to piece this thing together, in case he did something wrong. Of course, I'd like to cover it up, but I'm trying to get all the facts together, right? As it turned out the kid did absolutely everything, everything within his power, as being right."

Tammy and Mike, Habib's older brother, took over trying to comfort him, while Howard talked to Kevin Woods, 32, a neighbor who lives near the store and was a customer while the robbery was happening. Woods told Howard the robber had a gun, and he chased the robber as he was heading for the getaway car. Woods backed off when the robber turned and pointed the gun at him.

The stock clerk, Amy Smith, 27, was another witness. She told Howard she came out of the bathroom during the robbery. All she saw was Habib with his hands in the air and the guy with the gun. She froze. She saw the robber raise the gun, heard shots, and thought he was shooting Habib.

The police officers roped off the store with crime scene tape, while detectives interviewed the witnesses and collected evidence. Tammy was in the office trying to comfort

Habib, who was still in shock, while his father called the family lawyer, who happened to be in New York. The lawyer recommended Habib not give a statement to the police at the time. He did give a statement later in the week after the lawyer returned to Toledo. When they left the store that night Habib's younger brother, John, drove him to St. Anne's Hospital, where he was given a sedative.

The police never found the robber's gun. The getaway driver took the robber back to the house where his girlfriend was staying. They changed his clothes and put the bloody clothes in the trunk of the car. Then the getaway driver drove him to Toledo Hospital and dropped him off. The police estimated the robber and his driver had about twenty minutes to get rid of the gun before arriving at the hospital.

The police caught up with the driver and arrested him a short time later. Detective Paul Tetuan said a warrant for the robber was issued that night. He was identified as Jose Custodia-Mota, 23, of Columbus, Ohio. His getaway driver was believed to be Alberto Martinez, 32. Technically Custodia-Mota was arrested when he was released from the hospital. Tetuan thought Custodia-Mota was in the hospital for about a week. "He was shot pretty good. He almost died," the detective said.

Custodia-Mota is Hispanic and comes from somewhere in Latin America, Tetuan says. He speaks Spanish, but not much English, and is very dark skinned. He was described as black in the initial police report. "If you just passed him on the street without speaking to him or anything else, you'd probably think he was black," the detective said.

Custodia-Mota had been arrested previously in Columbus, where he was living, Tetuan said, but he didn't think the arrest was for anything as serious as robbery.

He believed Custodia-Mota was probably in the country illegally and may have pulled a couple of robberies in the Columbus area, but nothing was proven.

Tetuan thought Custodia-Mota and Martinez were visiting one of the girlfriend's relatives on Mother's Day. "I think they were up here visiting, and they needed cash to get back to Columbus, so they went and did the robbery—tried to, anyway," he said.

Both were indicted a few days later on charges of aggravated robbery with a firearm specification and robbery. In September Custodia-Mota pleaded guilty and on October 29, in Lucas County Common Pleas Court, Judge Ruth Ann Franks sentenced him to six years in prison. The charges against Martinez were dropped for lack of evidence.

Detective Paul Tetuan said witnesses corroborated Habib's account of what happened. The only thing about the incident that puzzled him was why Custodia-Mota raised his gun as he was leaving.

"Was this guy responding to something Habib said or did when he turned and pointed the gun, or was he going to shoot Habib? In most robberies that doesn't happen; they just want the money, and once they have the money they're out the door. This guy had the money and was at the door when he turned and pointed his gun. That's when Habib took action and drew his weapon. I guess the only thing that's not a hundred percent clear in my mind is why would this guy do that? Did Habib say something to him? Did he pull his gun first or make a motion that he was going to pull a gun, and this guy felt threatened so he pointed the gun at Habib? I don't know."

Habib said he never said anything to the robber and didn't think the man could see his hand on his gun.

He believes that if he had not shot Custodia-Mota, the robber would have shot him.

"Bottom line is that this guy shouldn't have been doing what he was doing, obviously," says Tetuan. "He's out there breaking the law, committing an armed robbery, and Habib fortunately was able to win the gunfight so to speak. So the good guys won. In that regard I have no problem with anything Habib did. I mean legally, morally, or anything else, I think it was a justified action on his part."

Tetuan said he has seen situations where clerks or store owners have resisted robbery attempts and have been killed. He cited a case that happened three or four months before the robbery at Howard's, where a carryout owner in Toledo was shot and killed. Two robbers entered the store, one armed with a handgun and the other with a semi-automatic rifle. The man with the handgun fired a shot into the ceiling. This apparently caused the man with the rifle to fire, said Tetuan. The bullet hit the owner in the head, killing her.

In another incident, which was caught on video, the robber came in, pointed his gun at the clerk, and it went off, the detective said. Fortunately, the bullet only nicked the clerk in the neck. When they caught the robber, he claimed the gun went off by accident, Tetuan said.

"Within just a few months' time-frame we had several robberies of carryouts where shots were fired," he added.

It took Habib several days to get back to normal. He took the day following the robbery, Monday, off and went horseback riding with his girlfriend, staying away from the store. On Tuesday he went back to work for about three hours.

"I couldn't stand it because something felt wrong. I just shot somebody there like forty-eight hours prior. Psychologically I wasn't fit, I guess, to be there, so I called my brother. He came in," Habib said.

On Wednesday he took five or six hours off, and his brother covered for him. On Thursday Habib felt better and returned to work full-time.

A lot of people were very supportive after the shooting, his father said. He even received a letter from a lawyer in Dallas, Texas, congratulating him on handling the situation and himself well. Some anti-self-defense people reportedly said the store would lose business, but it didn't, his father reported.

Months after the shooting the incident was still with Habib and bothered him occasionally. "I think about it at the store every once in a while," he said. "I get shook up every once in a while, but psychologically, do I feel bad for what I did? No."

Asked if he was scared during the robbery, Habib said, "I think I was more scared of the gun being pulled than shooting the guy. When it was happening, I think I was just blank. Afterwards, I went into shock."

He is more aware of what is going on around him since the shooting, he said. He goes to the range once or twice a month to practice, mostly by himself. He normally practices using both hands on the gun, but he thinks he only used one hand when shooting at the robber. He also does not remember using the sights when shooting.

"Just point and shoot," he said.

Reflections

In retrospect, Habib wishes his aim had been better and that he had used the sights. It never occurred to him to take cover behind the counter, and he had not practiced that.

When Habib said he couldn't take his eyes off the robber's gun, he was describing tunnel vision. David Ham, a San Antonio aikido instructor, refers to it as "the mind captured by the weapon." Firearms instructors teach their students to glance to right and left after shooting to break this tunnel vision. If your mind is captured by your attacker's weapon, you are not aware of what else is happening around you. Bad guys often operate in pairs.

While the police had his Taurus for evidence, Habib carried a Baby Desert Eagle with nine rounds of 9 mm in the magazine and one in the chamber. He acknowledges he should have had more rounds in the Taurus during the shooting, and they should have been hollow-point self-defense rounds. He should also have been armed with a gun that was reliable and would not jam even if the magazine were fully loaded.

Perhaps the most important training Habib received was, at his father's insistence, practicing with his brothers what to do if a robbery occurred. Howard explained the plan he devised to keep his sons safe.

"The way the convenience store is situated, as you're facing the customer, you've got an aisleway where you can walk sideways. You take five steps from the register away from the bad guy, if he's robbing you. I always taught them to put their hands straight up in the air, which gives the bad guy the confidence that he's won the war. In other words, you've surrendered. As you take five steps, the bad guy's supposed to reach in the register with his gun in his hand, and then you would have the entire torso as your target, which is the best target to shoot at.

"But what happened, the bad guy foiled our plan. The first time he [Habib] walked away, the bad guy told him: come back to the register and put the money on the counter. So he had to sidestep again to the left with his hands up in the air, he dropped one hand down, took his money, and put it on the counter. And then again with his hands straight up in the air, he's walking from left to right. That gives the bad guy a direct view of his left arm up in the air. Now, as soon as you're four to five feet away from him, he loses track of where your right arm is at. Then your right arm goes down to your gun, undoes the safety, and you're ready for action, in case the guy does something.

"Now he's approximately twelve to fifteen feet away, and there's a door that leads into the office. You can A, duck into the door for shelter; B, in case the guy decides to shoot his only witness, blast him away, because you've got your gun ready to go. That's how it went down."

Bill Davison, owner of Tac Pro Shooting Center in Texas, teaches armed self-defense to police officers and civilians. He is an experienced firearms instructor who was in the British Royal Marines. He might have been referring to the Toledo shooting when he tells his students: "The reality of self-defense is: it is here right now, and you've got to do something about it. The thing that comes out all the time is that you should have a plan and, as we know, all plans are forfeited by first contact with the enemy. So when it actually happens, the plan that you had will not work. Good, the fact that you had a plan means that you have already started the progression of getting the problem sorted out."

And that is exactly what Habib Howard did that May evening in 2004.

One beneficial result of the shooting incident concerned the parents of Habib's girlfriend. They are liberal Democrats, and the incident changed their attitudes about guns and concealed-carry, he said. "When it hits somebody that you know, you look at it in a totally different way," Habib said.

On the very day of the shooting, Mother's Day 2004, the optimistically named Million Mom March held a rally in Washington, D.C. It was anti-gun, anti-self-defense. Organizers managed to dredge up only a couple of thousand people to support their gun-confiscation agenda.

Habib Howard is one person who is glad he had a gun that night. He believes that had the members of that rally been successful in forcing their agenda on all of us, he might well have been killed.

Chapter 6

Hotel Holdup:
Steve Robey

You won't find "home invasion" as a category of crime in the FBI's annual reports of crime statistics. It is a relatively new term.

People often confuse robbery with burglary or theft. They say, "I was robbed," when criminals break into their homes and steal things when they are away. What they are actually talking about is burglary and theft, which are classified as non-violent or property crimes. Robbery is a crime that includes violence or the threat of violence and involves a confrontation with the victim by the robber. We have coined the term "home invasion" to describe a particular type of robbery.

We frequently read in our newspapers of home invasions when a couple of decades ago they would have been called robberies. Infrequently we read or hear of criminals forcing their way into someone's temporary home, such as a hotel room. There are advantages to this type of crime from the perpetrator's point of view. Travelers usually have money with them. They are not local and will be moving on quickly from the city, the state, or even the country where the hotel-room invasion took place. This means that victims may be reluctant to return as witnesses if later the robbers are caught.

In August 2002 42-year-old Phillip C. Nelson, known as "New Wave," and his daughter's boyfriend,

Ernest Henry Major, 22, had this figured out. The two were suspects in three hotel-room-invasion robberies in Fort Myers and North Fort Myers, on Florida's west coast.

One of these occurred on August 11 at a Motel 6 in North Fort Myers. The victim was an Episcopal nun, Sister Carol Andrew, of the Convent of St. Helena in Augusta, Georgia. Sister Andrew was in North Fort Myers visiting her mother, who was in poor health. Major burst into her motel room and demanded money at gunpoint.

However, luck ran out for the two robbers when they tried to pull what was probably their fourth hotel-room invasion on August 24.

Steve Robey

On Friday, August 23, 2002, Steve Robey and his 16-year-old daughter, Sarina, checked into the Howard Johnson Express Inn on North Cleveland Avenue in North Fort Myers. They had been house hunting. At the time, Robey lived in New Smyrna Beach, nearly two hundred miles north on the Atlantic coast. They had moved from Cape Coral about five months previously but didn't like New Smyrna Beach. They wanted to return to Cape Coral, which is just west of North Fort Myers.

They had started looking for a house earlier in the week. Steve had $9,000 in cash with him in a zippered pouch, in case he wanted to make a down payment on another house. The money was the proceeds from the house in Cape Coral Steve had sold before moving north to New Smyrna Beach.

That evening Steve and Sarina had driven around jotting down the addresses of houses that interested them and the phone numbers of the realtors trying to sell them.

Steve and Sarina shared room 104. She occupied the bed nearer the bathroom, while he slept in the bed nearer the door. Steve was awakened that Saturday morning by a maid knocking on the door. He told her that he was not ready to get up, and she apologized.

He tried to go back to sleep but couldn't so he got up and turned on the television. He also took his medication for high blood pressure. Little did he know that his blood pressure would have cause to escalate before the morning was over.

Sarina was still in bed. Her father told her he was going to the motel lobby for the continental breakfast. She asked him to get her a glass of orange juice. He returned a few minutes later with a plate of sweet rolls and the orange juice. Steve told Sarina it was time she got up. He turned the television back on.

The Incident

Shortly after 9:30 A.M. there was a knock on the door. Steve assumed it was the maid returning and went to the door. Sarina was still in bed trying to go back to sleep. He opened the door to find two black men standing one at each side of the door. One was in his early twenties and the other in his early forties. The younger one was over six feet tall and weighed nearly two hundred pounds. He was later identified as Ernest Henry Major; the older man was Phillip "New Wave" Nelson. Major towered over Robey, who is five feet five inches tall.

Major asked Steve for a loan of couple of bucks. Steve replied that he didn't have any money: it wasn't exactly the truth. He started to close the door.

"I almost had the door shut, and they pushed their way through, and Major stuck a gun in my face," Steve said later in a deposition.

It was dark inside the hotel room, with the curtains closed and the only light coming from the television screen.

Major demanded money, while Nelson picked up a blue, zippered bank pouch which was lying on the bed. Inside the pouch were some bits of paper relating to the house hunt. It also contained $9,000 in $100 bills.

As Nelson was trying to unzip the pouch, Steve handed Major his wallet. This distracted the two robbers, and they never found the $9,000. In the wallet Steve had some photos of his 2½-year-old daughter, who lived in Ohio. They were the only photos of her that he had, so he asked Major for them.

The robber ignored him, rifled through the wallet, then passed it to Nelson, who dropped the bank pouch. The older man looked through the wallet then threw it on the floor. Steve had a bunch of keys clipped to his belt loop. Major unclipped them and took them. He ordered Steve to lie down on the bed with his face in the pillow.

Sarina poked her head out from under the covers, and Major realized that there was someone in the other bed. He screamed at Sarina to get into the bathroom. She got out of bed, wearing shorts and a T-shirt. Major grabbed her hard by the arm, hurting her. When she was 6-years-old she had cut her arm badly when she went through a glass door, and it still hurt. Major steered her towards the bathroom at the back of the hotel room.

"Who is he to you?" Major asked her.

"He's my father," Sarina replied.

All the while Major kept the small revolver he was holding pointed at Steve. The robber pushed Sarina into the bathroom. Once inside she locked the door.

Meanwhile, Steve turned to look at Nelson, who was standing beside him.

"Get your f---ing face in that pillow," Nelson yelled. It was a fatal mistake.

The older robber smacked Steve in the face, then he pulled up his shirt with his left hand as though to draw a gun. Steve did what he was told. He lay face down on the bed.

"I knew I was gonna' be killed, and I didn't know what they were gonna' do with my daughter," he later told Detective Mike Rakestraw of the Lee County Sheriff's Office. "I assumed that they were going to shoot me in the head or something, rape my daughter, and who knows. But I couldn't let that happen."

Under the pillow was Steve's Colt Combat Elite, a .45-caliber, semi-automatic pistol. He had a Florida concealed-weapons permit, but he carried the gun only when he was traveling. The gun held a magazine with seven rounds in it, but the chamber was empty and the hammer at halfcock.

Convinced that he was about to be shot in the back of the head by Nelson, Steve groped for the gun. He managed to pull back the slide and let it go forward, chambering a round without getting the pillowcase stuck in the action.

He rolled over and before he got up off the bed he started shooting in the direction where he thought Nelson was standing. Steve called it shooting blind and said his cousin, who had been a deputy sheriff in Albuquerque, New Mexico, had taught him the technique.

Phillip "New Wave" Nelson in an earlier booking photo.

He thought he fired two shots at Nelson, but deputies later told him he fired three. As soon as Steve started shooting, Major, who was still near the bathroom door, opened fire at him.

"I'm looking down the barrel of another pistol, and he started pulling the trigger, so I just emptied my magazine. And I'm not sure if I even hit him, because he never even blinked," Steve said.

He had four rounds remaining in the magazine, and he fired them all at the younger robber.

By this time Steve had reached the door leading outside. He assumed he had missed both men in the half-light, because they rushed him before he could get out of the door.

The fight was on.

"They were trying to get me on the floor, but I kept my back against the wall, and I just kept swinging my forty-five, and they were punching, and kicking, and biting me," Steve said.

Nelson bit Steve's left index finger to the bone. Deputies told him later the bite reflected it was Nelson, because the older robber had no bottom teeth.

"Yeah, it had to be Nelson, because Major had me by my head and was kicking me on my left side with his right knee. And one of them was stomping on my foot, and I don't know which one that was at all," he said.

Steve was fighting back. He was punching and kicking the two robbers and flailing about him with the gun. He hit Nelson with the gun and saw "flesh coming off his head."

Meanwhile, Steve was trying to unbolt the door and escape from the hotel room. The fight lasted for mere moments, but to Steve it seemed like hours. Finally Nelson collapsed at the foot of Steve's bed and Steve was able to get out of the door.

Sarina, still in the bathroom, heard Major yell: "Let's go, let's go. Let's get outa' here."

"I thought I heard the door open. So I slowly opened the [bathroom] door, and then I seen light, and then I seen a guy laying on the floor, and then I seen my dad in the parking lot, so I just came out of the room," Sarina later recalled in a sworn deposition.

Steve's Jeep was parked right outside the hotel room, and he stepped towards it while Major ran to a late-model, champagne-colored Ford Taurus. He got into the car and accelerated towards where Steve and Sarina stood.

"He was trying to run over us in the parking lot, so I shoved my daughter and told her to get to the office and call the police. And then I started yelling at all the people that were standing out there to call the police," Steve recalled.

Major escaped from the hotel parking lot and headed across the bridge over the Caloosahatchee River for the house on Barker Boulevard in Fort Myers, where he had been staying with Nelson and Nelson's daughter, Shalona Stafford.

The Aftermath

By the time deputies from the Lee County Sheriff's Office arrived, Major was long gone. When the officers arrived at the hotel, they found Phillip "New Wave" Nelson lying on the floor at the foot of the bed with his head pointing towards the door. He was taken by ambulance to Lee Memorial Hospital where he was pronounced dead from a gunshot would to the chest.

Jean-Paul Galasso, the assistant state attorney who prosecuted Ernest Major, said the shot that killed Nelson hit the middle of his chest, rupturing his aorta.

Steve Robey was treated at the hotel for the bite on his finger, a swollen foot, and neck injuries.

Crime Scene Technician Philip Puglisi was in charge of collecting evidence and documenting the scene. His report states that a nine-shot, .22-caliber revolver made by New England Firearms Company was found on the floor between the two beds. This was the revolver used by Major to shoot at Steve Robey. While it could hold nine rounds in the cylinder, it contained only six: four empty casings and two live rounds. Three of the bullets fired by Major hit the door and the fourth hit the wall to the left of it above the light switch. None of them hit Robey.

Steve fired seven rounds, emptying his Colt Combat Elite .45-caliber semi-automatic. As the deputies were arriving, Steve placed the empty gun on the hood of his 1999 Jeep. Investigators found a line of five empty casings on the floor between the two beds. Two more .45-caliber casings were found on the bed nearest the door.

Puglisi documented the locations of six .45-caliber bullets. The first three rounds Steve fired at Nelson. Two bullets went through the wall of room 104 into room 103.

According to Galasso, a maid was working in that room at the time but was not hit. The other bullet was the one that hit Nelson and destroyed his aorta. Steve fired the other four rounds at Major. Two went through the wall into the bathroom, missing Sarina. The other two hit just to the left of the bathroom in the vanity area.

Shalona Stafford, Nelson's 17-year-old daughter, told Detective Mike Rakestraw about Major's return to the house on Barker Boulevard after the shooting.

"He pulled in the driveway, and he said he been shot and New Wave dead. That's all he said, and he kept blanking out, but I tried to wake him up. And that's all he kept saying: New Wave's dead."

Major told her to call 9-1-1. Stafford told the detective that the Ford Taurus Major was driving had been rented by her mother, Velda Royals, from Enterprise Rent-A-Car.

Shortly before 10 A.M. Lee County Sheriff's Office received a 9-1-1 call from the house on Barker Boulevard, according to an affidavit signed by Rakestraw. As a result a Lee County Emergency Medical Services ambulance took Major to Lee Memorial Hospital, where he was treated for gunshot wounds.

Prosecutor Galasso said Major was shot in the stomach, shoulder, and shin, which broke his shinbone in half. One bullet took off the last knuckle of his little finger, Galasso added. He said that Robey's Colt was loaded with round-nosed, full-metal-jacketed bullets, not hollow-points. Galasso figures that if Robey had been using hollow-points, Major would have died.

Back at the hotel Detective Rakestraw took sworn statements from Steve Robey and his daughter Sarina. Later that afternoon, Steve identified Nelson and Major as his attackers from a photo line-up. His daughter, Sarina, identified Major, but said she did not get a good look at Nelson.

Ernest Henry Major was booked after being released from the hospital.

Galasso said Robey was not arrested or prosecuted, and he didn't go before a grand jury.

"Our office looked at it, and there was no reason to suspect that he had done anything wrong. He was lawfully in the room. There wasn't much doubt what had occurred. That's it. There was never any allegation that there was any wrongdoing on his part, not even by the defendant."

Major recovered from his wounds and was charged with attempted murder, attempted robbery, and second-degree murder. In Florida a person can be charged with murder if someone, even an accomplice, dies during the commission of a felony. He was also charged with robbery in the hotel-room invasion of Sister Carol Andrew, the Episcopal nun from Augusta, Georgia. She too identified him as her attacker from a photo line-up.

Major was also suspected of pulling a couple of other hotel-room invasions with Nelson in August 2002, but was never charged. Major had been released from prison in 2001, after serving two years for grand theft auto and robbery. Nelson had served three terms of imprisonment on charges of theft and carrying a concealed weapon.

Major was tried first on the charge of robbing Sister Andrew at gunpoint in her hotel room. He was convicted in October 2003 and sentenced to life in prison. In 2004 he was tried on the charges resulting from the Howard

Johnson hotel-room invasion and found guilty. He was sentenced to twenty years minimum mandatory consecutive, said prosecutor Galasso, which means he serves all twenty years consecutive with the life sentence. In Florida a life sentence lasts for life, he added.

Reflections

During the deposition Major's lawyer asked Robey if he used the peephole in the door to check who was knocking before he opened the door.

"The peephole was about a foot taller than I am," Steve, who is five feet five inches, replied.

However, he said he thought it was the maid or someone from the office asking whether he would be staying another night. So he probably wouldn't have checked, even if he had been able to reach the peephole.

It is important to know who is knocking on the door and why before opening it. Many hotels post checklists of safety advice, which usually include putting on the chain and using the deadbolt when you are in the room. Steve could have looked out of the window to see who the visitors were. If you are in any way suspicious and the people at the door claim to be working for the hotel, call the office and check.

People like Ernest Major and New Wave Nelson can come up with all sorts of inventive reasons for you to open the door: from "the previous occupant complained about the air-conditioner, and I need to check it," to "I have an envelope for you from the office." If you do open the door, at least be certain the security chain or other safety device is in place.

One of the problems with this attack was its timing. I'm sure Steve would have been more wary had the knock come during hours of darkness. But who expects a robbery at 9:30 in the morning? The hotel-room invasion serves as a reminder that attacks can happen at any time and one must always be alert to that possibility.

Steve had a Colt Combat Elite, a fine single-action semi-automatic. He said he bought it at a gun show in Ohio about three years before. He had the gun under his pillow, which shows he was alert to the possibility of bad things happening. However, he told Detective Mike Rakestraw that he had one magazine containing seven rounds and one containing four. Although he did not have time to reload, a second full magazine would have been an asset. According to the prosecutor, the magazines were loaded with full-metal-jacket bullets. He would have been more effective with hollow-points, which create a larger wound channel, but don't tend to penetrate as far.

One of the basic safety rules is to know what is behind your target. A couple of Steve's bullets penetrated through the wall into the bathroom, where his daughter was confined. Two more went through another wall into the room next door, where a maid was working. Under the circumstances, there is little Steve could have done to prevent the risk to Sarina and the maid. He was fighting for his life and, as they say, it is better to be tried by twelve than carried by six.

All but one of the bullets Steve fired were found at the scene. Therefore, the shots that wounded Major went through him instead of stopping in his body. This is another argument for hollow-point bullets which are designed for self-defense. Hollow-point bullets rupture when they hit flesh, expanding to more than twice their original size. This slows them down more quickly, so they are less likely to over-penetrate, and they make a larger wound channel.

Prosecutor Jean-Paul Galasso speculated that, if Steve had been shooting hollow-points, he would not have prosecuted Major, because the robber would have been dead.

In the semi-darkness of the curtained room, Steve thought all his rounds had missed, because they did not seem to be having any effect. In fact, he shot well, hitting Nelson once and Major four times. Good shooting. However, it is worth noting that Nelson was able to keep fighting for some time with his aorta ripped apart, and Major kept fighting despite his serious wounds.

Robey told Rakestraw he carried the Colt only when he was traveling. He had acquired the carry permit to make it easier to buy guns at gun shows and elsewhere. It would be interesting to know if he carries his gun more frequently since the attack.

I was unable to find Steve Robey. He mentioned in his deposition that he had made himself hard to find. Most of the information for this account came from police and court documents.

Chapter 7

The Risks We Take:
Mark Wilson

Are we a nation of cowards? Have we become brainwashed by big government, big media, and big academia into believing that personal risk is unacceptable in a civilized society—that dignity and self-respect must bow to safety at all costs? Jeffrey Snyder certainly thought so, as expressed in his excellent article, "A Nation of Cowards," which appeared in the Fall 1993 issue of *The Public Interest*, a quarterly journal of opinion published by National Affairs, Inc.

As he pointed out, if we do not fight crime on a personal level we are abdicating our personal responsibilities as citizens and condoning evil. Yet for decades we have been told by big-city police departments to give the criminal what he wants. Do not resist because you might get hurt. We have allowed our schools to demonize firearms, which are the most effective weapons for personal defense. We have been encouraged to rely on authority to protect us.

However, things have changed since 1993. One of the positive things that came out of the terrorist attacks in September 2001 and, more recently, Hurricane Katrina, is that people realized that the government cannot protect them. The veneer of civilized society is exceeding thin.

The other thing that has been happening in the past two decades is that concealed-weapons laws have rampaged through state legislatures. At this writing forty states have laws that make it relatively easy for law-abiding citizens to carry concealed handguns for protection. More than three million people have licenses to carry handguns concealed in public.

All the ordinary citizens who go to the expense and trouble of getting concealed-carry licenses are taking the first small steps toward being responsible for their own safety. They have taken a stand against the degradation and humiliation of being victims of crime. They have indicated that they are willing to take the risk of fighting back. Although the odds are with those who fight back with guns, there are still risks. But without risks there would be no heroes.

Mark Wilson

Mark Alan Wilson was never one to consider consequences. He was a Navy brat, moving constantly from place to place, as his father was transferred to different cities around the country. When the family arrived in a new city, the first thing his mother Lynn did was find the nearest emergency medical facility.

"I knew we'd be there shortly," she said. "When we lived in San Diego the guys in the emergency room knew him by his first name, he had been there so many times. There was no telling what he'd do."

One time, when Mark was in junior high, Lynn heard him come into the house and go into the bathroom. She heard the water running and asked if he was all right.

"He opened the door and he was standing there with blood all over him—I mean just covered with blood.

I said: 'Mark, what happened?' He said they were racing their bicycles, and they hit gravel, and he fell."

Lynn said she could see the bone in his ankle, and skin had been scraped off down the whole of one side of his body. They rushed Mark to the emergency room. After he had been patched up, he was still in considerable pain.

Lynn remembers the return journey. "It was the only time I've been able to hold him in my arms since he was two years old," she said.

From the time he was a toddler, Mark was always very independent. His mother recalled that when he was 4- or 5-years old, he laid down the rules to his grandmother. "When his grandmother came to visit, he said: 'Granny, you can kiss me hello and you can kiss me goodbye, but not in between.'"

If Mark saw something he felt was wrong, he would not think twice about getting involved, said Lynn. Typical was an incident that happened when the family was living in Durham, North Carolina.

Mark was born in January 1953 and his sister Melody in December of that year. Another sister was born in 1958, but Mark and Melody were particularly close.

"Sometimes every year we moved to a different part of the country, so we never really had any roots," Melody recalled. They moved from school to school, not staying long enough to develop real friendships. "So a lot of the time, it was just us," she said.

One evening in the spring of 1969, when Mark was 16 and Melody 15, they were dating a brother and sister who lived a couple of doors from the Wilsons. "We were just out on a double date, riding around looking for something to do," Melody said.

They spotted a sign that said "KKK Meeting" with an arrow beneath the words. "We saw this sign, and none of us had been exposed to anything like that. So we decided we would go and see what it was all about." They followed the arrow out into the woods until they came to the meeting. They parked their car among the others and got out. The Ku Klux Klan members were dressed in their white robes and hoods. A man was addressing the crowd from a platform at the front.

"There were a ton of people there, a lot of cars, and they had their torches all around. It was really quite frightening. We stood at the back—I'm sure our eyes were as big as saucers—and listened to this guy up there just spewing all this hatred. It was horrible, just horrible, because we were raised not to think that way."

After listening to the speaker spreading vitriol against blacks, Mark cupped his hands around his mouth and shouted as loudly as he could, "You're full of s--t."

"Of course we were immediately attacked. They didn't hurt any of us, but they grabbed us and physically threw us out," Melody recalled. "They just grabbed us and manhandled us out. I was quite concerned that they were going to harm Mark, but they didn't."

Melody remembers being afraid that their mother would find out what had happened. There was an article in the local newspaper the next day about a group of unruly kids disrupting the Ku Klux Klan meeting, but there were no names in the story.

Lynn said it was some time before she heard the story. "I take credit for some of this. I raised those kids that nobody is better than anybody else. They might be smarter, they might be richer, but they weren't any better," she said.

In 1973 Mark followed in his father's footsteps and joined the Navy. However, instead of making the service his career, he received an honorable discharge in 1977.

Tyler

By 2005 Mark had moved to Tyler, a city of 87,000 in East Texas known nationwide for its annual Rose Festival. He was working as a project and quality control manager for Sealtite Building Fasteners, a local company that manufactures bolts, screws, and other hardware used to hold metal buildings together.

He was living in a second-floor apartment that overlooked Spring Avenue and the Courthouse Square. From the four windows of his apartment he had a clear view of the east entrance to the Smith County Courthouse, a yellow-brick building built in 1954 in the shoebox style of architecture. In more than a decade of living in Tyler, Mark had become well known for his participation in community events, such as the Festival on the Square, and his volunteer work for charities.

In the mid-1990s Mark had owned and operated an indoor shooting range called On Target, on Southwest Loop 323, where the emphasis was on self-defense-style shooting. He wanted to provide a range where law-enforcement officers and responsible civilians could practice. Being something of a perfectionist and wanting to get the range just right, he spent most of his operating budget building the range according to one of his friends. He lost the range due to subsequent financial troubles.

Living between the courthouse and the Smith County Sheriff's Office, and through his ownership of the range, Mark knew many law-enforcement officers.

*Mark
Wilson,
when he
owned On
Target
Indoor
Shooting
Range*

*(Photo courtesy
of Lock & Load
Indoor Shooting
Range)*

"We knew Mark and thought a lot of him, and Mark was an exceptionally good shot," said Major Mike Lusk of the Smith County Sheriff's Office.

Mark also had a Texas concealed-handgun license.

David Hernandez Arroyo

When Tyler Police Officer Luis Correa reflected on first meeting David Hernandez Arroyo about 1990, Correa wrote in a statement that David appeared to be a very happy man: "I was always under the impression that everything was well with his family."

Arroyo and Correa knew each other quite well, and the officer felt David trusted him and looked on him as an authority figure. Arroyo often talked of buying a ranch in East Texas and raising horses. He also showed a strong interest in guns, so Correa explained Texas gun laws to him.

Arroyo told the officer that in Guerrero, Mexico, where he came from, there was little law enforcement and, consequently, the man of the family handled any enforcement problems.

"Knowing David Arroyo as long as I did led me to believe that all he wanted to do in life was to be what I would call a modern-day cowboy, like Texas had a hundred and fifty years ago," Correa stated.

After losing touch with Arroyo for some time, Correa saw him in mid-2004 in the lobby of the police department. Arroyo's vision of the American dream had soured. After two decades in Texas he had become an embittered man. "I saw a different David Arroyo," Correa stated.

Arroyo had lost weight and moved as though he was in constant pain. He told Correa he was in bad health and was taking pain medication for back problems. He was separated from his wife, who was then 40, and said he was having trouble with his son, who was 21. He claimed the pair were trying to set him up so he would be arrested on family-violence charges.

He also had to go to the hospital for treatment of head injuries he said were inflicted by David Jr. He was behind in his child support and was afraid of losing his 10-year-old son Abraham. He was receiving disability checks and was unable to work. In his statement Correa made it clear that he was only getting Arroyo's side of the story. The officer advised him to get a lawyer to handle his divorce and child-custody problems.

Arroyo twice met with Correa at the Tyler Police Department when there were outstanding warrants for him. On one of these occasions he asked Correa about getting a bullet-proof vest, perhaps a used one from the police department— or perhaps the officer would sell him one. Correa asked him why he wanted one. Arroyo said he wanted to be a police officer.

David Hernandez Arroyo

"David laughed and said he was just joking," Correa recalled. He added that he wanted the vest in case he was hit by a stray bullet from a hunter while out riding.

According to court records, Arroyo was divorced from his wife, Maribel Estrada, in 2004. He was charged both with assault causing bodily injury to Maribel and with failure to pay child support.

Arroyo's court-appointed lawyer, Peter Milne, told investigators his client received a disability check of $898 a month and could not work. He was supposed to have been paying $240 a month in child support for more than a year. He had paid only $350 in total.

By 2005 Arroyo was on probation for the assault charge and was seeking custody of his 10-year-old son. He was less concerned about his teenage daughter.

Maribel's brother, Julian Estrada, remembered that his sister had told him Arroyo had threatened "to kill everybody" before he would pay her child support.

An initial court appearance for the 43-year-old Arroyo on the child support charges was set for February 17, 2005, but it was postponed because his mother died on February 12. Relatives told police that Arroyo took his mother's death hard and became very depressed, and Arroyo's older son later told investigators his father had started wearing a bullet-proof vest.

The date for Arroyo's court appearance had been rescheduled to Thursday, February 24.

February 24, 2005

February 24, 2005, started as a very ordinary day for Mark Wilson. He left his loft apartment overlooking the courthouse square by the back stairs to reach his Dodge Ram pickup in its assigned spot behind the building at 119 East Erwin Street. He drove to his job at Sealtite Building Fasteners on Reynolds Road, just inside East Northeast Loop 323, arriving about 7:45 A.M.

Initially Mark had gone to Sealtite to remodel some offices. When he had finished the work, he was offered a permanent position. "In doing their offices, they liked him so much they kinda' made this position for him," said his friend Robert Lloyd. "He was a real perfectionist. Everything was always in order. It's just the way he thought, and then it's the way he worked."

His friend and supervisor at Sealtite, Jim Carter, said Mark supervised a couple of operations for the company, in addition to being responsible for safety and quality assurance at the plant.

For Mark and Jim that morning was just the first half of a normal business day. Carter doesn't remember anything out of the ordinary. They would have seen each other several times and conversed about normal business issues, he said.

They would go for lunch together on average four days a week. That Thursday was no exception. About 11:40 A.M. they left in Carter's vehicle and drove to the Potpourri House on Troup Highway just off Southeast Loop 323. It was an upscale restaurant that sold antiques on the side. At lunchtime it was usually filled with middle-aged women. Mark and Jim would eat there perhaps once a month. The food was good, and Mark liked the chicken Caesar salad.

During lunch Mark asked Jim if he knew anybody who wanted to buy a gun. This was an unusual topic of conversation between them. Although Carter knew Mark used to own On Target shooting range and was a federally licensed firearms dealer, they had only talked about guns perhaps half-a-dozen times in the years that Jim had known him. Mark explained that he had to sell so many guns a year to retain his gun-dealer's license. Jim said he didn't know anyone in the market for a gun.

They discussed Mark's upcoming operation. He had injured his hip some years before in a traffic accident and was planning to have a hip replacement operation, but he had been putting it off. He liked to play tennis and racquetball, but had not been able to play tennis for about six months. He also talked about taking up golf as something that would be easier for him to do after the operation.

"He ultimately could have played tennis or racquetball after the operation, but he realized that he would probably be a little more restricted, so we were talking about golf clubs and golfing and that sort of thing," Carter said.

Although Mark had never married, he was never short of girlfriends. His mother Lynn said he had never married because he was too picky.

"He wanted beauty; he wanted personality; he wanted brains; he wanted everything. And he wouldn't settle for anything less than perfect," she said. "He was too particular. I've met so many of them, and they were all lovely girls, and all of them were career-type people—professional dancers and teachers and attorneys."

He was an old-fashioned romantic, putting the woman on a pedestal and inundating her with flowers. But when he broke up with one, they usually remained friends, his mother said.

At lunch that February day Carter said Mark hinted that he had a hot date for the coming weekend. Jim said his advice to Mark when he was on this date was: "Just don't be yourself." They both laughed.

After lunch Jim drove them back to the plant. They arrived at Sealtite about 12:45 P.M. Mark said he was going to visit the East Texas Fasteners building where the fasteners are plated. The company is owned by Sealtite and is about a mile-and-a-half east of the courthouse on East Commerce Street.

"He would have had reason to go over there—maybe it was about a compressor—I really couldn't tell you why, but that wasn't out of the ordinary for him to have gone over there," Carter said.

Although not on a direct route from Sealtite to East Texas Fasteners, Mark's apartment was only a short detour. He wasn't planning to stay long, because he parked on the street in front of his building.

"I am assuming that he probably went home to check an e-mail, maybe it was about this date or something, on his home computer," Jim said.

The Shooting

David Arroyo knew that February 24 would not be an ordinary day for him. He had made preparations to ensure that it wouldn't be. When he left the shabby mobile home with an add-on at the end of a dirt road called Indian Trace, he left it in disarray. He left food on the stove and on the kitchen table. It appeared that no one had cleaned the inside or the outside of the residence in a long time. Gang graffiti was painted on the walls.

A blue mattress lay folded in half on the living-room floor and on it were several empty Wolf-brand boxes for 7.62 x 39 mm rifle ammunition. In the master bedroom a loaded Savage .410-caliber single-shot shotgun stood leaning in a corner.

When Arroyo drove his maroon step-side Chevrolet pickup away from his residence that day he was ready

Flowers on the sidewalk indicate the spot where Mark fell. The east doors of the courthouse are on the far side of Spring Avenue. (Photo by Robert Langham)

for battle. He was wearing a bullet-resistant vest and a military flack jacket under a black-leather jacket.

With him he had a MAK-90, a Chinese-made, semi-automatic, AK-47-style rifle. He had a forty-round magazine and several thirty-round magazines, all loaded with full-metal-jacket military-style rounds. He also had a loaded Remington .243-caliber hunting rifle with a telescopic sight.

Arroyo drove downtown to the courthouse, parked in a loading zone on the east side of Spring Avenue outside Levine's department store, and waited. Spring Avenue on the east side of the courthouse is three lanes wide with angle parking on both sides. Next to the courthouse the parking is for law-enforcement vehicles only. On the opposite side, in front of shops and offices, is public metered parking.

Shortly before 1:30 P.M. Maribel Estrada and her son, David Hernandez Arroyo Jr., arrived. David, who was driving, parked in one of the diagonal spaces on Spring Avenue, north of where his father was waiting.

Exactly what happened in the next ten minutes or so is the subject of some speculation. The Tyler Police report lists 167 civilian witnesses to parts of what occurred. Some witnesses heard shots but saw nothing. Others saw parts of the incident, and their descriptions of what they saw vary, as eyewitness accounts always do. No one but David Arroyo Sr. saw the entire incident, and he isn't talking. What follows is the best account gleaned from witnesses, police reports and video, autopsy reports, and interviews.

As Maribel and David Jr. crossed the red-brick-paved street heading for the east entrance of the courthouse, Arroyo Sr. got out of his pickup with his semi-automatic rifle and started to walk towards them.

As Arroyo Sr. reached the center of the street he raised his rifle and opened fire. He hit his former wife in the chest, mortally wounding her. He hit his son in the right knee and the right lower leg. They both fell at the bottom of the steps leading to the east entrance of the courthouse.

Arroyo Jr. told police he attempted to cover his mother with his body. He also said at one point he stood up and yelled at his father: "You shot me; now let's talk."

Other witnesses said that Arroyo, still trying to shield his mother, raised one or both arms in the air and pleaded with his father to stop shooting.

By this time several law-enforcement officers were responding. Smith County Deputy Sheriff Sherman Dollison was providing security in Judge Randall Rogers's courtroom. He was first out of the east doors of the courthouse. Dollison, 27, ran across the wide steps to his right, exchanging shots with Arroyo.

Unfortunately, there was no cover in front of the steps, and the bullets from his 9 mm handgun made no impression on Arroyo's body armor. Dollison was hit four times and went down on the grass just south of the steps. Though seriously wounded. the officer kept shooting at Arroyo.

Another officer came out of the courthouse doors and turned to his left, trying to take cover behind a trash can. Arroyo's rifle bullets had smashed all the glass in the doors, and the shards lay like snow in the entrance. Several officers, mostly sheriff's deputies, fired at Arroyo through the doors that no longer had glass in them. Sheriff's Lieutenant Marlin Suell was nicked in the neck and ear by a bullet.

Tyler Police Detective Clay Perrett, 54, was sitting in the spectator section of a courtroom on the second floor waiting to give testimony at an appeal hearing into a 1998 double-murder case. When he heard the first gunshots, Perrett didn't recognize them for what they were. He looked out of the courtroom windows, but they faced west, and he saw nothing unusual.

He then heard screaming coming from the floor below and ran for the stairs. On the first floor he could tell the shots were coming from the east side of the building, and people were running towards the west exit. Accompanied by sheriff's deputies and court bailiffs he headed for the sound of the gunfire.

"I ran to the east-side doors and immediately saw a gunman on the far side of Spring Street. I saw him walking and firing," Perrett stated.

He saw Maribel Estrada and her son down on the steps of the courthouse and saw other people running for cover. Arroyo was walking south behind the cars parked on the far side of the street and more than a hundred feet from the detective. Perrett said the gunman was shooting at the courthouse, also to the south, and possibly to the north as well. He recognized Arroyo's rifle as a semi-automatic, AK-47 type.

"The way he was randomly firing and walking gave me the impression that everyone was a target. I came to the immediate conclusion that I had no choice but to try to stop him," the detective stated.

Perrett was inside the doors of the courthouse using a wooden post for cover. He is short and stocky and wished the post was wider. He had a clear field of fire through the now-shattered glass doors. "I took deliberate aim at center of mass and fired. I tried to remain calm and focused on what I was doing," he said.

Perrett was fully aware that behind Arroyo there were offices and businesses, almost certainly with people inside them. He had no intention of spraying rounds from his 9 mm-caliber Beretta Model 92.

The detective fired a second shot, and Arroyo returned fire in his direction. The gunman walked over to his maroon pickup, possibly to reload, as an empty forty-round magazine was found in his truck. He had his back to Perrett when the detective fired again.

Arroyo turned and fired more rounds at the courthouse doors. Perrett fired two more rounds, then something hit him on the left side of his head. It appeared to have been a piece of glass or other debris dislodged by one of Arroyo's wild shots.

In addition to Perrett, several sheriff's deputies were shooting at Arroyo from the courthouse. Tyler Police Officer Mike Gray, who first broadcast details about the shooting on the police radio, was also shooting at Arroyo from Spring Avenue and Ferguson Street. None of the rounds seemed to be having any effect.

"None of us knew at the time that he was wearing body armor. Frankly, for me, at the distance I was firing at, to do a head shot at that range would have been a terrific shot. I was trying to place my shots in the body," Detective Perrett said.

Mark Intervenes

Mark Wilson was in his second-story apartment when he heard the first shots. His apartment overlooked Spring Avenue and the east entrance to the Smith County Courthouse. It appears he had been sitting at his computer checking his e-mail. From the tall windows in his living room and dining area he had a perfect view of what was happening. He undoubtedly saw Arroyo's wife and son go down at the north end of the courthouse steps.

From his apartment window, Mark Wilson had a clear view of Spring Avenue, the east entrance to the courthouse, and the place where he would eventually lose his life to Arroyo's bullets. (Photos by Robert Langham)

Mark Wilson's Colt .45-caliber semi-automatic Tactical Officer's Model

Leaving his cell phone and his keys on his desk, he grabbed his Colt .45-caliber, semi-automatic pistol and headed downstairs. The lightweight Tactical Officer's Model contained a magazine holding eight Hydra-Shok hollow-point rounds and one in the chamber for a total of nine. He hurried down the thirty shallow steps to the street.

Skip Mason, a hairdresser in the Rage Salon on Erwin Street at the corner of Spring Avenue, saw him walk across the front of the store. He did not see a gun in Wilson's hand. Mark was probably walking so as to avoid attracting Arroyo's attention. "He was walking at a very normal pace," Mason said. "He looked to me like he was just walking to his car."

Wilson passed out of Mason's sight, crossed Spring, and walked up the street until he reached Arroyo's truck. He probably did not realize it was the gunman's escape vehicle.

Ron Martell saw more of the courthouse shooting and its aftermath than anyone but Arroyo himself. Martell, 52, a veteran of the U.S. Air Force, who runs a telephone-installation business, was driving south on Broadway Avenue on the other side of the courthouse when he heard shots. He was driving his white GMC Safari van and was heading to a bail-bond company at Spring and Erwin to do a network cable installation. He looked around trying to figure out where the shots were coming from, but could not see anyone shooting. "I figured this is just a jailbreak," he said.

The Smith County Sheriff's Office and the jail are a block south of the courthouse, so Martell turned left. He passed the sheriff's office and couldn't see anything unusual, so he turned left again onto Spring Avenue. He drove up the steep hill and stopped at Erwin Street.

"Arroyo was right there in front of me shooting at the courthouse," Martell said. "I saw what was going on, and I was looking around, trying to keep my wits about me, to make sure there wasn't somebody else involved in this thing, but I could tell this guy seemed to be the bad guy."

Ron Martell had a Texas concealed-handgun license. He reached under the seat of his van for his SIG Model 229, semi-automatic handgun in .357 SIG caliber.

"I had one foot on the concrete, my gun out between the doorjambs, aimed his way in case he spun around. I was coming in kinda' behind him at a very oblique angle. He wasn't looking back, he was very focused, and of course he was engaged in a frontal gun battle with the police over there that were hiding behind cover at the courthouse," Martell said.

He saw Mark Wilson wearing a red shirt taking cover behind Arroyo's pickup. He did not know Mark and thought he was a police officer in plain clothes. As he watched, Mark took aim at the gunman, who had his back to him while still loosing off rounds in the direction of the courthouse. Arroyo was backing up towards the open driver's side door, but was still close to the tailgate. Wilson aimed over the truck bed using a classic two-hand hold. He fired several fast shots at Arroyo, knocking him down.

Mark turned away and started to walk towards the sidewalk. He could not see Arroyo because he was on the other side of the truck. Mark was probably trying to go around the front of the pickup where he could check on the gunman while using the engine block as cover.

At that point Mark may well have thought he had killed Arroyo or badly wounded him. But as Mark turned away, Martell watched in horror as Arroyo scrambled up and fired at Mark, hitting him in the back on the right side. Mark fell face down alongside the pickup with his head against the curb. Arroyo stepped around the back of the pickup and fired another shot, hitting Mark in the back of the head, killing him.

Ron thought Mark fired three rounds at Arroyo, but police said he had fired five and had four rounds remaining in his pistol. Martell also thought the gunman had fired at least half-a-dozen rounds at Mark, though he hit him only twice.

"I saw Mark go down, and then Arroyo got in his truck after that, and he backs out, and I'm just stunned. I'm watching this whole thing, and I'm going, Oh my gosh, this guy has body armor, and he's just killed either an off-duty policeman or a plainclothes policeman, because Mark's engagement was very sound," Martell recalled.

Wisely, Ron figured he was outgunned and didn't intervene as Arroyo drove north on Spring Avenue, not seeming to be in any hurry.

Meanwhile, Detective Clay Perrett was aware of the gunman backing up his pickup and driving off northbound still firing his rifle at the courthouse through the open driver's side window. With blood pouring down his face, the detective got to a bathroom and made a compress out of paper towels. He was later treated at the hospital.

The Pursuit

Ron Martell put his van into gear and followed Arroyo's maroon pickup north on Spring Avenue. When he reached Ferguson Street two police officers were out of their cars and didn't seem to realize the gunman was in the pickup. Martell said he rolled down his window and yelled at them: "That's the shooter, that's the shooter." They got back in their cars and followed the pickup north on Spring Avenue. Initially some officers thought the shooter was in the white van, but this was quickly corrected over the radio.

"I had seen what this guy was capable of doing, and all I went along for was back-up for them," Ron said.

A procession of police cars, sirens screaming and lights flashing, accompanied by Martell's van, followed Arroyo north on Spring Avenue, east on Oakwood Street, and north on Beckham Avenue, with more police cars joining the pursuit as it progressed. It was not really a chase, as Arroyo was driving about forty miles an hour most of the way, firing shots back at his pursuers as he went. He seemed to be heading back to his mobile home on Indian Trace outside the city limits to the northeast.

Sergeant Rusty Jacks

When Officer Mike Gray first broadcast news of the shooting at the courthouse in a matter-of-fact tone, Sergeant Rusty Jacks was at the police department seven blocks west of the courthouse. Jacks was the commander of the Tyler Police Department SWAT team, and he was standing at the back door to the building with his rifle in his hand. The rifle was a Colt Commando, a full-auto variant of the M-16, with an 11-inch barrel. It was equipped with a C-More red-dot optical sight and was loaded with Federal .223-caliber, 55-grain soft-points.

Jacks ran to his patrol car and raced east along Ferguson Street to the courthouse. He turned south on Broadway Avenue and squealed to a stop on the west side of the courthouse in the middle of the street. Jacks got out with his rifle. He started to run around the north side of the building thinking that the suspect was still on foot. He hitched a ride on the hood of Officer Wayne Allen's patrol car.

Allen had been working red-light enforcement on Broadway Avenue a

Smith attempted the PIT maneuver, but Arroyo swerved.

couple of blocks north of the courthouse when he heard about the shooting. He saw Arroyo's truck heading north on Spring Avenue. Right after that he picked up Jacks and his rifle. When he heard on the radio that the suspect was heading north on Beckham, he stopped the car and Jacks got into the passenger seat.

They caught up with the pursuit on Beckham just north of the railroad overpass before it turns into East Gentry Parkway. They overtook all the other pursuing vehicles, because with his automatic assault rifle and a driver, Jacks was best equipped and probably best trained to deal with

Smith rams Arroyo's truck and fires, but Arroyo stops and gets out.

This photo sequence of Arroyo being pursued and killed is excerpted from a video recorded by a camera in one of the police cars involved in the event.

Arroyo fires his rifle at Smith's patrol car, as Smith accelerates past the truck to get out of the line of fire.

the suspect. As Allen and Jacks got directly behind Arroyo's truck they were overtaken by Deputy John Smith in his patrol car.

Immediately Smith attempted to perform the Precision Immobilization Technique or PIT maneuver. This involved using the officer's front-left fender to make contact with the pickup's rear-right quarter just ahead of the bumper. The officer would turn left into the truck and accelerate. If done correctly, the suspect vehicle is flipped around 180 degrees and ends up facing the direction from which it came.

As Smith closed on the pickup, Arroyo started weaving, throwing off the deputy's maneuver. Smith rammed the pickup in the back-right bumper, while firing through

Arroyo turns to step back into his truck.

the window of his car with his left hand. Most of his shots went through the back window of the pickup. Arroyo braked and stopped in the middle of the highway in an area with heavy timber on each side of the road. He got out of his truck holding the semi-automatic rifle.

Smith, whose gun was empty by then, accelerated past the pickup, but not before Arroyo fired a shot at him hitting the light bar on the roof of his patrol car.

When Arroyo stopped, Wayne Allen pulled his patrol car to the right towards the curb. Even before he stopped Rusty Jacks was out of the car and lining up his rifle's red-dot sight on the suspect. Initially, Smith's patrol car was in his line of fire. As soon as Smith accelerated away, Jacks heard the explosion of Arroyo's shot at Smith. Then Arroyo turned to get back into his truck.

Jacks, his Colt Commando on semi-automatic, fired as Arroyo's head disappeared behind the cab of the truck. Not sure whether he had hit the suspect or not, Jacks fired two more rounds through the back window of the pickup, but they were not needed. The first round went through the back-right corner of the extended cab

Arroyo's truck continued to roll after Jacks shot him in the head. Smith stopped the truck from becoming a traffic hazard as police officers advanced on Arroyo.

and split into two pieces. Both bits hit Arroyo in the head, just behind his right ear. He dropped like a sack of potatoes falling off the back of a truck.

After Arroyo hit the pavement his truck was in gear and continued to roll forward. Smith accelerated away from Arroyo then executed a neat U-turn and stopped the truck with his front bumper.

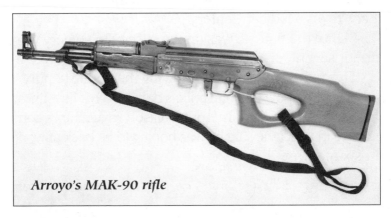

Arroyo's MAK-90 rifle

Wayne Allen got out of his patrol car and approached Arroyo at gunpoint. The gunman was lying on his back barely alive. Allen moved Arroyo's rifle out of his reach, while another officer handcuffed him. It wasn't until after Arroyo was down that Jacks realized the man had been wearing body armor.

Tyler's bloodiest incident in living memory was over.

Heroes

There were many heroes that day, but most of them were law-enforcement officers paid to put their lives on the line for their communities. Two men stand out for their actions and sacrifices.

The first was Deputy Sherman Dollison, who was first to run out of the courthouse doors and take on the shooter. Due to Arroyo's body armor Dollison got the worst of it.

Lieutenant Craig Shelton, the sheriff's office SWAT commander, and Doctor Mark Anderson were within a block of the courthouse. Anderson was a tactically trained SWAT officer and a physician, said Major Lusk. Anderson and Shelton were together going over some training issues when the shooting started. They drove to the scene, grabbed Dollison, put him in the back seat, and Anderson started working on him as they drove to the East Texas Medical Center.

"Until the time he was on the gurney in surgery was about seventeen minutes," Lusk said.

He credits Anderson with saving the young deputy's life. The high-powered rifle bullets damaged his intestines, bladder, and one lung. In April Dollison gave a news conference in which he said he was hoping to be back at work in six months.

"He did exactly what he had been trained to do; did it extremely well," Lusk said. "He did a tremendous job even after he was struck. He fired back, got back up on one knee, and continued to fire."

The other man, civilian Mark Alan Wilson, 52, made the supreme sacrifice. He died trying to protect others from harm. He would probably have succeeded had Arroyo not been wearing body armor.

Tyler Police Chief Gary Swindle commended Mark's actions that day. He credited Mark with probably saving the life of David Arroyo Jr. by distracting the gunman's focus away from the courthouse. His intervention may also have saved some of the officers and deputies who were around the east doors to the courthouse, the chief added.

"Mark was a hero. We hear stories like this where people jump in and save lives, and this is a perfect example of that. Sad thing is that Mark lost his life," Swindle said. "He's going to be remembered forever in Tyler, and this event will be remembered forever because in my twenty-three years, and it probably goes back to the 1800s, I'm sure there was never a shootout in Tyler, Texas, that was ever anything like this. And Mark was right in the middle of it."

Detective Wayne Thomas said David Arroyo Jr. acknowledged to him that Mark Wilson had probably saved his life.

Detective Clay Perrett also had high praise for Mark: "Mr. Wilson certainly was a hero in my opinion. He confronted the guy with a handgun. Of course, most of us confronted the guy with a handgun, and clearly a handgun was not what was needed out there that day. But yeah, he was definitely a hero."

Major Mike Lusk agreed.

"You can't Monday-morning quarterback his actions at all. You just can't do that. Somebody might say, well not a good move to go into an assault rifle fight with a pistol but, in my feeling, that's not appropriate," Lusk said. "He saw a threat. He was there, and he did what each and everyone of us do, he went to the threat, while most people go away from it."

Reflections

Mark did what he believed was right, but we would not do his sacrifice justice if we did not learn from his experience. Even Lusk said the sheriff's office had changed its tactics as a result of the courthouse shooting. "Even before then, but more so afterwards, we adjusted some of our training techniques," he said. "You know, double tap to the torso, once to the head, things like that."

Lusk was referring to what competitive shooters call the Mozambique drill. A shooter fires two shots— the double tap—to the chest, and if that doesn't put the attacker down, follow up with a shot to the head.

If there are lessons to be learned from Mark Wilson and the Tyler courthouse shooting they are:
- Bad guys often wear body armor these days, therefore hits in the chest area may not be enough to stop an aggressor.
- A handgun is good, but in some circumstances a high-powered rifle is better. While most bullet-resistant vests will stop handgun bullets, they will not usually stop bullets from high-powered rifles. One result of the courthouse shooting is that city and county patrol officers rushed to arm themselves with AR-15 semi-automatic rifles.

Swindle is in favor of the law that allows licensed law-abiding citizens to carry handguns for protection. He was a deputy chief at the time the concealed-handgun law passed in Texas in 1995. Forecasts of uncontrolled mayhem in the streets preceded the law's passage—from the media, some officials, and some politicians.

"We haven't had any problems in Tyler. I carry my weapon when I travel, and I think it's a great comfort to honest people who work hard and want to defend themselves and protect the family. And this is a perfect example of when you can make a difference by being armed against some of the bad guys. We know the bad guys are going to have weapons."

While both Swindle and Lusk spoke favorably of ordinary people being armed and able to defend themselves, they warned that sometimes it makes things more complicated for law-enforcement officers.

"The primary thing is that the officer needs to know who the good guy is. Whatever means necessary, if it's verbal, if it's laying the weapon down and pointing to the bad guy, but we've got to know who the good guys and who the bad guys are," Lusk said.

On reports of residential burglaries or suspicious persons, dispatchers are instructed to tell people to stay in the house. Innocent people have been shot before when officers arrive and find someone outside with a gun and assume it is the criminal, he added.

Swindle said that an armed civilian may also have difficulty identifying who the criminal is. In the shooting outside the courthouse the identity of the suspect was very obvious, but that may not always be the case.

"You have to be careful, you have to be aware, and a lot of times I would recommend: be the best witness you can for law enforcement. But if law enforcement is

Mark's mother, Lynn Stewart, receives the folded flag at his memorial service, three days after the shooting. (Photo by Robert Langham)

not around, then you have to protect yourself or others," the chief said.

"Just use your good sense. Mark was, in my mind, trying to do what he knew he could do and that's handle a weapon and stop this guy. He was right there on the scene within seconds of it happening, and he's a hero."

While Lynn Stewart would have preferred a live son to a dead hero, she was not surprised at what happened. She said Mark lived life to the full and crammed as much into his 52 years as most people would experience in two lifetimes.

In Memory of

MARK ALAN WILSON

1953 - 2005

"Greater love hath no man than this, that he lay down his life for his friends."

John 15:13

Tyler resident Mark Alan Wilson fell here on February 24, 2005, after giving his life in an attempt to protect fellow citizens and end an armed gunman's assault on the Smith County Courthouse. Mr. Wilson, a resident of downtown Tyler, was among dozens who witnessed the gunman armed with an assault rifle and bulletproof vest shoot his ex-wife and son as they entered the Courthouse. Mr. Wilson responded by retrieving his weapon from his apartment overlooking the Courthouse and firing on the gunman in an attempt to end the assault. While he saved the life of the gunman's son, who lay wounded on the courthouse steps, Mr. Wilson was mortally wounded in the exchange. This memorial stands as a tribute to his bravery and sacrifice for the citizens of Tyler.

"It's not easy, but I'm so glad that if it had to happen it happened like that, and it wasn't some inconsequential thing. He died for a good cause," she said. "I guess I'm lucky that I had him as long as I did."

On September 16, 2005, the city of Tyler acknowledged Mark's heroic action by dedicating a plaque in his honor on the courthouse square where he fell.

During the ceremony, Mark's friend and neighbor, John Seiple, quoted author C.S. Lewis: "It is in the kind of risks that we take that our true character is revealed."Seiple added: "On that day in February, Mark's true character was revealed."

Chapter 8

Nursery Defense:
Barbara Thompson

In most jurisdictions in the United States it is legal to shoot someone if you believe you are in imminent danger of being killed or seriously injured. Each state has slightly different wording for its laws regarding the use of deadly force, but that is the gist of most of them. In some states, like Texas, it is also legal to use deadly force to protect property under some circumstances. However, most firearms instructors tell their students it's not worth shooting someone over a television set.

This is undoubtedly true in a single case. But at what point is deadly force acceptable to deter a rash of burglaries that could bankrupt a small business. Large companies can and do hire professional security guards. But small businesses generally cannot afford such a luxury. What about insurance? It is expensive and usually comes with a high deductible. Insurance companies like only customers who don't make claims. Homes and businesses that get hit repeatedly tend to have their insurance rates increased or their policies cancelled.

So how many thefts or burglaries are enough to prompt home- or business-owners to stand guard with a firearm to protect their property—five, ten, thirty? And how far should the defender go—or be prepared to go—to protect their property?

An explosion of juvenile crime rocked the United States in the early 1990s. Disaffected teenagers in big cities joined youth gangs, getting involved in drugs and drive-by shootings, beatings and burglaries. Teens were being robbed, raped, and murdered at parties, at homes, and on the streets. As a police reporter in San Antonio, Texas, I remember reporting on the results of drive-by shootings. I saw dozens of holes where bullets or shotgun slugs had gone through the front walls of houses, through the interior walls, and out through the back walls. Usually I was reporting on such incidents because someone in the house, often a child, had been wounded or killed.

Burglaries were out of control. Juveniles would break into homes, businesses, and vehicles looking for cash or anything that could easily be converted into cash, such as guns and stereos.

In 1999 then Attorney General Janet Reno was quoted as saying, "If the last decade's trends continue unchecked, juvenile arrests for violent crime will double by the year 2010."

Juvenile crime was just as bad in Fort Worth as it was in San Antonio. In an editorial headlined "When Will Enough Be Enough?" *The Fort Worth Star-Telegram* urged more money and resources be spent combating the gang problem in the county.

"How many more people of Tarrant County—from children to the elderly—must cower in fear for their property, their safety, and their lives because of the terroristic nihilism of young savages?" the editorial asked. It noted that six youths had been wounded in gun battles in the previous week alone and likened the gang problem to a cancer. The situation was obviously out of control. The gangs had to be dealt with, because they would not go away on their own.

"They must be confronted and transformed if possible, but eradicated if necessary," the editorial stated. Strong words indeed for a mainstream newspaper. The editorial did not make clear whether it was advocating the eradication of gangs or of gang members.

Two people who were not cowering in fear for their property or their lives were Barbara Thompson and her brother, who worked in the family business, Herrmann Tree & Landscape Company, on the east side of Fort Worth.

"That summer was just a horrible time," Barbara recalled. The Fort Worth Police Department was taking a zero-tolerance attitude towards gangs and gang members, she said.

"They pulled over people for anything, searched their cars, confiscated guns. If you got pulled over for speeding, your car got searched, and nobody complained." She thought there would be outrage from some activists in the community but there wasn't. "The community leaders here were: go for it," Barbara said.

Barbara Thompson

She was born and grew up in the Fort Worth area. Her father used to take her and her brother skeet shooting at ranges in the area, so she was quite familiar with shotguns. She never hunted.

In 1981 she married Dean Thompson, an officer with the Dallas/Fort Worth Airport Police. He was the chief firearms instructor and sniper team leader for the department's SWAT team, which specialized in aircraft hijackings and counter-terrorism. He introduced her to handgun shooting, but Barbara was always more comfortable with a shotgun.

Herrmann Tree & Landscape was a wholesale plant nurseryand a landscaping business. The company has since changed its name. Barbara's father, Herbert Herrmann Sr., started the business as a landscaping company. It grew and Herrmann expanded it to include a nursery to grow the trees and plants needed for the landscaping. Eventually the business produced enough excess plants to sell to other landscapers and to retail nurseries. In the early 1990s Barbara was responsible for the nursery part of the business, while her younger brother, Herbert Herrmann Jr., handled the landscaping.

The nursery covered four-and-a-half acres on the east side of South Hughes Avenue. It lay behind a row of houses and was reached by a gravel road that stretched from the street about one hundred fifty feet to a high, chain-link, double gate. Most of the nursery area was covered by two rows of large greenhouses. A gravel road ran between the wire fence on the west side of the property and the first row of greenhouses. The road curved around the north end of the first row of greenhouses, then came down between that row and the other row of greenhouses along the east fence. The greenhouses in the west row were a hundred-feet long; the ones in the other row were eighty-feet long. The walls and roofs of the greenhouses were made of thick, clear plastic. A large metal barn was located on the east side, south of the greenhouses, and a travel trailer stood in front of it on the side of the gravel road. The office was more than a hundred feet from the trailer.

The nursery was an easy target for burglars, because it was fairly isolated and normally no one lived on the place. Barbara and her brother had tried keeping dogs, but it was pointless if no one was there to hear them bark. The dogs were two fifty-pound mutts, Labrador mixes, but they were not attack dogs. When the burglars cut the high, chain-link fence around the property to get in, the dogs would get out. They were also injured from time to time and not always by the burglars. On one occasion they saw a neighbor hitting one of the dogs, Barbara said.

By the spring of 1993 Barbara estimated burglars had broken into the business about thirty times in the previous twelve months. They had broken into the office, the house trailer, and the big metal barn, stealing anything they could carry away. During a two-week period at the end of March and beginning of April the nursery was broken into three times.

Overnight March 25/26, 1993, thieves broke into a 1980 Chevrolet pickup parked in the nursery. They broke through a vent window that had been damaged during a previous burglary. They stole two circular saws, a cordless drill with drill bits, and other miscellaneous tools, as well as license plates from both a dump truck and the travel trailer. The police report stated that the nursery had been the subject of numerous burglaries.

The next weekend, between March 27 and 29, thieves broke into the nursery through the fence, broke into a car on the property by smashing a window, and stole a bag of socks, a hammer drill, socket wrenches, and ratchets. They also broke into the house trailer, ransacked it, and stole two liter-bottles of soda.

On Monday, April 5, Barbara's brother called the police to report another burglary at the nursery. He reported that during the weekend the office and the travel trailer had been ransacked. Three shotguns, each valued at between two and three hundred dollars, two airguns, some chains, a radio, and assorted hand tools were stolen.

After these three burglaries Barbara's brother had taken to standing guard and sleeping at the nursery. He slept in a room off the office that had a bed and a kitchen area equipped with a microwave. It seemed that anytime he wasn't there burglars would break in. "We assumed somebody was watching," she said.

The Incident

On Tuesday, May 12, her brother was tired and dirty, so Barbara suggested he go home, have a shower, and get cleaned up while she stood guard. He followed her advice.

Shortly before 11:30 P.M. she was sitting in the office watching a Texas Rangers' baseball game on television. The game was in California, so it was on late in the evening and the Rangers were losing, she recalled. "I had just turned it off and sat there just for a minute in the dark when it happened," she said.

There was an intercom, like a large baby monitor, connecting the office and the big metal barn. She heard a clattering noise, as though someone was throwing rocks at the metal roof of the barn and they were bouncing down the roof onto the ground. The noise was loud enough to start all the neighborhood dogs barking. "They just went crazy when they heard that."

Barbara looked out of the office window but couldn't see anything. Before calling the police she decided to step outside to make sure it was worth calling 9-1-1. She was wearing a small Smith & Wesson five-shot revolver in an inside-the-waistband holster, which was covered by a sweat shirt. Before stepping outside, she picked up her Winchester Defender, pump-action, 12-gauge shotgun and carried it with her.

She took a few steps outside the door and looked towards the barn. There was a light in the trailer and she could see two figures silhouetted against it. She couldn't see whether they were inside or outside the trailer. The trailer had been broken into before, and the windows had not been replaced since the last time. All anyone had to do was reach in through a broken window and unlock the door.

She returned to the office and called the police. After telling them the nursery was being broken into, she said she was going to walk to the main gate and unlock it so the officers could get in.

"So I went up to unlock the gate. When it unlocked, part of the chain fell, and it made a clang. I looked down, and there's two guys walking up the road. They hear the chain, they stop, and they look in this direction. They see me, and they take off, which is fine with me. I wasn't going to chase 'em."

The two youths ran north along the gravel road in the direction of the trailer and out of sight behind the nearest greenhouse. They were more than a hundred feet away, and Barbara assumed they were heading for wherever they had cut the fence to get in.

She walked over to where the gravel roads formed a crossroads, a few feet inside the gate, where she had a good view of the south end of the nursery. She knelt down on one knee beside a pile of railroad ties that would give her some cover. The police would catch her in their headlights as soon as they arrived.

But instead of leaving, the youths cut through the nearest greenhouse, bringing them a lot closer to her. She saw a head poking out of the end of the long, plastic-covered greenhouse. "So this head pokes out and goes back in. Somebody looks out again; somebody goes back in. Somebody looks out again, goes back in. You know, I'm kneeling there with a shotgun, and I'm going: there's no way they don't know I'm armed, and they don't care. That's not right; there's something wrong here."

She was perplexed because she was in the flood from the yard lights, and they could see she was armed. They could also see her long hair and knew she was a woman, so perhaps they didn't think she would shoot. All this was going through her mind.

As she watched, one of the youths stepped out and started edging along the side of the greenhouse towards her. He was keeping against the plastic trying to stay in the shadows away from the light. Obviously, he wouldn't be coming towards her if he didn't mean her harm.

She does not remember being afraid. She had a shotgun and knew how to use it. She remembers thinking that she had to do something. The youth was about twenty-five yards away and getting closer. "I think: that's it. So I fired one shot at him, and he jumps back into the greenhouse."

Again, she saw a figure step out of the greenhouse. She was perturbed: how could she have missed at that range? "I just remember thinking: great, I've got a gun, and I can't do anything with it. So I fired a second shot, and he ran straight down that road and disappeared into the dark." She aimed lower with the second shot, because she thought she had missed high with the first round. The youth ran north along the gravel road, directly away from her.

"So then I heard someone running through the greenhouse. I heard a flip, flip on the other end, so I knew there were two people."

The Hermann Nursery's trailer and greenhouse area is very dark at night.

She walked over to a truck that was parked near the office and stayed in the shadows until a police helicopter lit up the area and several officers arrived by car. Barbara put the shotgun on the ground, then as more officers arrived she put it into the truck.

The Aftermath

She told the police what had happened. She surrendered the shotgun to them and remembers the officer who unloaded it being surprised at how many rounds it held. The officer was used to shotguns holding five rounds, but the Defender magazine held seven. It was loaded with Number 1 buckshot. About a foot apart near the railroad ties the officers found the two empty casings from the rounds she had fired .

One officer asked her if she shot at the first guy who was coming towards her along the side of the greenhouse. She confirmed that she did shoot at him.

"He said, 'Do you know whether you hit him or not?'

"I said, 'No, I have no idea.'

"In fact, I thought I missed. He looked at me kinda' funny, and he said, 'You didn't miss.'"

Barbara thought at the time that she fired both shots at the same person. She hadn't. Her first shot hit 15-year-old Jody Dears, a black male, in the chest. He ran back through that greenhouse, down the gravel road, and through another greenhouse to the place where he and his friends had cut the east fence. He climbed back through the fence and crossed a ditch before collapsing in the adjacent field. He ran more than one-hundred yards and left a blood trail all the way. Dears was spotted there by an officer in the helicopter. He was pronounced dead just after midnight. Barbara realized he was dead from listening to the officers talking among themselves.

Dears had been hit with four shotgun pellets, in the chest, abdomen, left thigh, and right arm. According to a report by homicide Detective David Thornton, the pellet that hit Dears in the chest pierced his heart and caused his death. The medical examiner who performed the autopsy told Thornton that Dears's left side was facing Barbara when he was hit.

Her second shot had hit a 16-year-old youth in the legs. He was the one who ran away down the gravel road. Police officers found him a few blocks away in the parking lot of a supermarket on East Rosedale Street. He lived in an apartment building near the nursery.

When interviewed by Officer R.O. Ruiz, the teenager denied any knowledge of the incident at the nursery and said he had been shot by somebody at the nearby Monaco apartment complex. He claimed that he had been hit when two other people were shooting at each other. However, his wounds were consistent with the shooting at Herrmann's nursery, and no reports of shots fired had come from the Monaco Apartments. Officers also noticed he had blue stains on his hands consistent with the color of a dye used at the nursery.

The youth was taken to John Peter Smith Hospital by ambulance, where he was admitted for treatment of gunshot wounds. Several shotgun pellets had hit his left knee, and one pellet was taken from his left side. While Ruiz was at the hospital he talked to the teenager's mother, who confirmed that he had been with Dears that night.

The wounded youth had changed his story by the time Thornton interviewed him at the hospital the next day. He was being guarded by a uniformed officer, who had been sent there by the Fugitive Squad, as the youth was wanted on an unrelated robbery warrant. The youth told Thornton that he, Dears, and two other teens were walking along East Rosedale in the vicinity of "the plant thing" when one of them said he had to go to the restroom. He walked up a dead-end street that runs close to the east side of the nursery, presumably to find a spot to urinate. The others waited for him on Rosedale. A few minutes later he came running back yelling to the others to run. The wounded youth claimed he was being chased by a white woman with blonde hair, who shot him in the leg and Jody Dears in the back. He said both of them were shot on Rosedale Street.

Much the same story was repeated to Barbara. "Their story to the police was that they were just walking through a field and a crazy white woman shot 'em. We said: 'Fine, let the story be that a crazy white woman is going to shoot you if you come around here.'"

The police later told Barbara that five people were involved. The police burglary report identified three people, while the homicide report identified four. All were black males aged from 14 to 23.

After Thornton interviewed her at the scene, he asked Barbara to come down to police headquarters to make a statement. Before she left Barbara went into the back room of the office and took off her revolver. The officers never asked her if she had another gun, she said.

She signed a document stating she had been given the Miranda warning, then gave the police a voluntary written statement about what had happened. The police treated her quite well, she said. They asked her if she wanted to talk to the media, but she declined. She did mention to one officer that her husband was a police officer. She was irritated when she read this in the *Dallas*

Morning News the following day. She felt it sounded as though she was cut some slack because she was a police officer's wife.

After the shooting Barbara received an outpouring of support from members of the community. Her father estimated the family had about a hundred phone calls of support.

Barbara never received any threats after the shooting. However, about two weeks after the incident a car full of what appeared to be gang members drove into the nursery, around the gravel road, and out again without stopping. Barbara said she didn't know if they were looking for a confrontation or not. The car drove past several people working, perhaps without seeing them. For a while after that, she or her brother parked a car across the road, so anyone intent on driving around the D-shaped road inside the nursery would be stopped.

Barbara received a subpoena to testify at the 16-year-old's juvenile hearing, but it was cancelled. She was told the District Attorney's Office had other cases against him, therefore she assumed he was not prosecuted for breaking into Herrmann's. Juvenile records are sealed, so it was not possible to confirm this.

Barbara went to the grand jury proceeding when the 16-year-old youth she wounded appeared. She had not been subpoenaed, but she wanted to be able to identify as many of the burglars as possible in case they ever came into the nursery. "Any of them could walk in here the next day, and I wouldn't have known them from anybody. So the one that was wounded, he was there. He had to testify, so I got a good look at him when we met face to face—him coming out and me going in. He couldn't even look me in the eye."

The police closed their file on June 19, 1993. Barbara never heard whether the five had gang affiliations, but she assumed they did. "As far as I'm concerned, if you have five kids out at midnight they are a gang."

After several months of hearing nothing from the police or the Tarrant County District Attorney's office, she called to find out what was happening with the case. Eventually, she received a letter telling her that a grand jury would hear her case on September 8. She was not subpoenaed to the hearing, but was invited to attend if she wished to. She opted to attend, but did not have a lawyer present. Her husband Dean went with her.

Before Barbara went into the grand jury room, the prosecutor came out and spoke to her and Dean. She said she was not putting the case in for prosecution. Detective David Thornton, who investigated the case, testified first, then Barbara went in. The process was not adversarial. She told them what happened and some of the jurors had questions. One woman asked where Barbara's husband was at the time. The prosecutor abruptly stopped that line of questioning. Dean was actually out of town at the time of the shooting. The grand jury no-billed her, which meant there was no case for her to answer.

Reflections

Dean had wanted Barbara to carry a different shotgun, but she declined because she was unfamiliar with its type of safety lock. The safety was on top of the receiver and slid backwards and forwards. She couldn't remember which direction was on and which was off. "I wasn't comfortable with the safety. I said: 'I need to go with what I know.'"

She was familiar with the pump-action safety that is beside the trigger on the Winchester Defender. She preferred carrying that. "That is what I learned with, and that's what I revert to without a lot of practice. So I went back to the safety I'm familiar with."

It was a good call. It takes some three-thousand repetitions to program a movement to become instinctive or automatic. In a shooting situation, people tend to revert to their training.

At the time of the shooting Barbara probably hadn't shot skeet regularly in ten years. The last time she had shot was off the fantail of a cruise ship a few years before.

She thinks the burglars threw the rocks at the barn roof to see if they got a reaction. They probably didn't know anyone was on the property because she had put her car in the barn and it was not visible.

Was what she did legal?

She was cleared of any criminal action by the grand jury and no one sued her civilly. In Texas it is legal to use deadly force—that is, to shoot someone—if you believe you are in imminent danger of serious bodily injury or death. You can also use deadly force to prevent sexual assault, robbery, or murder. It is also legal in Texas to use deadly force in the hours of darkness to protect property from burglary or criminal mischief. The law appears to allow the use of deadly force in the circumstances in which Barbara found herself that night.

Would she have done anything differently?

She felt she was in danger and had to do something when the youth started creeping along the end of the greenhouse towards her. He was not approaching her to ask the time.

"I think tactically someone would say: 'You should have taken better cover.' The only place I could have taken cover, I couldn't've seen. I had to get in a position to cover three roads."

She also wanted them to see she was there and that she was armed, hoping to deter them.

"I was in the light, and I had a shotgun. My assumption was: they know I'm armed, and they don't care. Something's not right with this."

She had no doubt that the two she fired at would have done her harm if she hadn't shot them. It still puzzled her that, even though they could see she was armed, it didn't stop them. She speculated that perhaps they thought there was safety in numbers, because there were five of them although she didn't know that at the time. When they repeatedly looked out of the greenhouse at her, she thought they were making their plans and egging one another on.

She knew when the police asked her she should tell them she was in fear that her life was in danger. She said she knew that she was in danger—she could have been raped, robbed, or murdered—but she doesn't remember being afraid. "Logic tells you: if I don't respond to this [the threat], something's going to happen. It's not fear, it's common sense."

Asked if she was upset at killing the youth, she said: "No. I mean not as far as being able to look back and say I shouldn't have done it. I'm sorry that it happened. And I'm sorry that the choices they made put me in a position to make the choice I made. My choices were to do something or do nothing, and if I had done nothing, I might not have been able to finish it."

Did defending her property with a shotgun work for Barbara? There is nothing more likely to deter burglary than a dead burglar. From about thirty burglaries in the previous twelve months the rate plummeted. The nursery didn't suffer any more break-ins for quite a while.

"It was pretty quiet after that," Barbara said.

Chapter 9

Arkansas Attack:
Clarence Cochran

In his book, *The Myths That Divide Us: How Lies Have Poisoned American Race Relations*, author John Perazzo states that the FBI's Uniform Crime Reports indicate blacks are responsible for nearly 60 percent of robberies, while they comprise only 13 percent of the population. Many of these robberies involve convenience stores.

"Contemporaryblack males aged fourteen to twenty-four are among the most dangerous demographic groups in American history. Constituting just 1 percent of our country's population, they commit at least 30 percent of its murders each year," Perazzo writes.

Yet these figures are a well-kept secret. They remain hidden from the public, largely unaddressed by the self-censorship of the mainstream media. Many of the perpetrators in these accounts of self-defense, including this one, are black.

Perazzo writes that blacks account for 94 percent of the homicides against blacks and 81 percent of all other violent crimes against them.

Crawfordsville

The plains of eastern Arkansas near the Mississippi River are as flat as a Formica tabletop. When you drive west over them on U.S. Highway 64, about twenty miles out of Memphis, you can see a water tower and some trees less than a mile away to the south of the highway. The trees hide the hard-scrabble little town of Crawfordsville in Crittenden County.

Ken Heard, a reporter for the *Arkansas Democrat-Gazette*, described it as a typically depressed town in an impoverished rural area. Ben Krain, a photographer for the same newspaper, who has spent time in Afghanistan, went further. He likened it to a town in a third-world country, Heard said.

According to the 2000 census the town has a population of just over five hundred, mostly black. It has a post office, convenience store, and some boarded-up stores. The main industry is poverty. The houses are clapboard over wood frame, many with tin roofs. The town is a stereotype of the Old South of a hundred years ago. It has no police department. Law enforcement is handled by the Crittenden County Sheriff's Office, located about fifteen miles away in West Memphis.

Clarence Cochran

Clarence Cochran runs The Neighborhood Store, a tiny ramshackle convenience store on Green Avenue on the southeast side of Crawfordsville. The store reminded reporter Ken Heard of a shoebox. It is about fifty-feet long by twelve-feet wide, and the ceiling is not much above six feet. It sags lower in places.

Cochran and his wife live in a trailer that doubles as a warehouse for the store. It is crammed with canned food and other supplies. The trailer is about forty feet from the store. Clarence can keep an eye on the inside and outside of the store through a system of video display cameras that can be monitored from inside the trailer. The

Clarence Cochran in his store. *(Photo courtesy of Benjamin Krain and Arkansas Democrat-Gazette)*

cameras do not record what they show, just reveal what is happening in real time.

The front of the store has a porch, home to a couple of cats and an old stove. A solid door leads into the dimly lit store itself. As you enter the store you can see a counter to the right supporting an ancient cash register. A small video screen monitors the outside of the store. Across from the counter stands a refrigerator. Heading towards the back of the store shelves crammed with merchandise line the sides. At the back a door leads to a small bathroom. The rest of the back wall is taken up with a modern cooler that Clarence refers to as his drink box. It is filled with Cokes, Pepsis, and other soft drinks. It stands about six-feet high and is equipped with double sliding doors.

In addition to the soft drinks, Clarence sells crackers, potato chips, canned food, and candy for the kids who come by after school. Some of the merchandise, like Spam and Fanta Orange, seem to come from another era.

Store hours are 6 A.M. to 7 P.M. six days a week; on Sundays Clarence stays open until 11 P.M. to give his customers a chance to stock up for the coming week. Clarence's son, Tommy Turner, 33, helps him run the store. A daughter lives across the street.

"The guy's well liked around town. A lot of folks like the store because it stays open so late. It's a black community, and it's easy for them to go in there right near their neighborhood. They don't have to worry about driving to Earle or West Memphis," Heard said.

The Neighborhood Store has been robbed several times. The robbers came in, stuck a gun in Clarence's face, and he handed over the money. But he was getting tired of being a target. He had a couple of rifles and a shotgun that he kept in his trailer. He kept a small, .38-caliber revolver handy in the store.

Heard remembered Clarence's piercing eyes. "I mean he was a nice guy, he's very quiet, but there's a hardness to him. To me, he was almost like the steel of the gun itself."

Clarence has lived in Crawfordsville since the early 1990s. Before he opened his store in the late '90s he used to sell groceries out of his truck, delivering to people who had no way of getting into town from the farming area around Crawfordsville. He also worked as a maintenance man for the city and the school district.

The Incident

It was just after 8:30 on Sunday evening, the day after Christmas 2004, when a young black man came into the store. He started looking around as though he was going to buy something.

"I was in the store by myself, and I was filling up my drink box at the time. When I got through filling it up, I turned around, headed back to the door," Clarence said.

Clarence passed the young man but didn't pay him much attention as he headed back towards the counter. As he reached it, another young black man came into the store from the front porch. This man was heavy-set and about six-feet tall according to the police report.

He pointed a .45-caliber, semi-automatic pistol at Clarence and, without saying a word, fired four shots at him. One bullet hit the older man in the stomach; the other three hit the wall behind him. Clarence said he slid down behind the counter.

"He fired first, and when he shot, he hit me dead on with the first shot. I had my gun in my pocket. So after I figured he was going to kill me, I snatched my gun out, and I shot at his head. That's where I hit him, in his head."

Clarence was carrying the gun in his pocket as a precaution. He told his son he was tired of being robbed.

The other man, who had been at the back of the store near the drink box, ran past Clarence towards the front door. "He tried to run by me, but I popped him in the back," Clarence said. "He was just waiting on the other guy to kill me."

Clarence hit the second man in the shoulder. The would-be robber kept going and ran out into the night. The heavy-set robber who shot Clarence staggered back towards the door and collapsed on the threshold.

Tommy Turner was across the street at his sister's house. He was house-sitting for her. "Next thing I know I heard 'bang, bang,' and I thought it was a car backfiring," Turner said.

He didn't know what had happened until someone ran across the street and told him his father had been

Clarence Cochran was ready to protect himself.
(Photo courtesy of Benjamin Krain, Arkansas Democrat-Gazette)

shot. When Tommy got to the store his father was out-side walking around near the porch in front of the store. Tommy ran to get a blanket so Clarence could lie down on it.

"All he said was, 'ow, ow, ow,'" Turner recalled.

When Deputy Sheriff Duane Roberts arrived, a large crowd had gathered outside the store. The robber who shot Clarence was lying dead on the threshold.

A chrome-colored, semi-automatic pistol with black grips was lying beside him, according to Roberts's report.

Clarence was lying on the floor of the porch near his attacker. He told the officer that two men had tried to rob him and he had exchanged shots with them. He said that his gun had been taken next door.

The report stated that Tommy handed the gun to the police. It was identified as a Titan Tiger, five-shot .38 Special.

Clarence fired all five rounds. In addition to hitting the two robbers, as Tommy put it, he "killed the refrigerator."

Clarence was not just conscious, he was loquacious, Turner said. "That man gave a full conversation to those people. The only time he stopped talking was when they knocked his little butt out at the hospital."

When paramedics arrived Cochran was loaded into an ambulance and taken to where a helicopter landed. He was airlifted to the Regional Medical Center in Memphis, known locally as the Med. Clarence had never flown before. He was 80-years-old at the time.

The Aftermath

The dead man was identified as 20-year-old David Carson of West Memphis.

The wounded suspect was picked up, probably by a getaway driver, and dropped off at Crittenden Memorial Hospital in West Memphis. He was identified as Antonio Bass, 21, also of West Memphis. He was arrested at the hospital for aggravated robbery. He was later transferred to the Regional Medical Center in Memphis, where he was treated for gunshot wounds.

After Bass recovered, he escaped from the hospital and a year later remained at large. There was a warrant out for his arrest. "He just walked out," Ken Heard said. "He slipped away into Memphis and they couldn't find him."

Because of its layout, it is relatively easy to get into or out of the Regional Medical Center without being detected, he added.

Clarence stayed in the hospital for two months. The bullet that hit him went through his diaphragm and his liver. He had several operations before he was released on February 26, 2005, with instructions to take it easy. However, the day after he returned to Crawfordsville he was back at work. "I'm in the store, minding my business, and here he comes taking over," Tommy recalled.

Clarence said he's somewhat stiff as a result of the bullet wound, but the shooting has not intimidated him. "Well, I ain't afraid; I just be alert to 'em all the time," he said. "I can just about look at a fella' and tell what's on his mind."

Clarence said he keeps the money from his sales in a cigar box, but the robbers made no attempt to steal the money or anything else. He had never seen the two robbers before, and he has received no threats as a result of the incident, he added.

Shortly after he returned from the hospital, Clarence married his girlfriend, Debra Wright, who was 36 at the time. It was his first marriage, he said, though he claims five children and step-children. "I was just kinda' slow," he said.

The residents of Crawfordsville were very supportive after Clarence returned from the hospital. He still opens the store at 6 A.M. and doesn't close it until at least 7 P.M. When he isn't in the store he monitors it through the closed-circuit television system.

What makes him such a tough old bird? "I just come up tough, you know. I've always done hard work."

Reflections

It is unusual, but not unheard of, for a convenience store robbery to start with the murder of the clerk or owner. It may be out of sheer cussedness; it may be that the robber knows the victim is armed or likely to be armed; or it may be to ensure there are no surviving witnesses. Unless Antonio Bass can shed some light on the motive, it is unlikely we will ever know why David Carson started shooting at Clarence as soon as he entered the store. There was no doubt in Clarence's mind about what the robber intended to do. "He didn't say nothing. He just came in and shot me; that's all. Well, he's intent to kill me, what he's intent to do."

If Clarence had not been armed, he almost certainly would have been killed. As it was, his actions likely saved other citizens and store clerks from the trauma of being robbed at gunpoint had Carson continued with his life of crime.

It is interesting that the first gun-control laws were passed after the Civil War, specifically to disarm blacks and keep them easy victims for white racists, such as members of the Ku Klux Klan.

Secretary of State Condoleezza Rice has stated she is a Second Amendment absolutist. In the early 1960s when she was growing up in Birmingham, Alabama, her father and his friends used to stand guard with shotguns to protect themselves and their families from white nightriders during the civil-rights movement. Without their guns they would have been defenseless. Had they registered them the guns could have been confiscated.

It is ironic that leaders such as Jesse Jackson, who claim to represent the black community, support disarming law-abiding citizens, black and white. Perhaps it is because Jackson's livelihood depends on keeping blacks as victims. If they control their own destiny they don't need him.

Chapter 10

The Ozark Code:
Zelda Hunt

Zelda Hunt was born in the Ozark Mountains in 1925 to a father who was a World War I veteran of the Rainbow Division—the nickname of the U.S. 42nd Division. It was created in 1917 and comprised National Guard units from twenty-six states.

Zelda's father taught his three girls to ride, drive, and shoot. By the time he had finished their education they could shoot handguns, rifles, and shotguns. He told them not to come crying to Daddy if they chose to marry some guy who mistreated them or beat them up.

"We were taught to cover the ground we stood on, because there might not be anyone to help us," she said.

Zelda married a man who didn't mistreat her or beat her up. The couple had a daughter and two sons. In 1953 the family moved to Tucson, Arizona, where Zelda has lived ever since.

In 1997 she had been a widow for several years, but still lived in the home on the south side of Tucson, where she and her husband had raised their family. It is a large, single-story house on the frontage road of the highway to Nogales. She and her husband bought it in 1960 so they would have enough room for their three children and their pets. The house is on a lot about an acre in size where she used to grow strawberries.

In thirty-seven years, her house was broken into twice, but she wasn't at home either time. The first time she believes the burglars were kids. They broke in through a high window and climbed down across her bed. "They mostly took change and small things. That's the reason we assumed it was kids," Zelda said.

The second time she came home to find all the cushions from her couch on the floor, the mattress was pulled off her bed, and all the drawers in the furniture had been dumped out. All the ammunition that she and her husband had for all of their guns was stacked on a desk. However, the thieves hadn't taken their guns because they couldn't find them. They kept them hidden in a crawl space over a back bedroom closet.

"My husband and I both hunted. We both had our rifles, we had our shotguns, and we had our handguns. I hunted javelina and deer. My husband hunted birds and bow hunted," she said.

The Incident

On Saturday, September 13, 1997, Zelda Hunt was asleep when she was awakened about 6:30 A.M. by the sound of breaking glass. At first she thought it was kids breaking bottles. She got out of bed, wearing an old lady's nightgown—high neck, long sleeves, nothing fancy. She walked into the living room. It is a big room with the front door leading directly into it. The sun was just coming up.

"My house faced the east, and he was on my porch. His shadow was just completely on the window. I could see him through the curtains."

Zelda could see from the size of the shadow that he was a man, not a kid. There were small windows on each side of the front door, and he had broken one of them.

He was probably intending to reach through and unlock the door, she thought.

"I saw this shadow, and of course I was on carpeting, so I wasn't making any noise."

She thought: Damn thieves. I work for what little I've got. "I always thought what belonged to me was mine because I worked for it. And it wasn't there for someone else to take," she said.

Zelda, who was 72 at the time and suffering from diabetes, went back into her bedroom. She picked up her cordless phone and her Smith & Wesson .22-caliber revolver. With the gun in one hand and phone in the other she walked back into the living room and to the door.

"He was still breaking glass, taking his time."

The intruder was on Zelda's front porch. He was shielded from the street by honeysuckle and morning-glory vines that grew densely over the wire enclosing the porch. Zelda unlocked the front door and opened it. As she did so, she cocked the hammer on her revolver. A young man in his mid-twenties was kneeling by the broken window.

"What in hell are you doing?" Zelda demanded, pointing the gun at him.

"I'm fixing this window," the young man said. He was as cool as though she had just offered him a cup of coffee.

"I didn't have a problem with it before you got here," she retorted.

The young man calmly continued picking the glass out of the window frame. As Zelda began to dial 9-1-1 he stood up and started to speak.

"I have to . . . ," he said.

Zelda interrupted him: "Oh no, you're not going anywhere. Just get your ass on that chair and don't move."

She repeated the order and the suspect sat down on the white plastic lawn chair that was on the front porch. It was a chair she often sat in to smoke and watch the traffic go by on the highway.

"He was a young man, and I have grown children and grandchildren. I spoke to him like a mother. I told him to sit there and he did," Zelda said.

Zelda reached the 9-1-1 operator, who asked her for her name and address. The operator asked Zelda if she was okay.

"*No, I'm shaking like hell. I'm scared to death,*" she replied. She told the operator the suspect was on the front porch.

Zelda: "I've got the door open and my gun cocked. He's not going anywhere."

Operator: "You're armed?"

Zelda: "Yes ma'am, I am."

Operator: "Okay, I'm going to want you to put the gun down before I get units there, okay?"

Zelda: "Yes, as soon as I can see the officer at the gate, I'll put the gun down, yes."

Operator: "Okay."

This dialogue would become the subject of much controversy in the weeks that followed.

Zelda was impressed with the young man's appearance. "He was sitting there, just sort of twiddling his thumbs, and looking at his hands. He was such a nice-looking young man. He had his shirt off, and he had some kind of necklace on. He was just as clean as soap and water would make him—trim haircut. His tennis shoes were just sparkling white. His trousers were pressed, and had you seen him down the yard, you would have assumed he belonged there and was doing something. He was the calmest man I have ever seen."

The operator asked Zelda more questions about her and about the intruder.

Operator: "And your gun is loaded?"

Zelda: "Yes ma'am, it is."

Operator: "Just stay with me, okay? You don't have a heart condition or blood pressure problems do you?"

Zelda: "Yes, I have high blood pressure, and I have sugar diabetes. I'm shaking like a leaf."

The operator expressed concern and asked if she should be dispatching an ambulance. Zelda's answer is not intelligible. The operator asked what sort of gun Zelda had. She replied that she had a .38 but that she was holding a .22.

When the first police officer arrived, the operator told Zelda to put her gun down and to tell her where she had put it. Zelda said she had put it on the mantle.

The officers vaulted the gates in the four-foot fence around the front of the property because they were locked. They came running, she said. Police reports indicated that four officers arrived in their patrol cars.

Zelda told one of the officers that if an old lady with a shaking hand had been holding her at gunpoint she would have been worried. But the suspect remained calm throughout the incident.

"When the officers came in, he just stood up and assumed the position, hands behind his back ready for them to cuff him, and they did."

One officer asked the suspect something but he didn't answer, so the officer turned to Zelda and asked if the suspect spoke English.

"I don't know, but he understood every damn thing I told him," she replied.

The Aftermath

Two officers led the suspect off the porch into the front yard; a third officer went into the house to talk to Zelda.

Officer Daniel Mejia, who arrived after the intruder was handcuffed, read the young man his rights in Spanish. According to his report, the suspect was identified as Arturo Nolan Lopez, 25. Mejia asked him why he had no tools or glass to replace the broken window. Lopez did not reply. He declined to answer further questions, but had a request. "The request was that we would not notify his wife of this incident and that the car, a red Chevrolet Camaro, be returned to his wife," Mejia stated in his report.

The red 1985 Camaro was found parked on a side street. Mejia stated he later contacted Lopez's wife, who told him Lopez was a tile setter and the car belonged to a friend.

As soon as the young man had been arrested Zelda phoned her son, Bruce Hunt. His immediate reaction, according to his mother, was: "What have you done now, Mother?" She told him briefly what had happened, and he said he would be right over.

The officer who followed Zelda into the house asked her if she was okay. She told him she was. He asked her where the gun was, and she told him it was on the mantle. As he walked across the living room he asked her if she had let the hammer down.

"Of course," she replied.

The officer looked at the gun, but did not touch it or pick it up, Zelda said. "Had he, I would have cautioned about it, because I don't like for people to handle my guns," she added.

The officer asked her if she needed to be checked out by the hospital. She said she didn't think so. The officer stayed with Zelda until her son arrived. According to her the officer said: "I think your mother's great."

Bruce replied: "You don't have to live around her."

Lopez was charged with burglary and criminal trespass. He went to Pima County jail with bond set at $7,500. A detective called Zelda, and she agreed to press charges, but she didn't think it ever went to court. The last time she spoke to a detective he said investigators were overloaded with new cases.

Later in 1997 Zelda was presented with a certificate from Brassroots, Inc., a national civil-rights organization. It honored her safe and prudent use of a firearm in defending herself.

In October 2004 she was honored with a Human Right of Self-Defense Award at a banquet in Phoenix, celebrating ten years of concealed-carry in Arizona.

Her family members wanted her to get a permit to carry a gun, but she said she didn't need a permit.

"If I wanted to carry a gun I carried it. It used to only be a $25 fine if you got in trouble for carrying a gun. I wasn't up at that point to going to the school and getting the permit. My son and daughter-in-law both have them," she said.

Reflections

Initially, Zelda spoke to a reporter from the *Arizona Daily Star*. Speaking from memory she said the 9-1-1 operator had asked her to put the gun down before the police arrived. She said she would do so only when she saw the officers come through the gate.

The story also included a quote from Officer Daniel Mejia: "She had a weapon, and she used it wisely. It's something we prefer not to have people do, but it's becoming more prevalent."

Mejia's brother, Sergeant Eugene Mejia, was quoted as saying the police preferred civilians not to confront criminals. When this was reported in the newspaper it caused howls of protest on talk radio, in letters to the editor, and in calls to the police department.

In a letter to the editor of the *Arizona Daily Star*, Edward J. Owen castigated Officer Daniel Mejia, calling his quote absurd. Owen wrote: "What does Mejia prefer, that Hunt did not have a weapon? That she should use her pistol unwisely: That non-cops never use available weapons to stop a crime, as Hunt did?"

As a result of the public outrage at the 9-1-1 operator telling Zelda to put her gun down before the officers arrived, the Tucson Police Department asked for and got a "Clarification" from the newspaper. Four days after the initial story ran, the newspaper stated: "A police dispatcher did not instruct Zelda Hunt to put down the gun she held against a would-be robber, as reported in a Page One story Sunday. Instead, the dispatcher told the 72-year-old woman, who interrupted a man allegedly trying to break into her home, that she would need to put down the gun when the police arrived."

If that was true the Arizona desert gets ninety inches of rain a year. The following day the *Arizona Daily Star* corrected the record and clarified the clarification. It printed most of the tape of the 9-1-1 call. On the tape the operator did indeed say: "I'm going to want you to put the gun down before I get units there, okay?"

After slipping down the slope from truth and honesty, the police department made an attempt to regain the high ground. A spokesman said the statement had to be taken in context. It was true that, when Zelda replied firmly that she would put her gun down when she saw an officer at her gate, the operator said, "okay," and didn't push it.

Essentially the dispute was a quibble over one word: "before." However, "before" was the key word. Only an idiot would have followed the operator's instructions and put her gun down before the police arrived. Zelda was no fool. She was an independent-minded, tough grandmother who grew up in the Ozarks. "I was raised in the hills, and you don't wait for the cops to come and help you. We were raised to help ourselves," she said.

As for the police officers who said they prefer ordinary citizens to leave the crime fighting to them, most police departments repeat this mantra at least in their public statements. Along with "leave it to us" usually goes the "give the robbers what they want and don't resist because you might get hurt."

This is not good advice. In his book *More Guns, Less Crime: Understanding Crime and Gun Control Laws*, Professor John R. Lott Jr. of the American Enterprise Institute contends that it is bad advice. His research shows that a woman who defends herself with a firearm is 2.5 times more likely to survive a violent confrontation with a criminal without serious injury than if she were not to resist at all.

We tend to admire the people like Zelda, who fight back against criminals, rather than those who roll over and submit to the indignity of robbery or worse.

However, Tucson Police Chief Doug Smith said in a letter to reporter Scott Wood: "It is not our intent to dissuade citizens from exercising prudent and reasonable methods in defending themselves or their property."

From the time Zelda reached the 9-1-1 operator to the time the first officers arrived at her house was four minutes. This is a good response time, but still time enough for the suspect to have raped, robbed, or murdered Zelda, had she not had a gun and been prepared to use it.

If the suspect had just run away, would she have shot him? She said she would not, "because if you shoot someone that's fleeing, shoot 'em in the back, then you're in trouble."

Chapter 11

To Draw or Not to Draw: Robert Lawrence

Most states have laws that make it illegal to brandish a firearm or to threaten someone with a gun. In almost all jurisdictions, however, a person is justified in drawing or pointing a gun if the use of deadly force is justified. In other words, if you feel you are in imminent danger of being killed or seriously injured, or someone you are trying to protect is in the same situation, you can draw your gun, aim it at a would-be assailant, and shoot if necessary.

One of the most difficult decisions for a law-abiding, armed civilian is when—or whether—to draw a gun in response to a criminal threat. The hair on the back of your neck may be standing up, and this guy is moving into your space, but he hasn't shown a weapon. His partner may be moving behind you. How far do you allow him or them to proceed before you take action?

According to various academic studies, each year at least a couple of million ordinary citizens use firearms in response to criminal attack or threat. In only a very small percentage of cases is the gun actually fired. And in fewer cases still is anyone wounded or killed. So every year a massive number of people expose their guns, brandish them, or point them and successfully discourage an attack.

Most of these defensive uses of guns are not reported to police, so they do not appear in police crime statistics and almost never in the media. But they happen and they happen frequently.

The would-be victim has solved the problem. The attacker has remembered he has an urgent appointment elsewhere. The law-abiding citizen, who obviously felt threatened, is not certain what he or she did was legal: would the use of deadly force have been justified? This is where the law is murky, and law-abiding citizens can find themselves at risk, not only from criminals but also from the legal system. How well can you articulate the reasons that you felt threatened?

Another factor that may affect the result of many of these confrontations is who gets to tell their story to the police first. This is where a cell phone is useful. It is always a good idea to call police when you feel seriously threatened. The person who gets to tell the story to police first has a definite advantage. The first person to report a crime automatically becomes the victim or complainant when the officer writes the report. The other party becomes the suspect, and it can take a lot of persuasion to reverse those labels.

What happened to Robert Lawrence of Tempe, Arizona, is a cautionary tale of what can happen to a law-abiding citizen who attempts to ward-off an attack. Lawrence, then 59, recalled what happened to him on May 22, 2003, on a trip to the bank and the grocery store.

Robert Lawrence

It was the sort of day that makes people glad they moved to Arizona—a clear sky and temperature in the nineties. Lawrence, who is a native of New York, was feeling good as he drove to the bank. He had a check with him—a refund check from the Internal Revenue Service—and it was for a lot more than he had expected.

Due to an error made by his accountant, he had been expecting to get back less than $500. "I had gotten a letter from the IRS telling me there was an error, and I was going to be getting about $1,283 instead of $460," Lawrence said.

The check had arrived in the mail shortly after 1 P.M. and he was driving to the Wells Fargo branch where he banked in Tempe, a suburb of Phoenix.

As he usually did Bob was wearing a Colt Mustang .380-caliber, semi-automatic pistol with a 2³/₄-inch barrel. It carries six rounds in the magazine and one in the chamber. It was loaded with Federal HydraShok ammunition. He was carrying the gun in an Uncle Mike's Sidekick ankle holster made of black nylon with Velcro fastenings. It has a strap over the hammer, and he had the hammer down on a live round in the chamber. He had a concealed-weapons permit, which he initially received in 1994 shortly after they became available in Arizona. It is a four-year license, so he had renewed it twice.

Tempe is a pleasant city of about 160,000 people. Arizona State University is located there, and it is home to the National Football League's Arizona Cardinals.

Lawrence had lived in Tempe for about thirty years. He had worked for Motorola in Tempe, but in April 2000 he fell while lifting some equipment. This exacerbated an earlier spinal injury, leaving him in poor health and unable to work. His sole source of income was a disability check from Social Security. He used a cane when he walked, and he was in constant pain. He could neither walk, sit, nor stand for more than an hour at a time. Consequently, he tried never to be away from home for longer than an hour.

Bob drove to the bank about a mile from his house in his white 1991 Honda Civic station wagon. He had no indication that May 22 would turn into one of the worst days of his life.

He used the automated teller machine in the lobby, so he didn't have to stand in a line for a live teller. He deposited the check at 1:39 P.M. and withdrew a hundred dollars. He then drove to the local Trader Joe's, which is a small, upscale, supermarket chain. The store was relatively empty, and he was able to complete his grocery shopping quickly and easily. To celebrate his windfall, he treated himself to a purple butterfly orchid in full bloom. His neighbors knew him as "Botany Bob" because of his collection of rare and exotic plants.

The Incident

With his little station wagon full of groceries and the orchid, Bob prepared to head home. This Trader Joe's is on the southwest corner of McClintock and Guadalupe. Two exits open onto Guadalupe, which runs east and west. Bob took the exit further from the intersection. Because he wanted to head west, he waited for a gap in the traffic then pulled across the two eastbound lanes into the center turn lane. Speeding up to about thirty-five miles an hour, he waited for a car to pass him, then pulled into the leftmost of the two westbound lanes. He intended to move right, into the curb lane, so he looked back over his shoulder and signaled his intention.

"I looked back. The right lane was clear; I pull into it. The next thing I see, a car comes whipping out from behind the car that was behind me in the left lane, trying to pass them on the right, and I'm there. And they're about six inches off my bumper, because I had slowed down," Lawrence said.

He estimated the other car must have been doing fifty-five or sixty miles an hour. The speed limit there was forty-five. A young white woman was driving the green Chevrolet Monte Carlo, which also held two Hispanic men in their twenties—one in the front passenger seat and a younger one in the back.

"There were three people in the car shaking their fists at me, and about this time I speed up a little bit, get up to forty-five," Bob said.

Almost immediately he entered a school zone where the speed limit was thirty-five miles an hour, so he slowed down. The Monte Carlo pulled into the left lane where it could have overtaken him, but it didn't. It stayed about one-and-a-half car lengths behind him. Bob figured the occupants didn't overtake him in order to prevent him from reading their license plate number. Arizona vehicles have license plates only at the back.

"They were already ranting and raving and screaming: 'F--- you'—I can lip read. The woman was even doing this. The driver had a cell phone in her hand, was talking on it, and drinking from a drink she held in her lap."

Lawrence had his window half rolled down because his air-conditioner wasn't working properly. The man in the front seat of the Monte Carlo had his window all the way down and was leaning out of it.

"He has his whole torso out. The kid in the back seat is handing him things. He's throwing objects at the car trying to smash out the rear window." Bob thought one object was a stone, because it left a dent in the sheet metal next to his license plate.

"I actually thought I had something fail on the car. It was loud enough that I thought that a spring or something was broken, which really scared me, and I thought if something happens to the car, I'm coming up on an intersection which leads straight out of the school, and there are kids all over the place."

The green Monte Carlo then pulled alongside Bob's station wagon. Bob rolled the window all the way down and shouted to the front seat passenger that they were in a school zone and the speed limit was thirty-five miles an hour.

"And he goes: 'We're going to f---ing kill you old man.' At which point his wife [the driver of the car] hands him a fourteen-ounce Diet Dr. Pepper, which he throws and hits me square in the face with, as hard as he can. They're right alongside of me. I mean he could have reached out and touched me almost."

The soda was in a Styrofoam cup with a plastic lid. When it hit Bob, the lid came off, and the soft drink went all over his face and glasses, temporarily blinding him. The lid sliced into his forehead leaving a small cut that added some blood to the mixture, though at the time Bob did not realize he was bleeding.

They were about one-hundred-fifty feet from the traffic light at the school crossing. Lawrence drove on to the next street, Rural Road, and turned right, heading north. The other car swerved from the left lane, across the right lane, and into the turn lane to follow him.

"That's when I went: 'Oh crap.' That's when I got on the phone with the police, because it was obvious they were going to follow through."

Bob called 9-1-1 on his cell phone as he headed north towards the traffic lights at Baseline Road.

Operator: "Nine-one-one, what is your emergency?"

Lawrence: "(Unintelligible) just hit me in the face with a coke, threw it right in my face, threw other stuff in my car. He was speeding through a school zone."

Operator: "Okay, where sir, where are you?"

Lawrence: "He's driving a green Pontiac. He's got a wife, a kid, and a couple of other people in it. They are driving the same way I am."

Operator: "Sir."

The operator interrupts Lawrence who is talking fast and not listening to her. Panic is evident in his voice.

Lawrence: "On Baseline Road. Yes."

At this point, he is actually still on Rural but approaching the lights at the intersection with Baseline.

Operator: "Okay, so you're at Rural and Baseline?"

Lawrence: "I'm at Rural and Baseline. They're right behind me. He's got a woman in the car. He's getting out of the car now. He's coming towards me. I have a gun."

Fear is evident in Lawrence's tone.

Operator: "Do you have a gun?"

Lawrence: "Yes, I have."

Lawrence had an expandable baton in the station wagon, and he expanded it by flicking it downwards. Closed, the baton measured eight inches; opened it was twenty-one-inches long. As he saw both men get out of the Monte Carlo, he realized he wouldn't be able to defend himself adequately in the little station wagon with the baton so he dropped it.

"I could not in any way manipulate this baton without knocking out a window in the car. I just opened it because I thought I was going to get out, and if I had to, take down the one guy, but when the second guy got out I just dropped it."

He then reached down and grabbed his Colt Mustang from the ankle holster on the inside of his right leg. He normally shoots left-handed because he has neurological problems with his right hand from his spinal injury. But he held the gun in his right hand beside his ear with the muzzle pointing upwards. He needed to flip off the safety and cock the hammer before the gun would fire. He needed both hands to do that. He said he was not consciously trying to display or brandish the gun.

The two men could not see the gun because they were taller than Bob's station wagon, but the woman, who was driving the Monte Carlo, could see it through the vehicle's back window.

According to Lawrence, she screamed: "He's got a gun."

The two men hastily ran back to their car and got back into it. Bob reholstered his gun and, as soon as the light changed, he drove off, turning west onto Baseline Road. He estimated the gun was in his hand for no more than forty-five seconds. He never did take off the safety or cock the hammer.

Lawrence asked the operator if she heard the attacker at his window. The operator asked him if he still had his gun out.

Lawrence: "No, I do not. He threw a soda into my face. I have glasses. Luckily he didn't break them. He also hit the side of the car with something."

Lawrence drove west on Baseline, but slowed down to around twenty miles an hour trying to get the Monte Carlo to pass him so he could get its license number. He told the operator what he was doing. But the Monte Carlo stayed behind him and would not overtake.

Meanwhile, the operator asked Bob questions, trying to solicit more information about him and the people in the other car. He described the occupants as two Hispanics, a white woman, and a child. Lawrence gave the operator his name, his address, and cell phone number. He said the other car was not going to pass him. He added that he was going to turn on his emergency blinkers.

Lawrence: "He's turning around; I'm going after him."

Operator: "Okay Sir, don't, don't . . ."

Lawrence: "I'm trying to get the license plate number. I'm not going to . . . I'm not stupid, I just want the license. He's going into a red light. All I'm doing is going after a license for you because I have been accosted twice. He's going into a dealership."

The Monte Carlo suddenly pulled a U-turn and drove into the parking lot of Earnhardt Ford auto dealership. Bob also turned around and was able to read off the green car's license plate number to the 9-1-1 operator as he drove past the dealership.

He turned around again and continued driving westbound on Baseline Road. The operator asked where he was heading. Lawrence said he was heading home. During the drive to his home, Lawrence provided the operator with more information about what had happened, while she asked more questions.

The operator established that the other car was no longer following him. Lawrence told her when his attacker came up to his station wagon, the man tried to hit him in the face.

Lawrence: "I did have the weapon in my hand. I did not point it at him, and you did not hear a threat."

The operator told him to calm down—that she had officers trying to reach him. She asked him again for his address, and Lawrence repeated it.

Lawrence: "When two people get out of a car and come up and accost me, I did get the gun out. I did not have it cocked; I did not jack the receiver; I did not make any threats. I just said: 'Get back in the car and get away from me.'"

Operator: "Okay, you had the gun in your lap, but you didn't point it?"

Lawrence: "That's correct, ma'am. I don't point a gun at anything I don't want to kill, and I'm ex-military, Vietnam War vet, and I don't want to kill anybody. If I have to defend my life, I will. That's why I got it."

Lawrence told the operator he was going directly home, because he had a car full of groceries and didn't want to give his assailants the opportunity to get close to him.

He mentioned that he had limited use of his left arm. He said that he grabbed a baton when the two men approached his vehicle. He described both men as Hispanic skinheads and speculated they might have been gang members, because he did nothing to them. He just changed lanes after signaling.

Lawrence: "These people are dangerous. To throw something in the face of somebody when they are driving in front of a school—I was blinded temporarily. I'm soaked with soda pop right now. They hit the back of my car. They hit the side of my car. They were looking for something else to throw. I'm calming down if you notice. I'm now very close to home."

Lawrence said he carried a cell phone as a safety measure. He was scared to go out these days and would not have ventured out if he had not been out of food.

Lawrence: "If I had not had a weapon, I would have been attacked and dragged out of the car, because there were two of them got out to come after me, and I did not call them any names as you heard."

He said he speaks Spanish and is not prejudiced against Hispanics. The operator asked him where his gun was. He said it was back in its holster on his ankle. He repeated that he did not point the gun at anyone.

Bob told the operator he was pulling into his driveway. Several police cars were parked in the street in front of his house. Bob can be heard on the tape greeting them.

Lawrence: "How are you doing gentlemen? It's good to see you."

He then thanked the 9-1-1 operator and ended the call after sixteen minutes.

The Interrogation

At that point Bob Lawrence sighed with relief. He had been threatened and believed he had barely escaped a severe beating or even death. But he was home at the modest, single-story, brick-veneer house where he had lived for nearly twenty years. And the police—protectors of good, law-abiding citizens—were there. The front-seat passenger who threw the soda that hit him in the face would be arrested and charged at least with assault. He was sure everything was going to be all right.

He could not have been more wrong.

As he walked towards the first officer, a young blond man wearing glasses, he stuck his hand out and they shook hands. "I was just so glad to see them; I was home, I was safe, you know," Bob recalled.

He turned around to shake hands with another officer who said: "I don't shake hands."

According to the police report written by Officer Blair Wrigley, he asked Lawrence about his gun. Bob disputed this and said he was not asked but volunteered the information about the gun he was wearing. He said he sat down on the ground and pulled up the leg of his bib overalls so another officer could remove it from his ankle holster. He also handed the officer his concealed-weapons permit. He wore the overalls because they had shoulder straps and didn't need a belt. He had abdominal injuries that make wearing a belt painful. This was also one of the reasons he wore an ankle holster.

It soon became apparent that Bob was no threat to the officers, and several of them left.

Lawrence asked if he could put his groceries away. He had three gallons of milk, and the temperature was soaring towards one-hundred degrees. But the officers told him he couldn't go into his house, because he might have more guns inside. Bob said he did, but they were all secured in a gun cabinet. He had several other hand-guns: a CZ 9 mm, a Taurus .38, and a Ruger .22. He also had a Remington 870, pump-action shotgun.

"I was pretty adamant about it. I was upset now, because I came home, I was polite, I surrendered my weapon, I gave them my license, and this big burly guy steps up and says: 'You don't understand. This isn't negotiable. You're

not going in the house, or we're going in with you. And
I just got out of the Marines two months ago.'
   "I said: 'I'm a veteran myself, Vietnam War, Air
Force.' I said. 'Isn't the Marines motto: They'll make a
man out of you?'"
   "He said: 'That's right.'
   "I said: 'Well, God made me a man, so I joined the
Air Force.'
   "At that point everything went to hell."
   Bob said he had used the line frequently with
Marines when he was in the Air Force and had meant
it as a joke to lighten the mood. However, he admitted
he was starting to get angry at the treatment he was receiving, and it may not have come across as a joke. The officer certainly didn't take it as a joke.
   In his report Wrigley said: "Mr. Lawrence was talking very rapidly and was perspiring heavily. He seemed
to be very upset and said he had an 'adrenaline rush'
from the incident."
   Lawrence said the officers were welcome to come into
his house, but he had a 125-pound German Shepard in
the house. Two officers accompanied him into the
house and stayed with him while he put away his groceries. The dog and one of the officers hit it off immediately. "He and the dog were playing the whole time while
I was putting my groceries away. The other guy was standing behind me with his hand on his weapon."
   After putting away all the groceries Bob suggested,
because of the dog, they go back outside to finish the interview. He told the officers he needed to sit down or he would
collapse because of his medical problems. So he took
a folding chair outside and sat in it.

Wrigley's report stated that he talked with another officer, who was with the occupants of the green Monte Carlo at Earnhardt Ford on Baseline Road. The occupants were identified as Mario Garza, 28, who was the front seat passenger, his wife, Shirley Garza, 22, who was driving, and Jamie Castillo, 21.

> *Note: I have changed the names of the three occupants of the green Monte Carlo, as they were not charged with any criminal offense.*

The report continued, "I talked to Officer Kells on the police radio, and he advised that the parties he was with told him that Mr. Lawrence had pointed the gun at one of them and that he had tried to strike their car with an expandable baton as they drove beside him."

Wrigley said he asked Lawrence if he had an expandable baton. The baton was in his car and had been taken by another officer as evidence. Wrigley also said Lawrence told him he had attention-deficit disorder and was taking medication for it.

Lawrence later annotated the police report. He disagreed with much that Wrigley had written, noting what he thought were gross inaccuracies and more subtle changes that made him and his actions appear in a less favorable light. For example, Wrigley stated, "Mr. Lawrence refused requests by Tempe police dispatchers to pull over in a parking lot and meet with police. He advised the dispatchers that he was going home."

There is no indication on the 9-1-1 tape that the operator asked Bob to stop and await the police. There was no mention in Wrigley's report of his stated concern that his groceries would spoil if he didn't get them home. After he told the 9-1-1 operator that he was going home, she said, "So you're not going to stop?" although she never asked him to stop. Bob also provided the operator with his address and his vehicle license-plate number. In the report Wrigley gives the impression that police tracked Lawrence down by the plate number provided by the people in the green car.

Bob also said the only reason he mentioned his attention-deficit disorder was to explain to the officers that he sometimes had difficulty following what was being said. He added: "Especially when I am in a frightened or agitated state. I was in both. Death threats do that to one."

Wrigley's report continued: "He also told me that he was ex-military so he 'knew how to take care of himself.'"

Lawrence disputed that. He stated, "Actually I said I was a Vietnam War veteran and knew how to handle weapons and would never point a weapon at an individual unless it was required that I use it in my defense."

Wrigley's report further outlined Lawrence's account of the incident, though Bob noted additional inaccuracies. For example, the report stated, "As Mr. Lawrence continued to drive westbound on Guadalupe, Mr. Lawrence was hit in the head with something. He believes it was a cup of soda that was thrown by the front-seat passenger of the green car."

Lawrence's note: "No, I do not believe, I know. He was looking me right in the eye when he did it!"

The officer indicated a small cut on Bob's forehead that had been bleeding and asked him about it. Lawrence was unaware that he had been cut, but said that the object that hit him would have caused it. Officer J. Stone, the former Marine, took digital photos of the cut for evidence.

Wrigley left Bob with Stone and drove to Earnhardt Ford to hear the other side of the story. As heads differ from tails on coins, the account given by Mario and Shirley Garza and Jamie Castillo differed strikingly from Bob's.

Mario Garza told Wrigley he was the front-seat passenger in the green Monte Carlo that was being driven by his wife, Shirley. They were driving to his job as a life-guard and were westbound on Guadalupe. He told the officer they saw a car weaving from lane to lane.

Wrigley's report stated, "Mr. Garza's wife pulled up alongside the white Honda station wagon that was driving erratically. Mr. Garza had his window down, and the white male driver later identified as Mr. Lawrence also had his window down. Mr. Garza made eye contact with Mr. Lawrence and asked him if he was all right."

But Lawrence wasn't buying the Good Samaritan ploy. He noted, "The Garza car did pull alongside after they ran out of things to throw, but the only thing Mr. Garza said was that he would kill me, hardly rendering assistance."

Wigley's report continued, "Mr. Lawrence immediately started yelling obscenities at Mr. Garza and told him the speed limit was thirty-five mph. Mr. Garza tried to tell Mr. Lawrence that he was concerned for him because he was driving in two lanes of traffic."

Bob said he did tell Garza he was in a thirty-five-mile-an-hour school zone, but denied that he used profanity at any time.

Garza told Wrigley he was a certified lifeguard and emergency medical technician and wondered if Lawrence was having some kind of medical problem. Garza said Lawrence tried to hit the Monte Carlo with his expandable baton but couldn't reach it. This was another accusation Bob denied.

Garza also accused Lawrence of pulling in front of the Monte Carlo to block it from passing while going north on Rural Road. Lawrence stopped for a red light at Baseline, he said.

The police report stated, "Mr. Garza said that he then got out of his car and decided to approach Mr. Lawrence and talk to him face to face. He walked up to the driver's side rear corner of Mr. Lawrence's car. Mr. Lawrence stuck his right hand out the driver's window, and he was holding a silver/chrome small semi-auto handgun. The gun was pointed directly at Mr. Garza as he was walking up to Mr. Lawrence. Mr. Lawrence was yelling at him, but Mr. Garza could not hear what he was saying. Mr. Garza then stopped and walked back to his car and got in."

Lawrence commented, "My weapon is a Colt .380, a very small handgun, and it was never pointed in the direction of any human at any time. This is a blatant lie. Mrs. Garza can only have seen the weapon from looking in my rear window, as previously stated, and once the threat was gone, the weapon was holstered and never taken out until I gave it to the TPD [Tempe Police Department] officer."

Lawrence said Mrs. Garza could only have seen his gun through the rear window of the Honda station wagon.

Wrigley confirmed that Mrs. Garza called 9-1-1 and talked to an operator on her cell phone.

Mrs. Garza: "I have a guy driving in front of me who wouldn't pick one lane, and he slammed on the brakes in front of me, and he's got a gun, and he's like waving it around."

The operator questioned her about where she was and what the other vehicle looked like.

Operator: "Okay. And what color was the gun that this man was waving around?"

Mrs. Garza: "It was a silver, what was it, a twenty-two? Like a little silver twenty-two."

Operator: "Did he point it or just waving it?"

Mrs. Garza: "He pointed it."

A male voice interrupts: "Pointed it at me."

The operator told her to find a safe place to park with people around and wait for the police. She turned into Earnhardt Ford and waited for the officers to arrive.

Wrigley stated he asked Mario Garza what he had thrown at Lawrence's car. "I even bluffed him and told him I had an independent witness that had seen him throw something at Mr. Lawrence's car. He denied throwing anything at Mr. Lawrence or his car."

Wrigley reported that he spoke to Mrs. Garza who told essentially the same story as her husband. She told the officer she saw Lawrence point the gun at her husband. Castillo corroborated the couple's stories. Wrigley says he attempted to get Castillo to contradict Mario Garza's account. "I then bluffed Mr. Castillo and told him that Mr. Garza had told me that he [Mr. Garza] had thrown a drink at Mr. Lawrence. I asked Mr. Castillo if he saw if the drink hit Mr. Lawrence's car or not. Mr. Castillo said he did not see Mr. Garza throw anything out of the car, and he did not think that Mr. Garza had thrown anything or he would have seen it."

Wrigley then returned to Lawrence's house and questioned him further. Bob said they tried to get him to change his story, but he didn't.

It is obvious from the tone of Wrigley's report that he believed that the Garzas were the victims and were telling the truth, while Bob was the aggressor and was lying.

"They were calling me a liar and telling me I was harassing people. They had come up to render aid because he was an EMT [emergency medical technician] in training and was working as a lifeguard and that I had opened up on him with a burst of profanity and started waving my gun at them."

Carol Deodati lives next door to Bob and has known him for thirty years. She heard the officers aggressively questioning him and felt they were harassing him. She walked over from her house and stood at the entrance to his driveway until one of the officers came and talked to her. She said the police officer was making out that Bob had an arsenal.

"He said something about, 'well we found a lot of guns in his house,' or something like that. I mean I've been in Bob's house, there aren't a lot of guns there. I think he collects a few, but I don't think he's got an arsenal."

Carol said it sounded as though the officers intended to arrest Bob and throw him in jail. "They were talking about bringing him to the jail in Phoenix, and that's when we all got very protective."

She and other neighbors explained to the officers that Bob had not been well and was obviously stressed out over the incident. They were trying to talk the police out of arresting him.

The police asked if they could search the station wagon, and Bob gave them permission. He said they only searched in the front seat. A few days later he found the soda cup lid in the back, where it had landed after flying off the cup when the soda hit him in the face.

In addition to other ailments Bob has a prostate problem, which means if he drinks water he has to urinate frequently. So for an hour before he goes out he drinks nothing. He had had nothing to drink since before 1 P.M. and in the hundred-degree heat he was getting dehydrated.

Heat Exhaustion

He said he asked the police officers for a drink of water, but they ignored him. They kept him outside in the heat without water until he started going into heat exhaustion. "I'm sweating profusely, I'm white, my mouth is dry, my heart is racing, I'm getting chest pains. They call the fire department. The fire department checks my vitals, calls an ambulance," Lawrence said.

Southwest Ambulance got the call at 3:24 P.M. and took Bob to Scottsdale Memorial Hospital six miles from his home in Tempe. Unknown to Bob the young officer he shook hands with when he arrived home was in the ambulance standing behind him. The officer could not help but hear Bob telling the ambulance attendant the police were not stupid and they would figure out the truth. His trust was misplaced.

When he arrived at the hospital there had just been a major car wreck, and three helicopters landed with badly injured people on board. A woman came in to take Bob's vital signs but didn't have the right equipment so she left. Bob got up to get a drink and saw the young officer who was in the ambulance standing outside the curtain around his bed. When he came back after getting a drink of water a woman told him to get out of the hallway. Bob returned to the room and lay down.

He started to recover. He had been in an air-conditioned ambulance, followed by the air-conditioned hospital room, and he had had a drink of water.

He said Officer Wrigley burst into the room. He called Bob a liar and said they have witnesses. However, there is nothing in the police report about any witnesses except Jamie Castillo corroborating Mr. and Mrs. Garza's accusations. Lawrence told Wrigley that if there were any witnesses they were called by the Garzas and were lying.

Bob got up again to get another drink of water and again was told to get out of the hallway because the hospital had emergency patients arriving. He still hadn't been treated, so he told the woman he was leaving the hospital. He walked outside and saw Wrigley in his car making notes. He asked the officer for a ride back to his house. Wrigley refused and said it was against regulations. He advised Bob to get a lawyer. Bob said he couldn't afford one.

He used his cell phone to call his neighbor, Tom Hornsby, who with Carol Deodati fetched him and drove him home. During the drive Tom told Bob that the police said they were going to arrest him and put him in Tent City. This was the name for the encampment where the overflow from the Maricopa County jail was housed in tents. He arrived home at 5:40 P.M.

The Aftermath

That evening Lawrence made some notes about the incident while the details were still fresh in his mind. He had lived in Tempe for more than thirty years and had never had so much as a traffic ticket. His anger and frustration at what had happened was evident.

He wrote, "This is just unbelievable!! I am attacked and then presumed guilty. I want a receipt for my weapon and a full police report. Arrogant, ignorant, paranoid, great police we have here!?! Some are good, they must be, but I got the goon squad! So it goes. 2303 hr. Can't sleep, the more I think about the way I was treated by Tempe's finest, the more distraught I get." [The punctuation is his.]

The following morning Lawrence called the police department and got the case number. On May 28 the case was assigned for follow up to Detective Trent Luckow.

In the months that followed, Luckow's investigation progressed slowly. On June 10 Bob called the detective to tell him he had found the lid from a Wendy's soda cup in the back of his station wagon. It had been missed by the uniformed officers who searched only the front seats of the car on the day of the incident. According to Luckow's report he asked Bob about pointing his gun at Mario Garza. Lawrence denied doing so.

Three days later Luckow went to Lawrence's house and collected the cup lid as evidence. Bob again denied pointing the gun at Garza.

On July 2 Bob called Luckow wanting to know why the police were still holding his gun. Luckow told him it was evidence in a pending criminal investigation. The case was passed on for review to the Maricopa County Attorney's Office.

Bob later annotated Luckow's report and said it was the most accurate in recording what he had said.

Prosecution

After several more months Lawrence said that Luckow told him he would not be prosecuted. So it was with surprise and consternation that he received a summons shortly before Thanksgiving 2003. He was informed he was charged with disorderly conduct, a Class 6 felony, and had to appear in Maricopa Superior Court on January 7, 2004. He also had to be fingerprinted and photographed at the sheriff's office.

The arrival of the summons ruined the Thanksgiving holiday for him. "I was totally freaked out, because I'm here alone; I have no family; I'm living on Social Security disability, which isn't much."

He would have to find a lawyer and try to prove that he, not the Garzas, was the victim of the road-rage incident. After getting no help from a couple of lawyers, his pain specialist referred him to Alcock & Associates. His case was handled mostly by Tait Elkie.

A conviction on the felony charge would rob him permanently of his concealed-weapons permit, and under federal law he would be unable legally ever to own or possess a firearm again.

On December 8, 2003, he sent a letter to the court requesting special accommodation for his medical problems. He got a reply saying the court would make no accommodation, and if he didn't show up on time a warrant would be issued for his arrest. Elkie picked him up and drove him to the court.

Elkie told Bob he was going to negotiate a plea bargain, but Bob said no. He was not going to plead guilty to something he had not done. The lawyer said he had to negotiate a deal to be diligent to his client. Bob said he would refuse to accept it. Elkie did negotiate a plea deal, and Bob refused it.

In early January he received a letter from the Arizona Department of Public Safety demanding the return of his concealed-weapons permit. It had been suspended pending the outcome of the felony charge against him.

Tait made a discovery request for all material that related to the case. He initially tried to get copies of the 9-1-1 tapes from Tempe Police Department.

"We couldn't get it. They said there was a hold on it because supposedly it contained victim information and they don't want to disclose that. So we had to wait for, if I recall correctly, a number of weeks before we could actually get a copy of that from Tempe PD."

Arizona has a bill of rights that protects victims when going through legal proceedings. One of those rights is not having a victim's personal information divulged to the defense. Police normally provide all the tapes relating to a particular incident, and that would include information about the victims as well as witnesses.

Elkie said that was the reason for the delay. Tempe police said they would not disclose the tapes until the prosecutor had an opportunity to review them.

When recordings of the 9-1-1 calls arrived in his office Tait discovered more than just the calls made by Bob and by Shirley Garza. They included another 9-1-1 call from someone who had witnessed part of the incident. It was a lightening bolt that went right to the heart of the case.

The police had insisted all along that when Bob had said Mario Garza had thrown things, including a soda, at his car, he was lying. In the newly disclosed 9-1-1 recording a witness, who identified herself as Fiona and had provided her phone number, reported seeing part of the incident. The conversation was recorded at 2:16 P.M. on May 22, 2003.

Operator: "Nine-one-one, what is your emergency?"

Fiona: "I am driving on West Baseline, and there's a carload of guys; I don't know what's going on but they just like threw something at this older guy's car."

Operator: "Okay, where?"

Fiona: "It happened on Guadalupe Street."

Operator: "Guadalupe and what?"

Fiona: "Guadalupe and Rural."

Operator: "How long ago?"

Fiona: "About five minutes ago. A police officer just drove by, but I couldn't flag him down."

Fiona identified the car by its license-plate number. She said it was a green Monte Carlo with three or four people in it and the other vehicle was a white car with an older man in it. The operator solicited more information about the cars and their occupants. The call ended after Fiona identified herself and agreed to be contacted by police if necessary.

As soon as he discovered the 9-1-1 call from Fiona, Tait Elkie spoke to Deputy County Attorney Jeffrey Trudgian, who was handling the case. He pointed out the inconsistencies in the statements of the "victims" compared with those of Lawrence and of Fiona, the independent witness.

In a letter to the author Elkie wrote: "After meeting with his supervisor, Mr. Trudgian eventually agreed to dismiss the case against Mr. Lawrence. Quite frankly, I was surprised at the initial resistance I received from Mr. Trudgian, even after providing them with a copy of the 9-1-1 tape."

The case was dropped in April 2004, but Bob didn't get his pistol back until August. Tait tried to help Bob get the gun back. Tempe police said they didn't have the proper paperwork from the prosecutor's office. The prosecutor's office said that the prosecutor and his supervisor both had to sign off on it.

"It was several weeks before Bob was actually able to get it, and it was just a bureaucratic mess," Elkie said.

After the case was dismissed, the Arizona Department of Public Safety returned his concealed-weapons permit.

Reflections

Although Lawrence called 9-1-1 first, he got to tell the police officers what had happened to him after the Garzas had told their story. Tait Elkie believes that by talking to the police first, the three in the Monte Carlo probably swayed the officers in their favor.

"And I think the fact that Bob was the one with the gun, and you and I know that Bob is very excitable, especially in a situation like this—which I think anybody would be—he probably had some difficulty articulating himself, and the officers just took that to mean that he was probably the responsible person, and they proceeded that way."

Elkie said if the officers had paid attention to the evidence from Bob and the 9-1-1 call from Fiona, they would have realized that Lawrence was telling the truth.

The lawyer believes that whoever reviewed the case probably didn't listen to the 9-1-1 tape. He doesn't know if the prosecutor even had the witness tape at the time. He would probably have made the decision solely on the police report, which makes no mention of the independent witness in the case. He said he believes the sloppy investigation by police and prosecutor is not typical.

"I don't believe that it happens that regularly. I think that, to give them their due, they do the best investigation they can, but it kinda' fell short of what they could have done," Elkie said.

Did Bob do the right thing in showing his gun to the people he believed were about to attack him? His lawyer certainly thinks so. "I believe the fact that Bob had a concealed-weapons permit probably saved him from further harassment or possible violent injury. I think that with the right training and the right person having a concealed-weapons permit, having a weapon to protect yourself is a very important thing. And I think that when acting with responsibility, as Bob did in this particular case, you can avoid physical injury and possibly death.

"We don't know what would have happened had Bob not been able to display his weapon. I think he acted appropriately in two ways, first by calling 9-1-1 and advising the police what was going on immediately, but also having the ability to defend himself before the police were able to get there, I think, is extremely significant."

Bob maintains he did not display his weapon intentionally. He was about to use both hands to cock the Colt and take off the safety, and he was trying to accomplish that as discreetly as he could.

Although the system eventually worked, after a fashion, it would be an exaggeration to say that justice was done. The people who made a false report to police and who threw things at his car were not brought to justice. Detective Luckow told Bob they would not be charged. The case was not resolved before an innocent man was put through extensive financial and emotional turmoil.

"He really did have a horrible year emotionally with this whole thing. It put him under a huge amount of stress, and if the phone call hadn't turned up, who knows what would have happened? It would have been a lot messier for him," his neighbor, Carol Deodati, said. "There were other neighbors around here that were very upset at the way it was handled too."

The experience caused Lawrence to lose his trust in the police. All his life he had believed that the police were on his side and were there for his protection. That belief was severely eroded.

Lawyer Tait Elkie said he finds it most frustrating that the accused never gets compensated for the outlay in time and money spent in his defense.

"And in a situation where he acted appropriately. He truly did. He felt threatened by two men that were approaching his car at a stoplight. He didn't point the gun at them. He merely displayed it. He called 9-1-1 prior to that, and yet he still gets charged."

In October 2004 Bob Lawrence was among several recipients of the Human Right of Self-Defense Award, including Zelda Hunt, our subject in chapter 10. The award was presented to him in Phoenix at a banquet held to celebrate ten years of concealed-carry in Arizona.

Chapter 12

A Shot in the Dark: Judith Kuntz

As discussed in the case involving Deanna Eggleston of Arlington, in the United States residential burglary is a high-risk occupation. Usually burglary involves breaking into someone's home to steal. If somebody is home when the burglar breaks in, there is always a risk that the occupant may mistake the criminal's purpose or even object to his intentions. In Canada, Australia, and particularly the United Kingdom, there generally isn't much a law-abiding resident can do even if he or she would like to object. In those countries self-defense is officially frowned upon, and the most effective tools for self-defense—firearms—are as scarce as honest politicians. If an English homeowner is unwise enough to hit a burglar with say, a golf club, he or she will almost certainly spend more time in prison than the burglar. In 2004 Lord Goldsmith, the British attorney general, was quoted as saying that burglars have rights too and must be protected from violence.

This situation is familiar to residents of some uncivilized big cities in the U.S., such as Washington, D.C., New York, and Chicago. These cities appear to have passed a "Burglar Protection Act," which includes rounding up all the guns belonging to law-abiding residents so they cannot defend themselves effectively.

However, in the rest of the U.S., particularly in the South and the West where most households have at least one gun, burglars frequently take extra precautions to ensure no one is home before they ply their trade. Those who don't, face the distinct possibility of an early demise at the hands of a fearful resident. In many states a presumption exists that if someone forces his way into someone else's home the resident is in risk of serious assault, rape, or murder. This is justification for the use of deadly force.

Surveys by criminologists have shown that the one thing that criminals fear more than anything else is confronting an armed homeowner. But every once in a while a burglar, for whatever reason, will ignore the commonsense rules of his trade.

Judith Kuntz

Judy Kuntz loves living in Indialantic, a small town of about three thousand people on Florida's Atlantic coast. It is a beach town on the barrier island that extends south like a tail from Cape Canaveral. At Indialantic that tail is about a mile wide. The island is connected to the mainland and the city of Melbourne by a long bridge that spans the Indian River and the Intracoastal Waterway.

"When I go across the causeway every morning I just thank the good Lord that I live here because it's so beautiful," Judy said.

Indialantic is mostly a residential town of modest houses, but it is changing as developers race one another in erecting condos along the highway that parallels the beach. A mixture of subdivisions covers the area between the highway and Indian River. Judy lives in an older subdivision just outside the city limits in Brevard

County, where law enforcement is provided by the Brevard County Sheriff's Office. Judy has lived in the house on Avenida del Mar since the 1980s.

"It used to be that we could get up and see the sun rise and see the beach," she said wistfully. Now the condos block the view, and there isn't as much access to the beach as there used to be. "The quiet little place that it used to be is becoming surrounded by newer developments. But it's still a nice place to live. I go places and I'm always glad to come home."

Judy was an in-house nurse for Rockwell Collins, an aviation electronics company, but retired in the early 1990s when her husband retired so she could spend more time with him. She works part-time for a medical group in Melbourne, filling in for nurses who are sick or on vacation. She is a devout Christian who belongs to the Church of Jesus Christ of Latter-day Saints.

Judy grew up in Indianapolis, Indiana, in a family with three brothers. Her father was an outdoorsman who hunted and fished. "I was raised with guns. They were in our home, and my father taught me to respect them and to handle them safely." Long ago her youngest brother, Joel Burroughs, taught her to shoot. They used to target practice, but he moved to Louisiana some years back, and she had not practiced since.

In 2005 she was 64 years old, widowed, and living alone in the house she had shared for so many years with her husband. He died in 2000, but his son Jim lived right behind her house.

Living alone Judy is very conscious of her security. She always locks the door when she comes home. "I automatically lock myself in every time I go in the house. It's the way we have to live now unfortunately," she said. But she was security conscious even when her husband was alive. She had locked him out on more than one occasion, she admitted.

In addition to the deadbolts she had on her doors, Judy had other forms of protection. She kept a shotgun under her bed, and at night she slept with a handgun under her pillow. The gun was a Rossi, five-shot, .38-caliber revolver that had belonged to her mother, who died in May 2003. Judy had owned a larger revolver, but it was too big for her hands, and she traded it with her brother for her mother's gun. She had not shot it before.

The Incident

On the evening of Sunday, May 29, 2005, Judy went to bed between 9 and 9:30. She made sure that all the doors were locked. "I'm very, very, very paranoiac about that. I always lock my doors," she said later.

She was watching a NASCAR race on the bedroom television but fell asleep. Some time later she became conscious of the noise from the television and switched it off before falling asleep again. She was sound asleep when she was awakened about 10:20 by a loud bang. It sounded like something hitting the side of the house. She not only heard it, she felt it.

"It would have awakened the dead it was so loud, and I jumped. Of course it scared me, and I just went into a defensive mode right away," Judy later told Brevard County sheriff's investigators.

She knew what to do because years before her brother had taught her what action to take if someone broke in at night, and she had practiced. "He taught me how quickly someone can get you before you even have a chance to fire the gun," she said.

She grabbed her revolver from under the pillow and got up on the side of the bed nearest the door. She walked around to the other side, between the bed and the wall, facing the door.

"I hunkered down on the floor behind the bed with my arms on the bed and the gun in my hand. I could see the kitchen light come on, and I could see the flashlight playing around on the floor. And I just sat there scared half out of my mind," she told the investigators.

Meanwhile Jim Kuntz was sitting in the living room of his house on Palm Avenue eating a bowl of ice cream and watching the television.

"I heard a noise, and it didn't sound right," he said.

A door leads from his living room onto a back porch or patio area, where he had a clear view of the back of Judy's house. He stepped out on the porch and saw someone at her back door. "It looked like someone was trying to go in her door." Jim was wearing only a pair of shorts, so he came back into his house, put on a T-shirt, and grabbed a flashlight.

A few seconds after the kitchen light had come on, Judy saw the silhouette of a man with a flashlight in his right hand. He was standing in the doorway of her bedroom. She was afraid to say anything that would give away her location.

She knew she could not wait; she had to take action. She aimed the revolver as best she could at the dark shape in the doorway and squeezed the trigger. The noise in the confined space was deafening.

The man said, "Oh," then stumbled back towards the kitchen.

She waited. She kept seeing the play of the flashlight, so she didn't know if she had hit him; she didn't know whether he was still in the house; and she didn't know how many other intruders there might be.

With a shaking hand Judy found her telephone, which was also in the bed, and dialed 9-1-1. She told the operator that someone had broken into her house.

Judy: *"I think I shot him."*

Operator: *"Where did you shoot him?"*

Judy: *"I don't know. I shot at somebody who was at my bedroom door; I don't know. I'm not going to come out of my bedroom."*

Operator: *"Did the person scream?"*

Judy: *"Yes. Oh, I'm so scared."*

Operator: *"Okay, just stay on the phone with me, ma'am. I'm going to get somebody there."*

Judy: *"Please, please hurry."*

Wearing a T-shirt and grasping a flashlight, Jim Kuntz walked over to Judy's back yard. He had not heard the shot, or if he had he didn't recognize it as such.

"When I got there somebody was laying down in the back yard. He was breathing very erratically, and at that point I knew something was bad wrong."

Jim noted that the back door was open, and Judy's car was there, so she was probably home. He ran back to his house and called 9-1-1. He told the operator that a white man was lying in Judy's back yard, and he thought the man had tried to break into the house.

While Judy waited in her bedroom for the officers to arrive, Jim got on his bicycle and pedaled around the neighborhood checking for accomplices of the man lying in the back yard or perhaps for the vehicle he had used.

At the corner of Palm Avenue and Avenida del Mar, he saw a man sitting on the curb. The man was wearing shorts, a T-shirt, and flip-flop sandals. "He was sitting there, and he looked very out of place," Jim told investigators.

He asked the man who he was and what he was doing. The man replied that his name was Jason and he lived on Avenida de la Vista, two blocks to the north. He said he had been walking and had stopped to rest. Jim watched as the man got up and walked along Palm Avenue. At Avenida de la Vista he saw Jason stop at a truck parked in the yard of a house before entering the residence. Jim returned home to find that deputies had arrived. One of them told him to stay in his house until the investigators arrived.

The Aftermath

Deputies Brian Bomba and Sylvester Harris arrived at the house on Avenida del Mar about 10:30 P.M. Bomba saw a white man lying face down in the back yard of Judy's house. He was wearing a dark shirt and blue shorts. In his right hand he was grasping a flashlight that was still switched on, and his left was covered with a white sock. Bomba ordered the man to show his hands, but he didn't move. The deputy noticed a small pool of what appeared to be blood seeping from under the man's chest. He tried to find the man's pulse, but could not detect any heartbeat.

The back door of Judy's house was open, and the glass had been removed; it was found later on the patio, its frame bent. The two deputies announced themselves, and Judy met them at the back door. She told them what had happened, adding that, at the request of the 9-1-1 operator, she had put the revolver in a drawer in the nightstand beside her bed.

Judy went next door to a neighbor's house where she was later interviewed by agents Lou Heyn and Gary Harrell of the major crime unit. She told the investigators what had happened and that she kept the revolver under her pillow and the shotgun under the bed.

When she added that she also kept the telephone close in the bed Heyn said: "Sounds like you're ready for something like this."

"Well, I live by myself," she replied.

"Well, it's a good thing," Heyn said.

"I've never had to do anything like this, because I certainly wouldn't want to hurt anybody—ever."

Harrell asked her if she had been afraid.

"I was terrified," she said in a low voice, almost a whisper.

"Were you afraid he was coming to hurt you?" Harrell asked.

"Oh yes, yes."

Heyn showed her a digital photograph of the dead man, but Judy said she had never seen him before. Heyn's report stated that no identification was found on the body.

Judy told the investigators she had not had any previous problems with intruders.

The crime scene technicians took her handgun and a box containing forty .38-caliber shells. They took the blanket off her bed because it had powder burns on it. They did not take her shotgun.

Jason Louis Preston

Fingerprints were taken from the unidentified body the following morning at the Brevard County medical examiner's office. They were checked through the Automated Fingerprint Identification System or AFIS without a match, and were then faxed to the FBI by a crime scene technician later in the day. A description of the dead man was released to the media in the hope that it might result in his identification. He had tattoos on his arms, including one with four female names in it.

Five years prior to his death in Florida in 2005, Jason Louis Preston had been arrested in Clinton County, Michigan. These mugshots were taken in April and August of 2000.

About 6:30 P.M. Agent Heyn received a message to call a Karen Munro, who might be able to identify the dead man. The investigator called Mrs. Munro, who had been watching the television news. She said the description of the dead man matched her husband's cousin, Jason Preston, and that he had been missing since the night of the shooting. Mrs. Munro said Preston had been staying with her and her husband, Jason Munro, for about ten days, since he arrived by bus from his home in Eaton Rapids, Michigan. She gave Heyn the phone number of Preston's wife, Cassi Preston, in Michigan. When the investigator called her she identified the names on his tattoo as hers and those of their three daughters.

The following morning the FBI confirmed the identity of the dead man through his fingerprints as Jason Louis Preston, 33 years old.

Heyn called Jason Munro and asked him to drive to the East Precinct police station for an interview. Heyn and Agent Carlos Reyes interviewed him there. He told the investigators that Preston decided to come to Florida and stay with him and his wife in their house on Avenida de la Vista while earning some money. He had been helping Munro install hurricane shutters on houses in the area, as hurricane season was just about to start. Preston had been sleeping on the couch in the living room.

On the evening of May 29, Preston had received a call from his wife telling him she was thinking of moving in with another man. Preston was angry and agitated after the call and said he was going for a walk. He borrowed Munro's Ryobi rechargeable flashlight and took it with him, leaving about 8:30.

When Preston didn't return, Munro said he went to look for him. He walked south on Palm Avenue and eventually found his cousin running down the sidewalk in front of Hoover Junior High School. Munro told the investigators Preston had his flashlight in one hand while the other was wrapped in a sock. Later Munro told another investigator Preston said he intended to rob a crack house on Avenida del Mar.

Munro said he told his cousin not to do anything illegal, because it would cause him problems in the neighborhood. He told Agents Heyn and Reyes that Preston ignored him and walked down a bicycle trail that goes behind the houses in the area, including Judy Kuntz's house.

Munro started to walk back home, but stopped at the corner of Avenida del Mar and Palm Avenue to rest and consider what to do about his cousin. That was where Jim Kuntz found him just after the shooting and asked him who he was and what he was doing. Munro said he continued on home and fell asleep on the porch while waiting for Preston to return. Munro told the investigators he had no idea Preston was planning to break into Judy's house.

In the morning he called the county jail to see if Preston had been arrested. He drove around the neighborhood looking for his cousin because they had work to do. When he couldn't locate Preston, Munro went to work on his own, he said.

On June 1 Agent Heyn interviewed Karen Munro at her home on Avenida de la Vista. She essentially confirmed her husband's account of the happenings.

Two other burglaries took place in the area shortly before the shooting. A "weed-eater" and a small safe containing personal papers were stolen in a burglary on Palm Avenue; a boat motor was stolen from a home on Avenida del Mar. All three items were found hidden in

Karen and Jason Munro's yard. The Munros said they had nothing to do with the burglaries and didn't know the stolen items were hidden on their property. Heyn's report stated there was no physical evidence connecting the Munros to the burglaries.

Dr. Robert Whitmore, the Brevard County medical examiner, conducted an autopsy on Preston's body and confirmed he died of a gunshot wound to the chest. Agent Heyn said the bullet pierced Preston's heart. The autopsy report stated that Preston had tetrahydrocannabinol or THC in his bloodstream. THC is the active ingredient in marijuana. He also had benzodiazepine and cocaine metabolites in his urine. Benzodiazepine is a sometimes-abused prescription drug; cocaine metabolites were from crack cocaine, Heyn said.

Preston had a previous criminal record in Michigan. In 1993 he was convicted of felonious assault with a dangerous weapon and breaking and entering a building. He was sentenced to two-to-four years on the assault and three-to-fifteen years for the breaking and entering. The sentences ran concurrently, said Russ Marlan, a spokesman for the Michigan Department of Corrections. Preston entered prison in September 1993 and was paroled in February 1996. He was discharged from the corrections system on February 1, 1996.

In 2000 Preston was in trouble again. He was sentenced to three years' probation in April 2002 for another felonious assault with a dangerous weapon. His probation was terminated in September 2004 as a violator, and he subsequently spent three weekends in jail, Marlan said.

After the shooting Judy received nothing but support from her community. "Everybody, my neighbors, my congregation, the people at work, everyone was very supportive of me. No one ever found fault with what I did. It was amazing, as I didn't expect that."

The media kept her away from her home for three or four days. They staked out the house waiting for her to return so they could ask her questions. "Nothing can prepare you for that," Judy said.

She has not had nightmares as survivors of some shooting incidents do, and she has not suffered guilt about taking Preston's life. "I did what I had to do to survive. I feel sad for him, because he took the wrong course in life; he made the wrong choices and ended up where he is. I'm very sad for him, and I'm sad for his family."

However, Judy has suffered from the sense of violation that many crime victims feel. "Once the sanctity of your home has been violated—your safe haven from the world—once that happens, then you're never the same," she said.

"We live in a very dangerous world. Our homes aren't safe; we're not really safe anyplace." Judy thinks much of the violence is due to the breakdown of the family.

While sheriff's investigators did not take her shotgun, they did keep her handgun for almost eleven months before she was able to get it back. She said she called about three times to see if they had finished with her gun. "The sheriff's department treated me very, very well."

Judy Kuntz was cleared of any wrongdoing. In his report, Agent Heyn stated: "The evidence in this case clearly shows that Ms. Kuntz shot and killed the decedent to protect herself while in the bedroom of her home. . . . Ms. Kuntz was in fear for her life in her own home and was resisting the attempt of the decedent to commit a felony upon her when the shooting occurred."

Heyn briefed Michael Hunt of the state attorney's office on the case. He agreed it was a justifiable homicide.

Reflections

This is another example of a mortally wounded criminal being able to function for several seconds before collapsing and dying. Preston had been shot through the heart, but he was still able to find his way back through the kitchen and out of the back door before he collapsed. Had he been bent on destruction rather than flight he might have been able to do considerable damage before being incapacitated.

Agent Lou Heyn commented during his interview with Judy Kuntz that she seemed well prepared to cope with an intruder. She was. In the 1980s when she was living alone in an apartment, her brother Joel had showed her how quickly someone could reach her and attack her if he broke into her home. Under his direction she had practiced what action to take and how to be prepared for an intruder. "I practiced it enough to know what I would do if someone would break in on me and come into my home. And I knew that if they came through my bedroom door that I had to shoot them. If I waited any longer then it would be too late for me."

When she went to bed she was meticulous about making sure the house was locked. She had access to two guns—the revolver under her pillow and the shotgun under her bed. She also had a telephone ready to hand.

Not only was she prepared; she did what she had to do. "She was scared to death, but she didn't let panic control her," Heyn said admiringly.

She took cover behind the bed making herself a smaller target. She gave Preston no chance to attack her by telegraphing her position before she fired. Despite being terrified, Judy fired an accurate shot in the dark from a range of about ten feet.

"I feel very strongly that, yes, my brother taught me what to do and, yes, guns were not strangers to me, but I firmly believe that the Lord protected me that night."

She hasn't been shooting since Joel moved to Louisiana several years ago. She felt she was not in practice. "So I feel like divine providence made that bullet hit its mark. It certainly wasn't any skill on my part."

I think Judy sells herself short. Practicing what to do in an emergency stays in your subconscious until it is needed. An old saying among firearms instructors and other trainers is "you will do what you have practiced." Like Habib Howard in his convenience store, Judy did what she had practiced—and for both of them it worked.

"He broke in here violently. I mean he wasn't a cat burglar. He tried to kick the door down, and that's what woke me up. It was such a loud sound that you could feel the concussion of it. You could feel the house shake from it. And that just shocked me completely. My adrenaline just went through the roof. This guy was going to do me harm if he got to me."

A recent hurricane had blown the porch completely off the back of her house. The door he came in was not really an outside door, but it is until she gets her porch replaced. It had a barbeque grill in front of it, a ladder, and other things all covered with a tarpaulin.

"He had to move all that before he could even begin to break in the door." That is what he was doing when Jim, her stepson, saw him and called 9-1-1.

If she had been unarmed it is likely that even though he had only a flashlight Preston would have taken out his anger on her. He was obviously angry as a result of the telephone conversation with his wife and made absolutely no attempt to be stealthy. He made enough noise to attract the attention of at least one neighbor, Jim Kuntz. With two previous convictions in Michigan for felonious assault, Preston could certainly be considered dangerous even if he weren't armed.

What does she think would have happened if she had not had her gun? "I think he would have killed me," she said. "It was a horrific thing, and I feel terrible that it happened, but it wasn't my call. He came into my house where he did not belong. He started it, so I had to finish it."

Had she been living in England, Canada, or Australia, she would not have had the weapons to defend herself, and she might well have been murdered or at least seriously hurt. She might also have ended up in prison for defending herself.

"I believe in the Second Amendment, and I believe that if they take guns away from normal, law-abiding citizens that that's not going to solve the problem. I mean they're not going to keep guns away from the criminals. They're never going to be able to do it, no matter how many laws that they enact. It'll be us that'll be victims. We'll be victims even more than we are now."

She hopes that sharing her story will help someone else if he or she is ever faced with a similar situation.

"I never would want to hurt anyone. I'm a nurse; my business is to help people and to relieve suffering. I'm not into hurting people. But it's a horrible thing; it happened, and I'm just trying to move on now and try to make the rest of my life as meaningful as possible, and I thank the Lord every day for protecting me that night."

Chapter 13

Guns and Pizzas:
Ronald Honeycutt

Pizza is as American as apple pie. Each day hundreds of thousands of pizzas are delivered to houses, apartments, and businesses across the country, from Alaska to Alabama, Connecticut to California. Most pizzas come from the ovens of a few large chains such as Pizza Hut and Domino's. Pizza is the primary fast food eaten at home. While you can go to a Pizza Hut restaurant, order pizza, and eat it there, it is most often ordered by telephone and delivered.

Each evening an army mostly of young men fans out across the country to bring this supposedly Italian dish to the households of America. In most cases each young man is driving his own vehicle, but with a magnetically attached sign, called a topper, on the roof advertising the company for which he works. He delivers the hot pizza to the doorstep, takes the money, and often a tip, then drives on to the next delivery.

Sometimes pizza delivery, particularly in poor and minority neighborhoods, can be dangerous. The deliveryman always has some cash on him, usually less than a hundred dollars, and this attracts the parasites and predators in the poorer areas of any big city. The dangerous time is when the pizza company employee is returning to his vehicle after delivering an order. The predators know that he has at least the price of one delivery on him. Deliverymen have been beaten, robbed at gunpoint, and occasionally murdered. Sometimes it is a crime of opportunity with little or no advanced planning, and sometimes it is a planned ambush with the deliveryman being lured to a vacant house or apartment and attacked.

Despite the dangers, the big pizza chains do not allow their delivery people to carry guns, even if they may have concealed-weapons licenses and could do so legally. It seems they would prefer a dead deliveryman to an employee who is alive because he defended himself with a gun. The companies deny this, of course.

Ronald Honeycutt

Ronald Honeycutt started delivering pizzas in the Indianapolis area when he was a teenager. At 38 he had been delivering pizzas for more than twenty years. He was born and raised in the city and has always lived in the area.

By 2004 he had moved to one of the city's northern suburbs to get his two teenage boys into better schools. When they lived in Indianapolis with their mother they were two white kids in a mostly black school, and they got bullied, Ron said. "It escalated to the point of violence of course. They were fearful to even go to school. It got to the point where they weren't even going to school."

So Ron Honeycutt became part of white flight to the suburbs. He admitted to being somewhat prejudiced because most of the trouble he had had delivering pizzas had been from blacks. But most of the time he had been delivering in black neighborhoods.

"I'm a big country boy is what it boils down to, better known as a redneck. I'm a white guy in a black neighborhood, so I'm either crazy or I'm dangerous."

His older brother used to be in the pizza business but was robbed so many times he got out of it. However, Ron has never been robbed successfully. "I never have. I've always been a lucky individual, and I take notice of what's going on around me. After twenty years of delivering pizzas, I know quite a few people that's been robbed, beat up, hit with baseball bats, all for a pocketful of change. It's not just in the inner city; it goes on on the outskirts too." Ron has a concealed-handgun license and carries a gun. But at more than six-feet tall and weighing about two-hundred pounds people don't usually mess with him.

About ten years before, he bought his handgun—a Ruger semi-automatic in 9 mm caliber that carried fifteen rounds in the magazine and one in the chamber. His primary job then was working for the Indianapolis Star. He dropped off bundles of newspapers for the carriers while driving a company truck. Delivering pizzas was his second job then, as he had four children and was paying $1,100 a month in child support.

He bought the gun after another newspaper deliveryman had threatened him, Ron said. He was eventually laid off from his job at the newspaper, but he kept the gun and carried it all the time while delivering pizzas, which became his primary employment. It was dangerous work, and it made him feel like a target.

"You're like a bug crawling through a spider's web. They're not hunting you down, they're waiting for you to come into the web. You know what I'm saying?"

The Incident

It was Monday, May 17, 2004, and Ron Honeycutt was working his usual shift of 5 P.M. to closing time for a Pizza Hut outlet on the east side of Indianapolis. That night the store was busy, and he had left with four or five deliveries to make. It was about 11:30 P.M. when he arrived at the Wingate Apartments on Long Wharf Drive. It was his last delivery, but he wasn't anticipating any trouble.

He had just come from another apartment complex where some people on the street had given him a bad time about the vehicle he was driving. His usual vehicle was being repaired, so he was driving his secondary vehicle, a GMC Safari minivan almost twenty-years old. It had been in an accident previously, and the driver's door did not work, so he had to climb in and out of the passenger-side door. With two bucket seats in front, getting in and out of the passenger door was a challenge. The Pizza Hut topper was magnetically attached to the roof, but its light, which normally plugs into the cigarette lighter, was unplugged. However, the sign was easily readable.

Although some of the other deliverymen knew Ron carried a gun, the manager of the restaurant he worked for claimed he never knew—until that night. Ron was always careful to keep the big handgun concealed. In cool weather when he was wearing a jacket, he carried it in a shoulder holster which also held two spare magazines. This was his preferred method of carry, but wearing a jacket in the summer was too hot. Then he stuffed the gun down the back of his pants without a holster. He pulled his shirt out at the back to cover it.

"You use your butt-cheek to hold the gun up. Between your butt-cheek and your belt loop that gun will stay put. I always had it completely loaded, completely chambered up, completely ready to fire. When I pull the weapon all I've got to do is pull the trigger."

That was the way he was carrying it that night. He was wearing shorts and his Pizza Hut hat and shirt.

Although he knew the Wingate Apartments, he did not know the apartment for the delivery. The complex had several buildings. Ron used his million-candle-power spotlight to find the right building and check out the area before getting out of his van. He parked as close to the door of the building as he could.

"In rough areas you want to make sure you get as close as you can to your customer before you get out and walk around. If you're getting out and walking around trying to find stuff, you're looking for trouble."

As he got out of the van, Ron saw two young black men walking in his direction from another building in the complex. He also noticed a couple chatting outside the nearby building. He entered the building with the pizza inside the delivery bag to keep it warm. As he ascended the stairs he heard the door to the building open, and he saw one of the two black men follow him into the building. The young man did not look at Ron or speak to him, but went into one of the downstairs apartments.

Ron made his delivery, descended the stairs, and walked out of the building. He had thirty- to forty-feet more from the building door to reach the passenger door of his van. He was aware that the most dangerous part of a delivery was returning to his vehicle. That was when he was most likely to be robbed.

"After I make the delivery I always check my back. I've been on the road delivering pizzas for twenty years. I'm very street smart; I'm very street conscientious. My instinctive mode kicks in when I'm out there.

When you get scared, that's your instinct telling you you've got a reason to be scared, whether you do or you don't. I wasn't scared, yet I understood my surroundings before I went in on the delivery. When I come out I want to see the exact same thing or less. So in other words I had the lady and the other black gentleman at the northern part of the non-conjoining building still up there sitting and chit-chatting, but the two black males that were heading my way were nowhere around to be seen."

Just before he reached his van Ron looked back and saw the guy, later identified as 20-year-old Jerome Brown-Dancler, who had followed him into the apartment building. He was about ten feet behind Ron, and he was holding a semi-automatic pistol in his left hand pointed at the ground.

Ron turned around to face the gunman; his eyes locked onto Brown-Dancler and the gun. Ron had the delivery bag under his right arm. Ron is left-handed so he turned slightly to open the van door with his left hand.

He opened the door and started to climb into the van at the same time reaching with his left hand for the gun in his waistband at the back. The would-be robber was about five feet from him and raised his gun, pointing it at Ron.

"Hey, my guy," Brown-Dancler said.

Before he could say another word Ron's gun was out, and he was standing in the door of the van firing over the door and down at the robber. He was shooting with his left hand and still clasping the delivery bag in his right hand. He said he tried to aim each round not just spray and pray. He said he was conscious of seeing the sights and taking aim each time the gun came down out of recoil.

Brown-Dancler didn't move but continued to point the gun at Ron, so Ron kept shooting, aiming at the man's torso. He fired the gun until it was empty. He knew it was empty because the last two times he pulled the trigger the hammer clicked on the empty chamber. Ron said the slide didn't always lock back as it should when the Ruger was empty.

"He's still standing there and still pointing a gun at me. I don't know if I missed him, hit him, or what's going on. I feel pretty confident about the hits."

Ron was debating whether to get another magazine from inside his van or to charge Brown-Dancler, when the robber fell to the ground on his left side. He hit the ground hard, and the gun flew out of his hand. Ron dropped the delivery bag into the van, stepped down out of the vehicle, and picked up the suspect's gun.

"I just wanted a pizza," Brown-Dancler croaked as Ron approached him.

Ron got back into the van without saying anything to him. He put the robber's gun in the center console of his van and drove off. "I leave him there. I've got his gun. I know I'm not in a safe area. I know nothing about this area is safe. I just found out the hard way it's not safe. You know what I'm saying?"

Before he left he saw the couple he had noted earlier running into the apartments. They must have seen the whole thing, Ron thought.

Ron slapped another magazine into the gun and racked the slide immediately after he left the complex. He put the gun in the pocket behind the passenger seat. It was uncomfortable to drive with it in his waistband at the back. He drove back to the Pizza Hut restaurant at

Thirty-eighth and Post, about a mile-and-a-half from the Wingate Apartments.

"I was completely calm during the shooting. I was calm; I was alert; I was instinctive; I was at my finest. And my weapon backed me up on all that."

However, while the 9 mm operated perfectly, Brown-Dancler did not go down until after he had absorbed most of a magazine of hollow-point bullets. With all the shooting he was doing, Ron could not tell whether Brown-Dancler had fired at him or not, but he assumed that he had. And because the range was so short Ron could not believe he hadn't been hit. He had to check himself over to make sure.

When paramedics arrived at the Wingate Apartments they rushed the 20-year-old to Methodist Hospital, where he died shortly afterwards.

The Aftermath

Ron arrived at the restaurant before the police. He had no cell phone, so he could not call them until he reached the Pizza Hut. As he entered the restaurant he yelled for the staff to call the police. It was a good move. The police were already on the phone, and when he spoke to them it was obvious from their questions that his customer at the Wingate had called them. Because he had left the apartment complex instead of waiting there for the police, Ron felt he might have been accused of fleeing from the scene of a crime.

The Wingate Apartments complex was outside the Indianapolis city limits, so it was deputies from the Marion County Sheriff's office who arrived at the restaurant within five minutes of Ron's return. The officers asked him what had happened. He explained about the attempted robbery and why he had driven off.

"Once I went through the scenario with them they were friendly; they were understanding; they were saying I did what needed to be done."

Ron's concealed-weapons license kept him from being arrested. He was legal to carry a handgun. The deputies did not search him, but did take his gun. They also interviewed the restaurant manager, Mike, and asked whether he knew Ron was carrying a gun. The manager said he didn't, because Ron had never told him. Some of the other deliverymen did know, Ron said.

He turned Brown-Dancler's 9 mm semi-automatic over to the deputies. After examining the gun they told him it had a full magazine containing fourteen rounds, but he had neglected to rack the slide to put a round in the chamber. Either Brown-Dancler was not familiar with the workings of a semi-automatic pistol and didn't realize he had to chamber a round, or he never expected his victim to fight back. Either way it was a case of terminal stupidity.

"The way the scenario should have played out, had he had one chambered up, we would both have been dead at the scene. He was trying to shoot his gun as mine is going off."

Ron's manager, Mike, and he were friends and colleagues at work, but didn't socialize. Ron was a loner outside work. "I've been badgered by society to the point where I'm withdrawn. I go to work, and I come home. I go to the grocery store, and I come home. My off hours I'm at home. I don't associate with people outside of work."

Mike wanted to know what had happened. Initially he thought Ron had taken the robber's gun from him and killed him with it. "Had that scenario played out, I might still have been working there. But once I explained it to him, he knew that I would have to be fired, and sure enough I was fired."

Ron had broken the company rule that forbids delivery drivers to carry guns for protection whether or not they could do so legally. Mike shook his hand and told him, "nice work," Ron recalled. He too had been robbed at gunpoint. There was no animosity between them.

For almost two weeks Ron was in limbo not knowing whether he would be charged in the case. He said most of the information he received was from the media, not from the sheriff's office or the Marion County prosecutor's office.

"I was under scrutiny for overkill. I was under scrutiny for shooting a guy while he was down. They're quick not to believe self-defense," he said.

Jerome Brown-Dancler had already been booked prior to his fatal confrontation with Ron Honeycutt.

Deputy prosecutor Barbara Crawford said the case was not about whether Honeycutt was justified in using deadly force to protect himself. She did not quibble about his right to shoot under the circumstances.

The young man who was with Brown-Dancler admitted that they had agreed to rob Ron, but that he had chickened out.

"As soon as he saw Mr. Honeycutt with a gun he turned and ran so he didn't see the shooting," Crawford said.

Nobody else apparently saw the shooting or was prepared to admit to investigators having seen it. But Crawford acknowledged that Brown-Dancler had a gun and intended to rob Ron.

"He took it out, pointed it, and had the intention, or at least certainly Mr. Honeycutt could have that perception: that he had the intention to use it. That was very clear," she said. "So at that point I think the perception was, and it was a perfectly legitimate one, I don't have a choice, I have to shoot. This case didn't come down to that, the fact that he could shoot to protect himself. This case came down to the number of times he shot."

While Ron admitted firing sixteen rounds at his assailant, the medical examiner who performed the autopsy could not determine how many of those bullets had hit Brown-Dancler. The autopsy report stated that he was hit more than ten times but less than fifteen. It also indicated that some of the bullets fired by Honeycutt may have hit Brown-Dancler after he fell to the ground.

However, Crawford said it was impossible to tell which were entrance wounds and which were exit wounds because there were so many hits. The wound channels crisscrossed one another inside the body, so it was not possible to track the trajectory of each bullet. Most of the hits were in the area of the pelvis or below.

"It's unlikely that he was still shooting after the guy was down, but it's possible. We just don't know. That was one of the problems with the case," she said.

Brown-Dancler was not on drugs at the time of the shooting. He died primarily from blood loss, Crawford said.

Whether Ron Honeycutt was prosecuted or not depended on two things: was his use of force excessive, and if it was, was there enough evidence to support a successful prosecution?

While Crawford was obviously uncomfortable with the number of shots fired, she felt there was not enough evidence that Honeycutt had used excessive force.

"He gets the benefit of the lack of evidence; that is what it boils down to," she said.

So on Friday, May 28, eleven days after the shooting Barbara Crawford announced to the media that Ron Honeycutt would not be prosecuted. She was quoted in the *Indianapolis Star* as saying: "It's a clear case of self-defense. He did what the law allows him to do to protect himself."

For Ron it was a great relief.

It was several weeks after the shooting that Ron Honeycutt went back to work at a different pizza outfit. He would not deliver pizzas unless he was armed, and the sheriff's office took its time in returning his Ruger. Besides, based on his recent experience he felt the 9 mm handgun was not sufficiently powerful.

He bought a Smith & Wesson Model SW99 semi-automatic in .45 caliber. It carries nine rounds in the magazine and one in the chamber. "I spent my last $500 on that gun," he said.

Ron received threats but also support as a result of the shooting. He got a call from Pizza Hut because a young woman was trying to reach him. When he phoned her she thanked him on behalf of her father and herself for killing Brown-Dancler. She offered to testify on his behalf if his case ended up in court. The woman told him Brown-Dancler had pistol-whipped her in the face. She recognized him when his photo appeared on television. The attack happened about midnight in front of an apartment complex where she had gone to pick up her children from her cousin, who was babysitting for her.

She told him that Brown-Dancler had put a gun to her cousin's head while she was loading the kids into her car. He demanded money and threatened to kill her. When the cousin said she didn't have any money with her he turned his attention to the young woman. She said he pointed the gun at her stomach and demanded money from her. She told him to take her purse from the car. He pistol-whipped her in the face.

"She just wanted to let me know that she would be there for me if I needed her to testify. She just wanted to wish me the best," Honeycutt said.

Apparently the woman's father rode a Harley-Davidson motorcycle and hung out with other Harley guys who were actually looking for Brown-Dancler. If the police weren't going to catch him they were going to get him. She told Ron she had been living in fear because her attacker knew her identity and her address. She was afraid he might pay her a visit.

As was to be expected Brown-Dancler's family members didn't take his death as the just desserts of the incompetent predator that he was. "They were making statements that they didn't want their son to die in vain; that I hunted him down—like I'm the assassin. They talked vigilante crap," Ron said.

Honeycutt was working for another pizza company and was working in a same area as the shooting. Some of the people working at the pizza parlor knew Brown-Dancler's family, so word got out to them that Ron was working there. One night about six months after the shooting, some of the family members or friends called Ron numerous times to harass him accusing him of shooting Brown-Dancler in the back.

"I simply made remarks like: 'If that's what you think I did, then you need to call the feds and let them know what you think I did.' There was no back shooting or anything about the back. Whatever happened to the back were exit wounds, and they should be able to tell the difference. But they had their own beliefs."

After a few of these phone calls Ron stopped taking them. Brown-Dancler's friends and/or family members drove to the restaurant and followed Ron on a delivery. "It escalated to the point where I had three cars following me out on deliveries."

He pulled up to deliver a pizza, but didn't get out of the vehicle. He tried to drive away, but got into a dead-end street and to get away had to drive across some ruts bottoming out his car. He drove away to avoid having a confrontation, but he wanted to get the license-plate numbers of the vehicles that had been following him. When he got back to the restaurant he noticed the three cars pull into a store parking lot across the street. He followed them into the parking lot, stopped, and started to write down the plate numbers.

"Then one of them tried to back into me while I'm doing this—tried to back into my vehicle. But I already was successful in getting the plate numbers, so that's when I went ahead and left that parking area." He made it to a pay phone and called the police.

Since Ron was working at that pizza parlor only one day a week, he said, "To give up one day to not have a shooting was well worth giving up the one day for. I never went back to the one store and never heard from them since." He continued to work at the same company but not at that store, he said.

In the months after the shooting Ron had to pull his gun several times, but didn't need to shoot, he said.

Ron said he did not suffer the psychological trauma that affects many people after they have killed someone.

"I believe that my upbringing and my years of being on the street delivering pizzas like I have, delivering newspapers, working the third shift, being out there all night, has hardened me to the point where it doesn't affect me to kill somebody."

Pizza Hut did offer him a one-time consultation with a psychotherapist, but he turned them down. He said he didn't need psychological help.

"It did not affect me negatively at all. Matter of fact it didn't do anything but boost my spirits—boost my morale. After the shooting I came home and thought about what kinda' cool guy I am, and how cool it was to defend yourself; how cool it was to still be alive, and how cool it was to have a gun. It never dampened my spirits." Euphoria after a life-threatening situation is not an unusual response. It is the euphoria of still being alive. However, in many people it can be followed by feelings of guilt and depression that can last for months.

Reflections

The pizza-delivery shooting raises several interesting questions.

What options did Ron have when Jerome Brown-Dancler pointed the gun at him from a distance of ten feet or less? He could have attempted to run away, but the robber was too close, and no one can outrun a bullet. Even a Brown-Dancler could have hit him at that range—provided, of course, he had loaded the gun properly and it had a round in the chamber. Prosecutor Barbara Crawford confirmed that the robber had a fully-loaded magazine in the gun, but he had not racked the slide to put a round in the chamber. He could have pulled the trigger until Christmas and the gun would not have fired.

Ron could have succumbed and allowed himself to be robbed. If you are armed this is almost always a bad choice. You are at the mercy of someone who does not have your best interests at heart. You do not know the robber's intention beyond the robbery. He may shoot you because you have seen his face and could identify him.

He may shoot you accidentally. Robbers are often not familiar with the guns they use and certainly don't know enough to keep their fingers off the trigger if they don't intend to shoot. A robber with an unfamiliar gun in his hand, with his finger on the trigger, and an adrenaline rush, is quite likely to fire accidentally. And if he shoots you, it really doesn't make any difference whether he meant to or not; you are still shot.

Mindset has a lot to do with whether a person fights or flees. Some areas of our larger cities can be compared, probably unfavorably, with Baghdad. Delivering pizzas in what amounts to a war zone is not for the faint-hearted. Most people quit after they have been robbed once, Ron said.

It was obvious from talking to Honeycutt that he had made up his mind, probably many years ago, that he was not going to be robbed under any circumstances. "My scenario is: you point a gun at me you may as well pull the trigger, because I'm about to shoot you."

There was never any possibility of Ron fleeing or allowing himself to be robbed. His code wouldn't allow it. "The government don't give in to terrorists; I don't give in to the criminal. I'm not giving in, okay? If it's going to be my life, I'm taking you with me. There's plenty of room on that train for two of us, and we're both going. That's the one thing the criminal's not expecting, is someone willing to literally give up their own life to take their's."

In most cases a mindset like Ron's communicates itself to a person who might consider him a potential source of easy money, and it keeps him out of trouble. In the case of Jerome Brown-Dancler it obviously didn't. He either ignored the warning signs or believed that because he was holding Honeycutt at gunpoint he had control. Television and movies have taught us that, when you "have the drop" on someone, as they say in the westerns, he or she will not fight back. In real life, it ain't necessarily so.

Should Ron have kept shooting until the gun was empty? Prosecutor Barbara Crawford warned that ordinary citizens should be very careful about shooting in self-defense. The law has many nuances that enable authorities to prosecute if there is any doubt about the justification.

"I do not want under any circumstances to give the impression that that's an okay thing to do. It should be an absolute last resort for anyone, if they're intending to use a deadly weapon on another person," she said.

However, she said Ron Honeycutt was justified in using deadly force to protect himself from Jerome Brown-Dancler. She was satisfied that Brown-Dancler had used a gun to threaten Honeycutt. What concerned her most was that Ron emptied his magazine into his attacker—sixteen rounds of 9 mm hollow-point ammunition. The law in most states stipulates that you can use deadly force to protect yourself from imminent death or serious bodily injury—being held up at gunpoint counts. But the law also stipulates that you must use the minimum amount of force necessary to stop or neutralize your attacker. In other words you can't keep on shooting once he is no longer capable of carrying out his threat. What Crawford found difficult to believe was that this slight young man could have withstood this barrage of bullets without falling to the ground. Ron found this difficult to believe too.

"I was just flabbergasted that he was able to stand there and take it like no man I know. I don't know any man that would stand in front of sixteen rounds and not budge an inch, holding a gun on somebody, and that's what happened with him. He basically froze in his original position throughout the sixteen rounds."

It has been said that a handgun is what you use to shoot your way to where your rifle or shotgun is. This is because handguns are notoriously unreliable at stopping a fight instantly. There have been innumerable documented cases of people absorbing many handgun bullets without any noticeable effect for at least several seconds. They may die eventually, but often the bullets have no immediate effect.

This is why good firearms instructors tell their students to keep shooting until the assailant is no longer a threat. As long as he is standing and pointing a gun at you, he is a threat.

Ron estimated he was firing about two rounds a second, and it took him eight seconds to clean out the magazine. I suspect it was probably closer to five seconds or about three aimed rounds a second at a range of less than ten feet. Ron figured Brown-Dancler collapsed about two seconds after he had emptied the magazine. That would make seven to ten seconds after the first round hit him.

Where the bullets hit the assailant is also key to how effective they are. According to Bill Davison, whom I quote in *The Concealed Handgun Manual*, bullet placement is more important than bullet size in a gunfight. Davison owns Tac Pro Shooting Center in north Texas and says many American firearms instructors seem unduly fixated on the .45. He says you should carry whatever gun you can shoot accurately. Davison migrated from the United Kingdom several years ago after serving in the Royal Marine Special Boat Service. This is an elite special-forces unit similar to the U.S. Navy SEALs. He spent time fighting IRA terrorists in Northern Ireland where the standard issue handgun was a 9 mm, Browning semi-automatic.

"If you can hit the cardiovascular triangle [upper chest area] every time with your nine mil as fast as you can pull the trigger, then carry a nine mil," Davison told students attending one of his three-day pistol classes.

When he first came to the United States, everyone told Davison he shouldn't carry a 9 mm because the cartridge was ineffective, he said.

"I can honestly tell you, gentlemen, that I have never had someone not die because I shot them with a nine mil. They all died immediately, and I'm really pleased with the cartridge," Davison said.

Honeycutt hit his assailant at least ten times with his 9 mm Ruger, but according to Barbara Crawford most of the hits were low, in Brown-Dancler's pelvic area. Ron was aiming for his attacker's "center of mass," which is a little above the belt but lower than the cardiovascular triangle. He was standing on the van's floorboards in the doorway, which meant he was shooting down at Brown-Dancler. That may have accounted for the shots hitting low. Ron blamed the 9 mm bullets for their inability to stop the fight instantly, but bullet placement may have had more to do with it.

"After the end of the shooting, my response was: Oh, my God," said Ron. "Because he's still standing there pointing a gun at me, and I'm expecting to be shot to bits. I'm trying to make up my mind whether I'm going to jump on the guy or whether I'm going to go in for more ammo." Normally he would have been carrying an extra magazine in his pocket, but that time he wasn't.

"I wasn't expecting any problems. I was coming off a slew of deliveries; I was in a hurry; I grabbed the gun, but I didn't grab the extra clip [magazine]." He had four loaded magazines and some extra rounds in the van.

When Ron first bought the Ruger he practiced at a local gun range, but the ammunition was expensive and he could not afford to spend the money. He had four children to pay for and was working two jobs. One of his brothers had several acres outside the city and occasionally he practiced there.

Should Ron have left the scene of the shooting? The pizza-delivery incident was different from most other self-defense shootings, because Ron not only left the scene of the action but he took a vital piece of evidence with him. Neither action caused him a problem with investigators or prosecutors, as both appeared imminently reasonable under the circumstances.

Ron left the scene rather than wait around knowing that Brown-Dancler had at least one associate who might have involved him in another shooting. Staying around was not a sensible option. He did not have a cell phone, so could not call the police from the scene unless he found some resident to call for him.

He took Brown-Dancler's gun with him, because he believed if he left it there it would be stolen by someone before the police arrived.

"If I had left his weapon on the scene and it ended up missing, I'd have been prosecuted."

He is probably right. Without the gun he would have had no evidence that Brown-Dancler was armed. When he picked up his attacker's gun with his right hand he didn't take care not to obliterate the fingerprints. "I knew that as long as I had his weapon, I had evidence. I knew I had to have some kind of proof about what transpired; I knew that. And the only way I was going to get that is with his weapon."

Is it responsible for the big pizza chains to send their employees in harm's way and insist they be unarmed? Repeated phone calls to the Pizza Hut public relations department were not returned.

After word of the shooting spread there were calls on the Internet for a boycott of Pizza Hut because the company fired Ron for exercising a constitutional right. People claimed with some justification that Pizza Hut would prefer to have a dead driver rather than to allow employees to carry guns for self-defense.

The big chains like Pizza Hut and Domino's still do not allow their drivers to carry guns even though they are driving their own vehicles. It remains a condition of employment. They are concerned about their insurance and liability if one of their employees uses a gun inappropriately in self-defense or goes "postal" and shoots other employees. In our litigious society there are hundreds of lawyers eager to loot the deep pockets of any multi-million-dollar corporation found liable for someone spitting on the sidewalk let alone shooting someone.

This does not impress Ron Honeycutt. He believes that the Second Amendment of the U.S. Constitution gives every citizen the right to carry a gun for self-defense and that no business should be able to override that right.

"Even though Pizza Hut has a no-gun policy, my constitutional right dictates that I have a right to bear arms. I have a right to defend myself. . . . To me, no business has any right to tell you: you can't carry your gun," Honeycutt said.

How naïve to believe that the Constitution actually means what it says. To the layman the Second Amendment is quite clear: ". . . the right of the people to keep and bear arms shall not be infringed." It is also quite clear from the statements left by the founding fathers that they felt everyone should be able, even required, to carry guns. For example Thomas Jefferson said: "The constitutions of most of our states assert that all power is inherent in the people; that . . . it is their right and duty to be at all times armed."

In the years since those words were written, particularly in the past few decades, legislators, bureaucrats, and judges have whittled away at that right until, in many large cities such as Washington, D.C., Chicago, and New York, it has become as meaningless as a politician's promise.

While the big corporations try to protect themselves at the expense of their lowest-level employees, independent pizza-parlor operators are more sympathetic towards the dangers their drivers face. In the aftermath of the Brown-Dancler shooting the *Indianapolis Star* quizzed several independents. Most of them had no problem with their drivers carrying guns for protection, provided they had the required concealed-weapons permit from the county.

Jeff Callahan is president of the Association of Pizza Delivery Drivers, which represents two-thousand drivers across the country. He said there is a "wink and nod agreement" between the drivers for the big chains and their managers. The manager suspects or knows that a driver carries a gun but ignores it. If an incident occurs the manager claims not to know the driver was armed, and the driver gets fired.

"That's exactly the status quo and that's the best we can do," Callahan said.

Unless pizza corporations grow some sense of responsibility to their employees or get some legal protection from lawsuits filed by greedy lawyers the situation is unlikely to improve.

Meanwhile, Ron Honeycutt still delivers pizzas in Indianapolis. He told me in June 2005 he expected to have to defend his life with his gun again and he expected to be fired because of it. He was right on both counts.

In October that year he was working in another bad area of Indianapolis. Two black men tried to rob the pizza parlor where he was working. Ron managed to slip out of the back door, but one of the men came after him. As the man came through the door Ron pulled his gun and fired two shots. The first hit the bottom of the door frame; the second ricocheted off the door and hit the robber in the side. Ron exchanged shots with the wounded man's partner, but both of them missed, he said. The wounded man fled and was caught by the police nearby.

Again Ron was fired and at last report he was working in a much less dangerous area of the city where he hopes to be able to keep his gun holstered.

Chapter 14

Gun-Totin' Granny: Susan Gaylord Buxton

People who own guns and believe that the Second Amendment of the Constitution means what it says—that the right of the people to keep and bear arms shall not be infringed—have long accused the elite national media of a bias against guns and gun owners.

Professor John R. Lott Jr. of the American Enterprise Institute has written a book, *The Bias Against Guns*, devoting much space to this predisposition. Lott uses facts and statistics to back up his case that the national media are loath ever to show guns, particularly guns used in self-defense, in a positive light. In **The Concealed Handgun Manual**, I refer to one example Lott investigated. After a shooting at a Virginia law school that was stopped by two armed students, Lott found 208 stories about the incident in the media. Only four of those accounts mentioned that the students who stopped the rampage were armed with their own handguns.

There are several reasons for this attitude among members of the national media. The national newspapers and broadcasters are mostly grouped in the northeast of the country—New York City and Washington, D.C.—where few law-abiding citizens are allowed by their paternalistic big-city governments to have guns. Many people in these cities have been brainwashed into believing that the police will protect them—this despite several

Supreme Court rulings that the police have no responsibility to protect any individual citizen.

Most reporters and editors for these major newspapers and television networks have never faced the wrong end of a 12-gauge shotgun with a barrel the size of a four-inch sewer pipe or a .44-caliber revolver where each of the four visible hollow-point bullets looks like Oregon's Crater Lake seen from the air. These weenies who spend much of their lives hiding behind computer screens believe in the old saying that the pen is mightier than the sword. Of course nobody uses pens or swords much anymore, but you get the point. Anyway it wasn't the pen that Hitler, Stalin, and Mao used to exterminate millions of their disarmed citizens. Again and again it has been shown that reporters and editors of the liberal media would prefer to show a serial killer in a positive light rather than a law-abiding citizen who defended herself with a gun.

But every once in a while a case comes along that disproves the general rule. Such was the case of the Arlington—Texas, that is—gun-totin' granny.

Susan Gaylord Buxton

Sixty-six-year-old Susan Gaylord Buxton has four children, eleven grandchildren, and a gun—actually, several guns. She was born in Washington, D.C., but got to Texas as quickly as she could. Lee Harvey Oswald, the man believed to have assassinated President Kennedy, was in her second-grade class at Lily B. Clayton Elementary School in Fort Worth. She has the photo to prove it.

Susan is articulate, moves her hands a lot when talking, and smiles with the ease of someone who still takes life as a challenge. She and her relatives help maintain a mobile home park that is the family business and where her mother still lives in a brick house on the property.

Susan is a commercial artist and portrait painter who works from her home in Arlington, a suburban community between Dallas and Fort Worth. When she was divorced in 1975, she was an accomplished artist but had no credit rating. Even though she had paid the bills, it was her husband who had the credit rating. However, she had friends at the chamber of commerce, and one banker lent her $4,000 so she could pay it back the next week and start to establish credit. She never bought anything unless she had the cash in her hand, because she has old-fashioned ideas. She hates to pay interest.

She had no job so she started to do artwork for the chamber of commerce. She also painted portraits for local people and then not-so-local people. Susan has a collection of photos of herself with the subjects of her paintings. They include Dr. Henry Kissinger, 1993; Vice President Dick Cheney, 1995; former General and Secretary of State Colin Powell, 1996; former British Prime Minister Margaret

Thatcher, 1997; General Norman Schwarzkopf, 1998; and former Speaker of the House of Representatives Newt Gingrich, undated.

Susan lives in a two-story house built in the 1960s at the end of a quiet cul-de-sac, just south of Interstate 30 and east of the boundary between Fort Worth and Arlington. Through the trees from her back yard she can see the cars and trucks on the interstate. She has lived in the house since 1971, and like its owner, the house is hinting at its age.

Her back yard, graced with several large live oaks and pines, slopes gently down to a small creek, creating a park-like scene. The backyard is in the creek's flood plain so there are no fences separating her slice of stream bank from those of her neighbors.

Her Suburban sits in a carport at the back of the house beside what used to be the garage. Years ago it was converted into a room that Susan used as a studio. A concrete driveway runs to the back of the house where the former garage and current carport are invisible from the street. It is an unusual arrangement not much seen in new houses, where builders tack garages onto the sides of their houses to make the driveways short and cheap.

The former garage, like the ground-floor story of the house, is faced with brick veneer. It has glass windows where the big doors used to be. This gives the room a grand view of the back yard and the creek. It also gave Susan a good vantage point to keep an eye on the up-to-half-a-dozen grandchildren, whom she used to babysit during the day while her own children were at work.

"I used to teach them in the creek back there when they were little tots. I wanted them to learn about God's creations," she said.

She showed them the beauty in plants, trees, and animals. She taught them how to climb down the bank of the creek using the natural things that were there—tree roots and vines.

She instructed the children to collect rocks with interesting patterns on them and then used them for math problems. "It was a wonderful time. I can think about it now and I feel all happy again."

In the early 1990s one of Susan's granddaughters, who was 6 at the time, was almost kidnapped off her bicycle in the driveway of the house.

"Two Mexican guys tried to take her off her bike and kidnap her. They didn't do it. They put her down for some reason. She said she couldn't scream 'cause their hands were all over her mouth," Susan recalled.

This made Susan angry and also made her realize how vulnerable she was. The next week she bought a Smith & Wesson five-shot revolver in .38 caliber.

Susan had been taught to shoot by her younger sister, Judy Gaylord, who was the first woman recruited into the Navy Reserve in Fort Worth. "When she got in there she was the best shot of everybody, so she taught the men how to shoot," Susan recalled.

When Susan decided to purchase a gun, it was Judy who encouraged Susan to get a revolver, because it was simpler to operate, lighter, and more convenient to carry in a pocket or a purse. Even though Susan also has a 12-gauge, short-barreled, pump-action shotgun and a 9 mm, semi-automatic pistol, the little J-frame revolver is her favorite, and she is comfortable with it.

The sisters got their Texas concealed-handgun licenses together and renewed them together. In March 2005 when they were doing their proficiency test to renew their licenses, the instructor took Judy's target and held it up to the class. "You do not want to make this woman mad," he said. That sentiment applied to either sister.

Susan is a member of both the Texas State Rifle Association and the National Rifle Association.

By the fall of 2005 Susan's children were in their forties and her grandchildren were past the babysitting age. She had one granddaughter, 28-year-old Mandy Davis, living with her and sharing the house with her five fat Pomeranians, which she refers to as "my puppies," two cats, and two doves.

Despite looks that would make many Holywood starlets seem plain, Susan never remarried.

"I like men; I just don't want to be married to one. I've got my family; I've got grandkids; I can make my own living; I have puppies; I know how to shoot my gun."

The Incident

On Tuesday, November 8, 2005, Susan went to bed as usual at 10:30. Her five dogs were in her room sprawled over her king-size bed. Her granddaughter, Mandy Davis, was already in bed. She usually went to bed shortly after 9 p.m., since she had to get up at 5 A.M. to be at work in Dallas by 7.

Shortly after midnight, Merlin, one of Susan's Pomeranians, nudged her and licked her face, indicating that he wanted to go out. The previous day she had taken Merlin to the vet to get his teeth cleaned. The dog was seven-years old so the vet gave him a blood test before giving him an anesthetic. The vet called her and told her that Merlin's kidneys were in bad shape so he could not be given an anesthetic. The vet gave him some medication and told her that until the medication kicked in, if Merlin wanted to go out it would be wise to let him go.

So Susan got out of bed wearing a T-shirt and underpants and picked up her gun from the nightstand. She usually took the gun because coyotes roamed into her yard on occasion. She didn't want to kill any coyotes, but they could not attack her dogs. She didn't want one of her Pomeranians to end up as coyote appetizer.

She took Merlin out of the bedroom, shutting the door to keep the other dogs in. She walked along the hallway and noticed a light on in her granddaughter's room. It was unusual for her light to be on after midnight. "I stuck my head in the door and said, 'What are you doing up this late?'"

Mandy was sitting up in bed with the covers pulled up under her chin looking scared. She told Susan she had heard some glass breaking and some noise on the roof. She said she would have come and gotten her grandmother, but she thought it might have been a raccoon or opossum. It was not unusual for wildlife to come up from the creek.

"I didn't think a thing about it. I just said, 'Oh, okay. Well, I've got to let Merlin out.' I just had one thing on my mind—to let this puppy out like the vet told me."

Susan went down the stairs and walked into the kitchen. She picked up her spot light, turned the outside light on, and opened the back door. She noticed some mud on the concrete apron outside the back door. It hadn't rained for six weeks. Merlin stopped to sniff at it.

Mandy had followed Susan down the stairs and was close behind her. "Gigi, you know I'm really scared," Mandy said to her grandmother. All her grandchildren call her Gigi.

"I'm still not thinking anything's wrong," Susan said.

Merlin had disappeared into the yard and was doing what he needed to do. Susan looked at the mud more closely and realized it was a shoe print. It had a pattern on it like a running shoe. She and Mandy noticed there were several more shoe prints.

"You never think it's going to happen to you. It still didn't dawn on me that anything was wrong yet."

Mandy had been awakened by the sound of breaking glass, and she had been thinking about what was happening for a while. As they were talking about the shoe prints Mandy said, "You know Gigi, it's strange, the cats are out of the back room."

Susan shuts the two big cats into the back room each night because there are mice there and she wants them to catch the little rodents. The back room is an extension on the back of the house that was the garage before the carport was built. There is an outside door on the side of the back room near the back door, but it had not been used in years.

"They can't get out of the back room," Susan said.

"Well, there's Bob," replied Mandy pointing to one of the cats that was sitting close to the back door.

"We'd better take a look," Susan said.

They walked carefully through the kitchen and saw that the door leading from the back room into the rest of the house was open about six inches. They walked into the back room and looked around. They saw the frame of the door that led outside was ripped off the wall and lying against a heavy treadmill which had been pushed against the door. "It had to take some muscle to move that thing," Susan said later.

"Do you think we should call the police?" asked Mandy.

"No, not just yet." Susan still had her revolver in her hand. She suggested they look around a bit more and

The fugitive broke in through this door.

particularly at the window Mandy heard being broken. They went back upstairs to Mandy's room and saw the window was cracked. They looked into the next bedroom, which was used as a storeroom. Nothing appeared out of place or broken there.

Having helped raise eleven grandchildren in her house, Susan knew every hiding place. She and Mandy finished checking all the rooms upstairs then went back downstairs. They checked the ground floor, looking in all possible hiding places, including under the stairs. Susan was standing in the middle of her art studio and computer room, which is close to the front door.

"I shined my big spotlight around under the desk. We both kind of turned around at the same time and looked at the closet door right by the front door. And if anybody was in this house that was the only place left."

Susan put her spotlight on the floor of her studio pointing at the closet door. She turned on a light beside the front door.

"I still had my .38 in my hand, but this time my finger was on the trigger."

The closet door was closed. Susan approached it gingerly and pulled it open. The closet was filled with outdoor clothes hanging from a rod. The tan workcoat she often wore outside had slipped down so the bottom of it was on the floor but the top was hanging on something—or someone. She reached in and pulled the coat away.

"His face was right there. And that's when I pulled the hammer back, right in his face."

The man exploded out of the closet and lunged for Susan's gun. She jumped back and waved the gun around so he couldn't grab it.

"Get down on the floor. Get down!" she yelled at him. "Mandy, call nine-one-one."

The suspect, later identified as 22-year-old Christopher Lessner, was white, six-feet tall, and 162 pounds. He was wearing gray running pants and running shoes but had no shirt. He had tattoos around his arms, across his chest, and on his back. He looked athletic and muscular.

Susan is five feet five inches and weighs 120 pounds. She was still wearing only her underpants and a T-shirt that had printed on it: "Work for God. The retirement benefits are great."

As they faced each other, Susan had two things going for her: a few ounces of steel containing five hollow-point rounds and a belief that God would see her through this terrifying ordeal.

Mandy's call to the Arlington emergency operator indicates what happened next.

*E*mergency Operator: "Nine-one-one."
Mandy Davis in a panicky voice: "Hello, someone just broke into my house."

Operator: "Okay, what is the address?"
Mandy gave the address.
Operator: "Okay, are they still there? Ma'am?"
Mandy: "(Unintelligible) Hurry."
Operator: "Are they still there?"
Mandy: "Yes."
Susan screamed: "Get down."
Suspect: "I thought you . . ."
Susan yelled again: "Get down."
This is followed immediately by a shot.

"I kept saying, 'Get down.' I really didn't want to kill this guy, but if I had seen a knife come out of there I would have shot right in his chest," Susan recalled.

The suspect was paying no attention to her commands to get down on the floor. He kept lunging for Susan's gun, but she dodged back out of the way. He tried to get out the front door, but had difficulty because the closet door was open and blocking the front door.

"The configuration of these two doors, they tactically had him trapped," Susan said.

The front door opened inwards and the closet door opened outwards, so if the closet door was open he couldn't open the front door enough to get through it.

He was partly through the front door and still trying to grab her gun when Susan fired. The bullet went through the hollow-core door about six inches below the handle and clean through the suspect's thigh. He managed to get out of the door, turned to the right to run, and collapsed on the leaf-covered concrete a few feet from the front door. Susan followed him out and kept him covered with the gun.

Operator: "Okay, are they still there?
Mandy: "Yes."
Operator: "Do you know who it is?"

Mandy: "No. Hurry please."

Operator: "Is anybody injured?"

Mandy: "She just shot him. Hurry, please hurry."

Operator: "Okay, stay on the phone with me, okay. The suspect has been shot?"

Mandy: "He tried to bust in through my upstairs window."

Operator: "Okay, has he been shot? Has he been shot?"

Mandy: "He's been shot."

Operator: "Where has he been shot?"

Mandy: "I can't say. He's in the dark, laying in my front yard. Hurry, my grandmother's (unintelligible)."

Operator: "Okay, stay on the phone. What did she shoot him with? What kind of gun?"

Mandy: "What kind of gun, Gigi?"

Susan: "It's a .38 and (unintelligible)."

Mandy: "It's a .38. Please hurry, please. It's a .38."

Mandy described the suspect and what he was wearing.

The operator said the police and paramedics were on the way.

Operator: "And your grandmother is the one who shot him?"

Mandy: "She's got a gun pointed at him. Someone needs to hurry."

There was quiet except for the noise of the operator typing her notes.

Susan: "How dare you come into my house—you lousy sonofabitch." She was really angry.

The suspect said something like: "Let alone."

Susan told him to shut up and threatened to shoot him in the balls if he got up.

More typing could be heard.

Operator: "Stay on the phone with me, okay."

Mandy: "I'm staying; I'm staying."

Susan yelled something and this was followed by another shot.

Operator: "Did you shoot him, again?"

Susan: "Goddamn it. He got away; damn it."

Operator: "Tell her to stop shooting him. Help is on the way. She needs to stop shooting him."

Mandy: "Gigi, don't shoot him again."

Susan said afterwards that the suspect started to get up, and she fired a shot beside him not intending to hit him.

"I could have killed him. His back was broad enough to hit. I didn't want to kill anybody."

Later on the tape Susan could be heard saying: "I don't know whether I hit him when he ran away."

The wounded suspect ran around the side of her house into the back yard and disappeared into the darkness.

Near the end of the tape, Susan appeared to be talking to someone when she said: "I'm going to kill that bastard. He ran down here."

The police arrived about six-and-a-half minutes from the start of the 9-1-1 call. Susan saw the police officers running down the hill into the cul-de-sac. They saw her standing there in her underpants and T-shirt, still holding the revolver.

"They put their guns on me and said: 'Drop the gun, ma'am.' And I said: 'Oh yea, okay.' I just set it down and walked back into the house.

The police officers told her not to touch anything. The suspect had dropped several things during his flight, including a wristwatch and something that Susan thought looked like a pager, but police told her was a drug scale.

The Aftermath

The police had been chasing the suspect since about 11:15 P.M., before he broke into Susan's house on Northaven Court. An officer attempted to stop a black Chevrolet pickup for speeding in the westbound lanes of Interstate 30 where it runs through Arlington.

The officer gave chase, and the suspect took the exit ramp for Fiedler Road and turned north. He turned west on Packcrest Terrace, where he jumped from the pickup while it was still moving. The vehicle had been reported stolen from Euless, a suburb north of Arlington.

According to the police the suspect scaled an eight-foot fence, jumped over a chain-link fence, and ran into a wooded area just north of the interstate. The officer's description of the suspect matched the description of the man Susan and Mandy found in their house.

The police officer called for help. Additional officers and a police dog were dispatched to help in the search. A police helicopter from Fort Worth also was sent to assist.

The suspect apparently reached the creek that runs behind Susan's house and waded through it where it passes under Interstate 30. He climbed up out of the creek at the first house he came to, which was Susan's.

With his running shoes all muddy from the creek, the suspect apparently checked the back door leaving muddy shoe prints on the concrete beside it. He climbed up the back of Susan's Suburban and onto the carport roof. He tried to break in through Mandy's bedroom window on the second floor. He cracked the window but she awoke and turned the light on scaring him off.

The suspect crossed the roof of what had been the garage and jumped down to the ground. He kicked in the door leading into the old garage room, pushing aside a large cat box, a table with a television on it, and a very heavy treadmill.

He went through the door into the rest of the house letting the cats out inadvertently. He went into the kitchen and took a liter bottle of soda from the fridge. He found the coat closet next to the front door and hid in it behind the coats where he drank the soda. Susan later found the empty bottle in the closet.

"He could hear every word we were saying the whole time we were discussing calling the police; the whole time we were talking about checking upstairs; and he still didn't leave. He had every opportunity to get out of there when he heard us walk up the stairs to check her room. So that's kinda' scary. You think, it's a good thing it ended like it did, 'cause I don't know what he had in mind," Susan said.

The suspect climbed up onto the roof and tried to break in through a second story window.

After the suspect ran off into Susan's back yard and into the darkness, the officers resumed their search. Susan said it took them two or three hours before they found Christopher Michael Lessner, wounded and cowering on a neighbor's back deck two or three houses east on Northaven Court. He was arrested and taken to Harris Methodist Hospital in Fort Worth for treatment.

Lessner was later charged with theft of a vehicle, criminal mischief, criminal trespass, and evading arrest. He had been arrested previously for assault causing bodily injury, driving while intoxicated, retaliation, theft, and burglary of a vehicle.

The first thing the police wanted to know when they entered Susan's home was if there were any other guns in the house, she said. She told them she had a 9 mm, semi-automatic pistol in the kitchen. She also had a short-barreled, 12-gauge, pump-action shotgun. A former Arlington police chief had found the gun for her in the 1970s.

Several officers questioned Susan about what had happened. Suddenly she realized she was not suitably dressed to be talking to a group of men.

"Hold it; time out. I need to go put some clothes on," she told the officers and went upstairs to add some more modest clothing.

A female detective insisted on reading Susan her rights.

"I didn't do anything wrong," Susan said.

But the detective was adamant.

"I didn't do anything except protect myself and my granddaughter."

Susan wrote a statement about six-pages long while crime-scene technicians dusted for fingerprints inside and outside the house.

The detective told her to include as much detail as she could remember, but particularly what she was wearing and how vulnerably she was dressed.

Mandy called the relatives who lived close by and they came over, but the police wouldn't let them get close. They had to remain outside the crime-scene tape for two or three hours.

Before she left the detective said they needed to take Susan's gun for a couple of days, Susan said. The detective gave Susan her card and told her to call her and she would get the gun back to her. Susan said she took the woman at her word.

The Media

That morning Susan found she had become a media magnet. The local media were all over her like chicken pox. They had found a grandmother who had shot a man while defending herself and her granddaughter in her own home. She was not only willing to talk but she was articulate. Television loved it, and the story soon attracted the national media.

The morning of the shooting Susan had an appointment to take all her dogs to the vet for blood tests. She kept the appointment then brought the dogs home to find the news media still laying siege to her house. The usually quiet cul-de-sac had never seen anything like it.

Jacquielynn Floyd, a columnist for the *Dallas Morning News* known for her anti-gun sentiments, interviewed Susan and wrote an article that was mostly supportive of her. After a couple of paragraphs in which she refers to people "too stupid, too dangerous, or too hotheaded to own a firearm," Floyd hammered out a positive article about the incident. She ended it by saying that while she is not convinced, Susan does make a compelling argument for women to arm themselves.

Susan was interviewed by Charlie Gibson on "Good Morning America" via a satellite truck that came to her door.

She was also on Sean Hannity's radio show. She talked to him one day on the phone—she thinks it was Thursday. His producer called back and wanted to know if she would be on the television show he hosts with Alan Colmes on the Fox News network that night.

Fox sent a car to take her to a studio in Dallas and Mandy went with her. She said the interview arrangement was disconcerting because there was no image of the interviewer for her to respond to.

"You are talking to nothing but a black space and you are hearing the conversation on an earpiece," Susan said.

She was treated well and even Alan Combs, the liberal co-host of the show, didn't say anything bad to her, she added.

The next day Hannity called her again for his radio show and they talked for a while. Then he let her talk to people who called in from all over the country.

Susan also agreed to go on the "Montel Williams Show," a syndicated, daily television talk show. She was flown to New York where the show is produced, put up at a hotel, and flown back to Texas over a three day period.

The only interview offer Susan turned down was one with Katie Couric, co-anchor of NBC's "Today Show." A producer of the show told her they would fly her to New York, but she declined. She said she turned down the interview because of Couric's reputation for being anti-gun.

"I didn't want the hassle of traveling to New York for thirty seconds with someone who didn't like what I did anyway."

Her Gun

When Arlington police officers seized her gun after she had shot Christopher Lessner with it, Susan was told they needed it for only a couple of days. She gave them several days then called the female detective who had interviewed her. The detective who had given her a card and told her to call if she had questions did not reply to her phone messages, Susan said. She called another detective who was at the scene, but he didn't return her call either.

"Well, that's making me mad. They could at least call me back, because I left messages, and they won't even give me the courtesy of calling me back. And they had my personal property. Whether it is a gun or a skillet or a baseball bat, it's mine. And it didn't commit any crimes." Susan felt she was getting the run around. She called the police property room and was told police had the gun, but they couldn't release it until the female detective gave the okay. And she wasn't replying to Susan's calls.

She called Jill "J.R." Labbe at the *Fort Worth Star-Telegram.* Labbe is the deputy editorial-page editor and a columnist with the newspaper. Labbe, who also has a Texas concealed-handgun license, had written an earlier column about the shooting. Labbe wrote a second column that ran on December 11 headlined: "What One Woman Wants for Christmas: A Returned Gun."

Labbe found out that the District Attorney's office had instructed the police department to hold the gun until the legal process against Lessner was completed. She was told that Lessner's defense lawyer was blocking the return of the gun to Susan.

It is hard to see what part the gun could play as evidence in the charges against Lessner. As Susan put it: he was not charged with getting shot.

While she was deprived of her own revolver she borrowed a similar gun from her sister Judy Gaylord. The Smith & Wesson Chief's Special was not a light-weight revolver like hers, but it was handier to carry around than her 9 mm semi-automatic.

Susan got in touch with Albert Ross, an Arlington lawyer who is legal counsel to the Texas State Rifle Association. He promised to work on getting her gun back, but like molasses in winter, the legal system moved too slowly for Susan.

"I'm at the fuming stage now. They had my gun without cause. I'm one of these people who pays their bills on time. I don't owe anybody any money. And I was really starting to have some kind of a complex here and feeling that I have done something wrong. I don't like it because I have lived my whole life trying to be an upstanding citizen. So my kids will know what upstanding is, my grandkids. And I don't like being made to feel like a criminal."

It seemed as though she was not the only one outraged by what was happening. Labbe forwarded e-mails to her from all over the country from people writing in support of the gun-totin' granny.

Looking for help Susan got on the NRA web site. Under "Women & Firearms" she found her story posted. So she e-mailed the NRA and explained how she couldn't get her gun back.

About two days later she got a call from John Popp of *NRA News*. She had already talked to *NRA News* when the incident happened. Popp arranged to call the next day, and he interviewed her on the air. He said he would forward the information to the NRA legal counsel.

She received a four-page letter from Stefan B. Tahmassebi, deputy legal counsel for the NRA, citing four legal precedents that might be helpful in getting her gun back. The letter stated in part: "The state has a right to seize 'contraband' (illicit drugs, illegal firearms, etc.) and weapons that were used to commit a crime. If the property is not contraband, the police and prosecutor still have a right to use the property as evidence in a criminal prosecution, if said property is in fact necessary evidence of said crime. However, if these circumstances are not present, the state has no right to seize or to refuse to return seized property."

Ross confirmed that the assistant district attorney handling the case had dug in his heels and would not release the gun because the defense attorney wanted it held. There was no reason for the defense lawyer or the prosecutor to hold the gun as evidence, he said. If Lessner had touched the gun and had his fingerprints on it it would have been different.

Ross made it known that he was about to file a motion with the court to have the gun returned.

He discussed the case with Tahmassebi, the NRA lawyer who had written to Susan. One of the cases that Tahmassebi referred to left the government open to having to pay court costs if a citizen had to go to court to get property returned.

"Nobody wanted to take responsibility for making a decision on it—to give it back to her," Ross said.

Eventually, the prosecutor drafted a court order for the gun to be released to Susan, and on December 22 District Court Judge Mike Thomas signed it. No one thought to tell Ross or Susan that the court order had been signed. After Christmas Ross went deer hunting for a week and did not find out about the order until he returned.

296 ⌐ *Thank God I Had a Gun*

On January 10 Ross called the Arlington Police Department property room and was told he could pick up the gun on behalf of his client, Susan. However, when he arrived at the police department a few minutes later, he was told the court order said the gun was to be released to Susan Buxton, so they could not give it to him.

"I really think that the guys in the custodial room never thought that gun was going to leave their possession," he said.

He and Susan met at the police department the following morning at 9. "He's all happy, and I'm just elated that I'm going to get my gun back," Susan recalled.

Her elation was premature and soon was replaced by irritation. The police couldn't find the paperwork. The person who had the documents at 5 P.M. on Tuesday wasn't on duty in the morning. Finally the paperwork turned up. The officers had to check on the computer to make sure the gun hadn't been reported stolen. Then they had to conduct a criminal background check on Susan. Her concealed-handgun license apparently was not good enough.

Finally they brought out the little revolver in a paper-bag marked as evidence, and Susan identified it as hers. She was about to leave when Ross asked about the ammunition. The department had kept the three remaining live rounds that had been in the gun when Susan surrendered it. They said she couldn't collect the gun and the live rounds at the same time. She would have to take the gun out to the car and come back for the three cartridges. Eventually common sense prevailed, and she was allowed to put the gun and the container of rounds into her purse and leave. What should have taken a few minutes took most of the morning. It had taken two months and two days from the time it was seized for Susan to get her gun back.

Lt. Blake Miller, assistant to the Arlington police chief, said it is department policy not to give a gun and ammunition to a person at the same time. It is a safety precaution, he added.

Christy Gilfour, a spokeswoman for the Arlington Police Department, said the gun was initially seized as part of a criminal investigation. "Even at a police shooting, when an officer is involved in a shooting on the job, we take that officer's gun as part of the evidence. That's just routine," she said.

Anything police think they may need as part of a criminal investigation is seized as evidence. Later the gun was held at the request of the District Attorney's office, she said. "She [Susan] was made aware of exactly what was going on, and what was happening to her was no different than what happens to anyone in a similar situation," Gilfour said.

Once the District Attorney's office decided Susan was not going to be charged with anything, her gun should have been returned immediately.

"It was a screw up by the numbers deal, what I call a Chinese fire drill," Ross said. There was no real basis for the police to take the gun away from her, he said. "My position is that she did nothing wrong, and the gun wasn't going anywhere," he added.

Reflections

As the spokeswoman for the Arlington Police Department said, when a police officer is involved in a shooting incident investigators take his gun as evidence. It is part of the routine.

Michael McMains retired from the San Antonio Police Department after twenty-five years as a police psychologist. Before that he had five years as a psychologist for the U.S. Army. McMains has counseled about one thousand police officers, soldiers, and civilians who have suffered psychological trauma as a result of violent incidents.

At the 2006 annual meeting of the Texas Concealed Handgun Association, he talked about shooting trauma. He said that the San Antonio Police Department used to take an officer's weapon from him at the scene of a shooting. "What message does that send?" he asked. "You just went from being one of the good guys to one of the bad guys."

San Antonio changed the policy so that now the officer keeps his gun at the scene. When he arrives back at the police department, the crime scene technicians will take his gun but replace it with another one so he still feels like a police officer rather than a suspect. The San Antonio police policy manual states that a supervisor should take an officer's gun at the scene of a shooting only if absolutely necessary.

Obviously, a police department is not going to supply a civilian with another gun. However, civilians should not be lied to if their guns have to be taken as evidence. The department should not say "we need it for only a couple of days," when it may be much longer. If the situation changes, the department should keep them informed.

The days and weeks immediately after a shooting incident are when one would be most at risk for retaliation. When police seize a civilian's gun as evidence, it can leave them defenseless against either the attacker who survived or his friends. It may simply be revenge, or it may be that the attacker just doesn't want the citizen to testify against him. In Susan's case, Lessner had previously been arrested for retaliation.

Susan Buxton had other guns, but the one she was most familiar with and which she carried most of the time had been seized. In this case she was able to borrow a similar gun from her sister. It may be wise for the citizen gun carrier to invest in another gun of the same make and model as the gun she normally carries.

McMains also said that in the period after a shooting the person involved is very susceptible to the thoughts and responses of other people to the shooting. In Susan's case the insistence of the female detective who read her her rights made her feel like a suspect, although the investigators were generally supportive of her and what she had done. However, giving her the bureaucratic run around after the shooting and not returning her gun undoubtedly made the psychological trauma of the shooting incident worse for her.

"I felt like I was being treated like a criminal, because they won't return my gun," Susan Buxton said afterward.

It is inexcusable that Susan had to go to the expense of getting a lawyer in order to get her property back when a blind man with a stick could see that it was not evidence against Christopher Lessner.

Should Susan have given police a written statement right after the shooting? Investigators will pressure a civilian who has just shot someone to make a formal statement. In this particular case it didn't make any difference. Susan had done nothing wrong and it was obvious. However, the civilian is not an expert in the law, and there are many sinkholes in the legal system that can swallow up the innocent civilian who has just used a gun in self-defense. For example, do you know whether your state law requires you to retreat in the face of life threatening aggression? The wrong answer could send you to prison.

Commander Albert Rodriguez is the officer in charge of the Texas Department of Public Safety training academy. When he teaches concealed-handgun-license instructors about the use of deadly force, his advice to civilians who have just been involved in a shooting incident is: "Don't say a damn thing. Call an attorney."

Albert Ross, Susan's lawyer, echoes this advice. He advises his clients not to make a statement until they have talked to him.

Should Susan have called the police sooner? Most people don't call 9-1-1 very often. Most of us don't want to call the police without cause. Susan missed the warning signs, and like many crime victims—particularly first time crime victims—she didn't really believe it was happening to her. She wanted to make sure before she called the police that she had a good reason.

Should she have searched for the suspect herself? She was certainly putting herself at risk in doing so. But the reality is that people who are self-sufficient enough to get concealed-handgun licenses are not the sort of people who are going to call the police and say: "I think somebody may be hiding in my house. Would you send an officer to search it?"

Should Susan have cocked her revolver and had her finger on the trigger? Emmanuel Kapelsohn is a firearms instructor of police and civilians and a lawyer who has defended in court police officers involved in shooting incidents. He advises keeping your finger outside the trigger guard until you are on target and have made the decision to shoot. With adrenaline coursing through your system it is too easy to crank off a shot by accident if your finger is on the trigger.

Should Susan have left the house? Since the incident Susan has had several people ask her why she didn't just get out of the house immediately. Her answer is typical of the sort of independent Texan she is: "But you see, it's my house. I mean, my house. I'm the one who has the right to be here."

The police-will-protect-you argument of the people who hate guns and would prefer you to be a dead victim than a survivor who shot someone doesn't survive scrutiny in this case. It took Arlington police officers about six minutes to arrive at Susan's house, even though officers were all over the area looking for Lessner.

"That's how close they were, but they still couldn't get here in time to help me. If I hadn't known how to use my .38, I could have been dead or he'd have gotten it away from me. He could have hurt both of us. I mean he wasn't a heavy guy, but he was really muscular; he could have really hurt us."

Susan said people have criticized her for not shooting the suspect in the chest or in the face. Firearms instructors teach people to shoot for the chest area or the "center of mass," because that is where a shot is most likely to incapacitate a person.

However, it is hard to argue with success. She stopped the assault and successfully defended herself and her granddaughter without killing her assailant. She had a natural human reaction to the prospect of taking the life of another person. She is glad she didn't kill him.

"That's just another human being standing there really," she said.

Susan does not remember being scared during the incident. Listening to the 9-1-1 tape, one emotion comes across, and it is not fear—it is anger that this man is in her house.

She normally carries her gun all the time. Sometimes she carries the gun in her purse. When she isn't carrying her purse, she carries it in her pocket. She does not have a holster.

Albert Ross gave her credit for going to the range and practicing with the gun. He said she knows how to handle it. "I complimented her. I said, 'Susan, I give you A-double-plus for the fact that you go out and practice with it and don't just leave it laying around.'"

He said it is more and more difficult for ordinary citizens to find a place to shoot. "Part of it is the anti-gun environment that the national media has sold everybody— the idea that if anyone has a gun, it's just a matter of time until they rob a bank."

Should she have talked to the media? Susan obviously enjoyed her few days of fame, and she was able to put a positive spin on self-defense that was seen nationally. As a grandmother she was a sympathetic figure and, although she used deadly force, she had not killed anyone. She said her purpose in giving media interviews was to encourage more women to arm themselves. In Texas fewer than 20 percent of the concealed-handgun licenses are issued to women.

"I think everybody ought to be able to defend themselves," she said.

She made the front cover of the *TSRA Sportsman*, the journal of the Texas State Rifle Association. She was invited to sign copies of the magazine at the annual meeting of the association in February 2006. She was walking among the aisles of guns taking a break when a man pulled her aside. He said he wanted to thank her because both his daughters had gotten their concealed-handgun licenses as a result of what Susan had done. He added that his wife was planning to get her license too.

For Susan Gaylord Buxton this was vindication. It made it all worthwhile.

Afterword

You have now read fourteen accounts of ordinary people using guns to defend themselves and others. I hope you have reached the conclusion that a gun is a tool like a knife or an axe. It can be used for good or for evil depending upon the intent of the person holding it. It is the best tool for keeping you safe from attack whether you live in Arizona or Afghanistan, Delaware or Darfur, Los Angeles or Liverpool.

One hundred years ago travelers going from country to country or even county to county regularly took guns with them and no one thought anything of it. Now as governments take more and more control of our lives, they are uncomfortable with citizens who have access to guns, believing they are more difficult to control. The right to guns for protection has been eroded until it has disappeared in most countries.

In the United States the right of Americans to possess and carry firearms is under constant attack. If you want to preserve that right, I urge you to become involved in the fight to keep it. Freedom isn't free. Join the National Rifle Association and/or one of the other gun-rights organizations like the Second Amendment Foundation and Gun Owners of America.

Get a concealed-handgun license if you can. The more people who have these licenses the harder it will be for politicians to take away your guns and your ability to carry them. I know, you shouldn't have to seek government permission to exercise a constitutional right, but try telling that to a Massachusetts state trooper. It also puts you in a database as a gun owner, but then you are probably in someone's database for that reason anyway.

Women benefit more from possession of a gun for self-defense than men do, according to Professor John Lott. In his book, *More Guns Less Crime: Understanding Crime and Gun Control Laws*, he contends that a woman who defends herself with a gun is 2.5 times more likely to survive an attack unscathed than if she does not defend herself at all. The risk is higher if she fights back with something other than a gun. If a man defends himself with a gun he is 1.4 times more likely to be uninjured than if he behaves passively.

Despite benefiting more from being armed, women do not seek concealed-handgun permits as frequently as men do. In Texas only about 18 percent of licenses are issued to women. In Florida it is about 15 percent. At a time when individuals seem to be ceding more control of their lives to big corporations and to government, women speak of how empowering it feels to possess a gun and to know how to use it in self-defense.

Husbands, teach your wives how to shoot for the pure fun of shooting. Deanna Eggleston enjoyed shooting once her husband persuaded her to try it. Then urge them to seek formal firearms instruction and to apply for a concealed carry license.

It is also important for parents to teach their children safety around guns, and the best way to do that is to interest them in shooting. Take them to the range when they show an interest in guns. Just as with safe and responsible sex, today's mothers and fathers cannot rely upon the school system to educate our children about weapons skills and their safe and responsible use.

If we don't raise a new generation of hunters and shooters, we will lose the right guaranteed by the Second Amendment. Become involved.

Give the Gift of Knowledge
to Yourself or Someone Else

CALL TOLL-FREE AND ORDER NOW

 1-888-700-4333

Please have your card ready.

Orders by mail: Privateer Publications, P.O. Box 29427, San Antonio, TX 78229. Make checks and money orders payable to: **Privateer Publications**.

Please send _____ copies of **Thank God I Had a Gun** at $19.95 each, plus $5 each for shipping. Texas residents add $1.65 each for sales tax.

Please send _____ copies of **The Concealed Handgun Manual** at $21.95 each, plus $5 each for shipping. Texas residents add $1.81 each sales tax.

Name: _____

Organization: _____

Address: _____

City, State, ZIP: _____

Phone: _____ email: _____

Total enclosed or authorized to be charged: $_____

Card # _____ Exp. Date: _____

Three digit check # on signature panel: _____

Signature: _____

I understand that I may return any books for a full refund for any reason, no questions asked. Please phone 210-308-8191 for information on quantity discounts.

Visit our web site for more information at:
www.privateerpublications.com